PROMOTING YOUR SCHOOL

HOW TO ORDER THIS BOOK

BY PHONE: 800-233-9936 or 717-291-5609, 8AM–5PM Eastern Time

BY FAX: 717-295-4538

BY MAIL: Order Department
Technomic Publishing Company, Inc.
851 New Holland Avenue, Box 3535
Lancaster, PA 17604, U.S.A.

BY CREDIT CARD: American Express, VISA, MasterCard

PERMISSION TO PHOTOCOPY–POLICY STATEMENT

Authorization to photocopy items for internal or personal use, or the internal or personal use of specific clients, is granted by Technomic Publishing Co., Inc. provided that the base fee of US $3.00 per copy, plus US $ .25 per page is paid directly to Copyright Clearance Center, 27 Congress St., Salem, MA 01970, USA. For those organizations that have been granted a photocopy license by CCC, a separate system of payment has been arranged. The fee code for users of the Transactional Reporting Service is 0-87762/93 $5.00 + $ .25.

PROMOTING YOUR SCHOOL

A **PUBLIC RELATIONS** HANDBOOK

Irene M. Lober, Ed.D.

Professor and Chair
Department of Educational Administration
School of Education
State University of New York—College at New Paltz
New Paltz, New York

TECHNOMIC
PUBLISHING CO., INC.
LANCASTER · BASEL

Promoting Your School

a **TECHNOMIC**® publication

Published in the Western Hemisphere by
Technomic Publishing Company, Inc.
851 New Holland Avenue, Box 3535
Lancaster, Pennsylvania 17604 U.S.A.

Published in the Rest of the World by
Technomic Publishing AG
Missionsstrasse 44
CH-4055 Basel, Switzerland

Printed in the United States of America
10 9 8 7 6 5 4 3

Main entry under title:
   Promoting Your School: A Public Relations Handbook

A Technomic Publishing Company book
Bibliography: p. 313
Includes index p. 317

Library of Congress Catalog Card No. 92-62396
ISBN No. 0-87762-687-1

To my mother, Beckie Moss,
who was an unending source of encouragement,
and to my husband, Sol,
and my children, Clifford, Richard, and Lori,
and their families, who are my inspirations.

CONTENTS

FOREWORD

"*S C H O O L S* today are experiencing pressures that have never been faced before, and these pressures are having devastating effects on the operation of the schools." The beginning to this fine text by Dr. Irene Lober signals the two most important features of her materials: first, Dr. Lober writes a treatise concerning school public relations at a time when school/community relationships are at their nadir in the United States; and second, Dr. Lober intends this text to be a practical body of knowledge for use by administrators, supervisors, and by those currently involved in graduate work in educational administration. Moreover, this text is highly usable by teachers and community members as well, in what should be their verve to understand rational ways in which schools and communities may work effectively together.

Dr. Lober writes much of this text from her own experiences, which are as rich and varied as they can be. She has been an elementary school teacher, as well as an adult basic education teacher. She has been the principal of both elementary and secondary schools, as well as a consultant to the U.S. Office of Education. She was the Superintendent of Schools for University City, Missouri as well as for Danbury, Connecticut. Finally, she has had ten years of college teaching experience.

Although there are many admirable features to this text, the one that most appeals to me as an administrator is Dr. Lober's articulate manner of interweaving research with practical information throughout the book. Not a simple intersection of data with practice, Dr. Lober is indicating by means of her own work what is essential to excellence in school/community relations in particular: it is essential that administrators observe their own communities (school and local) and combine those careful observations with what current research indicates before making important administrative decisions. As dean of a school of education, I admire this approach, and it is my hope that this text will continually serve as a reminder that at the very heart of proper administration is this kind of careful analysis.

There are other fine features to this book that should be depicted in this foreword. The majority of the practices suggested by the author are consistently applied to real world situations, or result from her direct and varied experiences. Additionally, much of the exhibited research is drawn from the highly desirable combination of her own intern students' work at New Paltz as well as from research in the most current literature. Moreover, although each chapter contains a number of case-study documents, the book ends with a series of major anecdotal "showcase" descriptions which put the book in a particularly optimistic light. I encourage the reader to refer to these studies prior to the final reading. Dr. Lober's point seems to be that with the proper leadership and instruction, many school systems would be able to exhibit exemplary administration.

As I observe, then, this handbook, the current status of school/community relations, and our own training of administrators, teachers and intelligent, liberally educated community members at the University College at New Paltz, I have for the first moment in quite a while, an optimistic sense that the nadir I referred to earlier in this foreword may be on the wane. Experienced administrators such as Professor Lober are observing the apparent disjointedness of focus among schools and the communities they serve and are committing themselves through teaching and research to enabling the next generations of education leaders to improve the current situation. It is my hope that the many subjunctive statements in this foreword become reality and that readers of this fine text are able to translate Dr. Lober's practical experience and fine summaries of research into a plan that would force me to use the word "acme" instead of "nadir" in the foreword to future editions of this landmark textbook.

Philip A. Schmidt, Ph.D.
Dean of the School of Education
SUNY, The University College at New Paltz

INTRODUCTION

S C H O O L S today are experiencing pressures that have never been faced before, and these pressures are having devastating effects on the operation of the schools. In district after district, the public is voting down budgets, bond referenda, and propositions that would fund various aspects of the school operation. Members of the public are exercising their right to vote in larger numbers, mainly because of their disappointment with the perceived performance of schools.

Very often members of the public do not know how their schools are doing; they reflect on the information that they have gleaned from newscasts and new reports addressing education in general and its failure to produce a literate, well-educated graduate. They continue to hear about the high dropout rate, the need to set goals and standards, and the need to reform education.

The status quo is no longer acceptable, regardless of how well the school district may be doing. Not knowing how their district is doing, voters respond negatively. The situation today can be likened to a national disease that is hitting most districts. We find that the three R's in education are no longer reading, writing, and arithmetic, but reform, revise, and refocus. Many taxpayer groups are clamoring for revolts, refusals, and reductions. The repeated budget defeats are forcing school districts to go back to the drawing boards and make changes.

Budgets do pass, however, in districts where the public has been informed and knows what the district goals and objectives are, how the students are performing, and where the dollars are going. Unfortunately the public is informed in far too few districts. The vast majority of the public does not have the slightest idea as to what is going on in the schools. Very often, attempts to find out are met with negative responses on the part of the administration. A feeling seems to prevail that the public does not need to know, that the educators make the decisions, and that administrators know what needs to be done.

Conditions today dictate otherwise! Times have changed, and we find that state after state is now mandating site-based management and shared decision making that involves not only administrators, but teachers, parents, community members, and students.

The need to share information is critical; the need to tell the district's story must be a high-priority item. There is no way that site-based management and shared decision making can take place without the sharing of information, facts, figures, goals, and directions. Included in the information must be a report of how the students are doing, what the dropout rate is, and where the money is being directed and spent.

Unfortunately, few preparation programs for educators and administrators include an emphasis on the value and need for public relations. The how-to's were not, and generally are not, included in course content. As educators, we tend to concentrate on the running of the schools, as well as what is happening in them. Public relations has not been a prime concern.

This book addresses the issues facing schools from the vantage point of the practitioner. This is not a theoretical treatise on public relations. The book offers a hands-on, practical approach of proven techniques used by many districts throughout the country. The ideas presented here can be used by all schools and school districts. They are not necessarily expensive and do not require large sums of money or large numbers of people to accomplish. What is required is a commitment to share your story with your community so that they will be informed, know what you are trying to do, see how well you are doing, and understand where the tax dollars are being spent.

Chapter 1—Opinions and Attitudes Are Influenced and Shaped indicates that opinions and attitudes are influenced and shaped by what a person hears, sees, reads, and experiences. Confidence in the source of the information tends to give credibility to the information. The many ways by which parents and non-parents learn about schools are presented, as are the Gallup Poll results related to the prime sources for parents and non-parents. Decisions as to which audience(s) you would like to reach can be helped by reviewing the data presented.

Chapter 2—Public Relations: Whose Job Is It? discusses the responsibilities of boards of education, their policy statements, their treatment of the public and staff, as well as the responsibilities of the various positions held by individuals working for the system, from superintendent of schools through middle management and professional, clerical, and support staff members.

Chapter 3 — Dealing with Our Publics identifies the two key publics that need to be addressed as we share information about the school/district: the internal public and the external public. In addition to identifying who these publics are, why we need to concern ourselves with them, and what they want to know; strategies for communicating with the students, staff, and community members are shared.

Chapter 4 — Establishing Trust and Confidence addresses the importance of two-way communication, communication breakdowns, and how trust and confidence are built. Speaking and use of the telephone; the need for active listening; the importance of non-verbal communication to include facial expressions, eye contact, hand and arm gestures, body posture, appearance, and distance; and suggestions to assist in writing are offered.

Chapter 5 — Involving the Public shares information on how to work with groups of various sizes, the need to involve key communicators, advisory groups/councils, and the need to very specifically charge these groups/councils. Examples of charges to three different groups — task force, committee, and advisory board — are shared.

Chapter 6 — Meetings and Conferences goes into detail on the planning of a meeting (why, who, when, where) and on conducting successful meetings. Additionally, carefully delineated steps are given on how to plan a major meeting/conference. Every detail that needs to be dealt with is identified and explained, and suggestions are made to assure that the meeting/conference is successful.

Chapter 7 — Elections addresses the issue of national, state, and local elections. It includes school board elections for board members, bond referenda, budgets, and tax levies. The specifics for running a successful school district election are identified, examples and formats are shared.

Chapter 8 — Working with the Media recognizes the importance of positive press relations, as well as the need to work with the press and to understand the operation of the newspaper, radio, and television station. Press releases, the creation of tip sheets and public service announcements, and the use of photographs, press conferences, and press packets are discussed in detail. Dealing with crisis situations and dealing with critics are additional areas covered in this chapter.

Chapter 9 — Being Proactive Rather Than Reactive, Planning for

Public Relations provides the framework for you to determine the school/district's priorities and procedures to plan for public relations. Topics included in this chapter are surveys, operational plans, themes and logos, target audiences, budget requirements, action plans, lead time, and a checklist for a principal's PR plan. The need to be proactive in terms of crisis management is identified, as is a plan for doing so.

Chapter 10—Implementing the Plan—Channels of Communication discusses district-wide channels and building-wide channels. The "how-to" of accomplishing these channels is included, as are examples of districts that have put them in place. The need to deal with reality and implement a public relations plan is highlighted.

Chapters 11, 12, and 13 showcase three school districts. They are very different in size, in character, in location, and in organizational structure. Yet, they do an outstanding public relations job. They use the tools available to them and are very successful.

Take the time to read about the Fairfax County Public Schools in Fairfax, Virginia; the Orange-Ulster Board of Cooperative Educational Services in Goshen, New York; and South Central School District No. 406 just outside Seattle, Washington. Picture your school/district doing some of the activities they have done, and make a determination to join their ranks of excellence. You can do it, all you have to do is make the commitment to try!

CHAPTER 1

OPINIONS AND ATTITUDES ARE INFLUENCED AND SHAPED

J U S T what is public relations? The definition used by the editors of *Public Relations News* is:

> Public relations is the management function which evaluates public attitudes, identifies the policies and procedures of an individual or an organization with the public interest, and plans and executes a program of action to earn public understanding and acceptance.

The National School Public Relations Association (1986) defined school public relations as:

> A planned and systematic two-way process of communications between an educational organization and its internal and external publics designed to build morale, goodwill, understanding and support for that organization.

Dr. Philip E. Leahy, Superintendent of Schools of the Newburgh City School District, refers to the two-way process of communication by preferring to call it "marketing your schools, because the best form of communicating to the public is to demonstrate that your schools are doing an excellent job and to make sure people know about it" (Leahy, 1990).

From time to time you may see the terms public relations, public information, community relations, and school-community relations used interchangeably. The terminology is not nearly as important as the essential commitment to meaningful two-way communication between the school/district and the publics it serves. The prime thrust of an effective public relations program should be to assure two-way communication in order to develop an understanding of and support for the philosophy, goals, programs, and operations of the school district.

Public relations is a series of relationships between a school or school district and its publics that enables individuals to obtain and interpret facts, in order to participate intelligently in forming opinions and making decisions. All schools have public relations regardless of their efforts or lack thereof. A key concern is that all too often, the information received is by chance and from a variety of sources, resulting in a lack of, or distorted, understanding of the issues facing the school/district enjoying the confidence and support of its public.

What are the ways that parents and non-parents learn about school? Four graduate students at the State University of New York, College at New Paltz (SUNY – New Paltz) undertook a survey that paralleled to a large extent a survey on "Ways Parents Learn about School," done by Bonnie Sloan of the University of Toledo in 1973 and included in *School-Community Relations in Transition* (Saxe, 1984). In addition to surveying parents of students, the students surveyed non-parents in order to determine how they learn about school.

Ways Parents Learn about School

Three hundred fifty-eight parents were surveyed: 146 parents had students in elementary school and 212 parents had students in secondary school. For purposes of data analysis, "elementary" includes students in both elementary and middle schools, and "secondary" includes students in junior and senior high schools.

Respondents came from mixed socioeconomic backgrounds and represented several school districts. Respondents were asked to check as many sources as applicable.

Tables 1.1, 1.2, and 1.3 indicate the number and percent of responses identified for each communication channel used by the school/district to reach the parents. Table 1.1 summarizes the responses of parents of elementary students, Table 1.2 summarizes the responses of parents of secondary students, and Table 1.3 is a summary of all 358 parental responses. Table 1.4 rank-orders the communication channels parents used most frequently to learn about school, with "1" being the most frequent means and "16" being the least frequent means.

Eighty-seven percent of the parents of elementary school students (Table 1.1) indicated that their own children were their number one source of information about the school, with 76 percent identifying

Table 1.1. Ways parents of elementary students learn about school.

Communication Channel	No. of Responses	Percent
My child tells me	127	87
Neighbor children tell me	37	25
Conversations with adult friends and neighbors	96	66
School newspaper	71	49
Classroom newsletters	73	50
Teacher notes or phone calls	93	64
Parent-teacher conferences	111	76
Report cards	110	75
Notes or calls to school	67	46
Personal visits to school	89	61
Classroom visits or observations	41	28
PTA meetings	36	25
Local radio stations	48	33
Television programs	14	10
Local newspapers	86	59
Other	8	5

Number: 146 parents.

Table 1.2. Ways parents of secondary students learn about school.

Communication Channel	No. of Responses	Percent
My child tells me	133	63
Neighbor children tell me	40	19
Conversations with adult friends and neighbors	65	31
School newspaper	130	61
Classroom newsletters	46	22
Teacher notes or phone calls	64	30
Parent-teacher conferences	59	28
Report cards	173	82
Notes or calls to school	75	35
Personal visits to school	82	39
Classroom visits or observations	35	17
PTA meetings	43	20
Local radio stations	62	29
Television programs	15	7
Local newspapers	154	73
Other	13	6

Number: 212 parents.

Table 1.3. Ways parents learn about school.

Communication Channel	No. of Responses	Percent
My child tells me	260	73
Neighbor children tell me	77	22
Conversations with adult friends and neighbors	161	45
School newspaper	201	56
Classroom newsletters	119	33
Teacher notes or phone calls	157	44
Parent-teacher conferences	170	47
Report cards	283	79
Notes or calls to school	142	40
Personal visits to school	171	48
Classroom visits or observations	76	21
PTA meetings	79	22
Local radio stations	110	31
Television programs	29	8
Local newspapers	240	67
Other	21	6

Number: 358 parents.

Table 1.4. Ways parents learn about school (in rank order).

| Communication Channel | Level | | |
	Elem.	Sec.	Total
My child tells me	1	3	2
Neighbor children tell me	13	13	13
Conversations with adult friends and neighbors	4	7	7
School newspaper	9	4	4
Classroom newsletters	8	11	10
Teacher notes or phone calls	5	8	8
Parent-teacher conferences	2	10	6
Report cards	3	1	1
Notes or calls to school	10	6	9
Personal visits to school	6	5	5
Classroom visits or observations	12	14	14
PTA meetings	14	12	12
Local radio stations	11	9	11
Television programs	15	15	15
Local newspapers	7	2	3
Other	16	16	16

Number: 358 parents.

"parent-teacher conferences" as the second most frequent source of information, and 75 percent checking "report cards" as third. Children are the best messengers. Many teachers take a few minutes at the end of each day to review what was done over the course of the day. They send the student home with lots of information they can share with their parents. All too often the parents ask their children, "What did you learn in school today?" The answer invariably is, "Nothing." Many times the few minutes taken at the end of the day will give the children something positive to tell their parents.

Many elementary and middle schools schedule parent-teacher conferences at least once a year as a means of reporting student progress to parents. These conferences present an opportunity to talk to parents on a one-to-one basis, establish valuable working relationships, and share meaningful information with the parents. Educational jargon should be avoided.

"Conversations with adult friends and neighbors," "teacher notes or phone calls," and "personal visits to schools" were identified by 66 percent, 64 percent, and 61 percent of the parents. "PTA (Parent Teacher Association) meetings" and "television programs" were identified as the least effective means of learning about schools, having been identified by only 25 percent and 10 percent of the people, respectively.

Elementary school parents usually attend PTA functions. If parents are not coming to meetings, reasons for not coming should be determined. Are the meetings taking place at a reasonable hour? Is there a need to change the meeting time in order to accommodate the changing family structure and the working hours of the parent(s)? What are the meetings like—the content, format, timeliness of the topics? Consider your school community's needs before continuing to do the same old thing. Times have changed, and so must the ways in which we reach our parents.

Eighty-two percent of the parents of secondary students (Table 1.2) identified "report cards" as being their prime source of information about the school while 73 percent identified "local newspapers" as the second source of information.

Most secondary schools mail the report cards to the parents. Most parents do, therefore, have an opportunity to see the report card and have an indication of how their student is doing. Secondary parents ranked their own children third (63 percent) as a source of information. Most secondary parents do not see the information sent home from school because their children do not bring notices and papers home to them.

Only 7 percent of the parents of secondary school students identified television programs as being a source of school information. There is a sparsity of local news coverage by major networks. Local news is generally carried on cable networks at infrequent times. Many homes do not have access to cable television; others do not choose to purchase the service. Additionally, local news programs tend to compete with major network news telecasts.

Both groups (Table 1.3 and Table 1.4) identified "conversations with adult friends and neighbors" and "school newspapers" in fourth place. "Local radio stations," "classroom visits or observations," reliance on "neighbor children," "PTA meetings," and "television programs" were identified as least effective.

Other ways that parents learned about school were reading school calendars and monthly lunch menus, serving on boards of education, attending board meetings, calling the superintendent and administrators, going to open house, and attending programs such as one about the American Field Service.

As you plan to establish or expand your two-way communication with both parents and non-parents, recognize the changing demography of your school community. Estimates are that only 27 percent of the households have school-age children (Gallup and Elam, 1988) and that 60 percent of the children will be living in a single-parent household at some point in their lives. Families structured in the 1950s model, with two parents and the mother staying home full-time, make up only 18 percent of all families (Hamburg, 1987). More than 50 percent of women are in the work force today. Twenty-five percent (20 million) of households consist of people living alone.

Ways Non-Parents Learn about School

A total of 297 non-parents were surveyed in order to determine how they learned about schools. Results were obtained in three categories: ages 20−35 (Table 1.5), 36−55 (Table 1.6), and over 55 (Table 1.7). Table 1.8 summarizes the three groups and Table 1.9 rank-orders the three groups by communication channel.

Non-parents, ages 20−35, identified "conversations with adult friends and neighbors" (74 percent) and "local newspapers" (72 percent) as the two most frequent ways they learn about school. "Talking to children" (61 percent) and "school district newspapers mailed to the house" (47 percent) were also identified as being important sources of information.

Table 1.5. Ways non-parents learn about school (ages 20−35 years).

Communication Channel	No. of Responses	Percent
Children tell me	80	61
Conversations with adult friends and neighbors	98	74
School district newspaper mailed to the house	62	47
Meetings of clubs/associations	18	14
Visits to schools	26	20
Local radio stations	52	39
Television programs	33	25
Local newspapers	95	72
School posters in the community	23	17
Speakers at community meetings	6	5
Stories in magazines	12	9
Attendance at plays, games, etc.	32	24
Other	12	9

Number: 132 non-parents.

They identified "stories in magazines" (9 percent) and "speakers at community meetings" (5 percent) as being the least effective strategies in learning about schools.

In the 36−55 age group (Table 1.6) and the over 55 age group (Table 1.7), the most frequent sources of information were "local newspapers" and "conversations with adult friends and neighbors."

Policies and procedures for dealing with the print media need to be

Table 1.6. Ways non-parents learn about school (ages 36−55 years).

Communication Channel	No. of Responses	Percent
Children tell me	48	52
Conversations with adult friends and neighbors	63	68
School district newspaper mailed to the house	59	63
Meetings of clubs/associations	24	26
Visits to schools	15	16
Local radio stations	46	49
Television programs	27	29
Local newspapers	69	74
School posters in the community	22	24
Speakers at community meetings	8	9
Stories in magazines	15	16
Attendance at plays, games, etc.	16	17
Other	7	8

Number: 93 non-parents.

Table 1.7. Ways non-parents learn about school (ages — over 55).

Communication Channel	No. of Responses	Percent
Children tell me	23	32
Conversations with adult friends and neighbors	41	57
School district newspaper mailed to the house	31	43
Meetings of clubs/associations	13	18
Visits to schools	8	11
Local radio stations	28	39
Television programs	23	32
Local newspapers	51	71
School posters in the community	11	15
Speakers at community meetings	8	11
Stories in magazines	10	14
Attendance at plays, games, etc.	13	18
Other	1	1

Number: 72 non-parents.

developed in order to communicate with an ever-increasing non-parent constituency group. "School district newspapers mailed to the house" ranked third. Recognizing that few of these homes have school-age students, the reliance quite naturally falls to the media that the non-parents are able to access—the "local newspapers" and the "school district newspaper mailed to the house." It should be noted that not all of the school districts in which the respondents lived published a school district newspaper that was mailed to the house. Circulation of a school newspaper is an area that should be considered as part of a viable public relations plan.

Table 1.8 summarizes the ways all of the non-parents in the survey learn about school.

When combining the three groups there is very little change in the ways in which they learn about school. The "local newspaper" was identified by 72 percent of the respondents, with "conversations with adult friends and neighbors" (68 percent) ranked second, and "school district newspapers mailed to the house" and "children tell me" tied as the third most frequent way in which non-parents learned about school.

Table 1.9 was prepared in order to compare the rank order of the communication channels for the three age groups.

While "local newspapers" and "conversations with adult friends and neighbors" ranked highest as the sources by which non-parents learned about school, "speakers at community meetings" ranked lowest.

Table 1.8. Ways non-parents learn about school.

Communication Channel	No. of Responses	Percent
Children tell me	151	51
Conversations with adult friends and neighbors	202	68
School district newspaper mailed to the house	152	51
Meetings of clubs/associations	55	19
Visits to schools	49	16
Local radio stations	126	42
Television programs	83	28
Local newspapers	215	72
School posters in the community	56	19
Speakers at community meetings	22	7
Stories in magazines	37	12
Attendance at plays, games, etc.	61	21
Other	20	7

Number: 297 non-parents.

Table 1.9. Ways non-parents learn about school (in rank order).

Communication Channel	Ages		
	20−35	36−55	55+
Children tell me	3	4	5
Conversations with adult friends and neighbors	1	2	2
School district newspaper mailed to the house	4	3	3
Meetings of clubs/associations	10	7	7
Visits to schools	8	10	11
Local radio stations	5	5	4
Television programs	6	6	5
Local newspapers	2	1	1
School posters in the community	9	8	9
Speakers at community meetings	12	12	11
Stories in magazines	11	10	10
Attendance at plays, games, etc.	7	9	7

Number: 297 non-parents.

Other ways that non-parents learned about school were from recent graduates, sports pages, church, being friends with teachers, having a sister in school, discussions with granddaughters, school employees, and attendance at college classes.

"I do not know much about the schools" was indicated by thirty-nine non-parents, with twenty-six of them having checked other categories and thirteen checking no categories. Two-thirds of these respondents felt that, even though they did know something about schools, they really did not have much information about them. This subgroup represents 13 percent of the non-parent group.

It was interesting to note that several individuals in the over 55 category volunteered their ages – 76, 78, 82, 87, and 92.

In planning public relations programs, it is important to reach as many members of the community as possible, including the non-parents, by not restricting ourselves, and using many avenues to reach the various publics.

Gallup Poll Results

The 20th Annual Gallup Poll of the Public's Attitudes toward the Public Schools (Gallup and Elam, 1988) had a series of questions dealing with the sources of information people used to get their information about schools. The results of the survey done at SUNY – New Paltz paralleled the Gallup Poll in several areas.

- The prime source for non-parents was newspapers (55 percent, Gallup Poll; 72 percent, SUNY – New Paltz).
- A prime source for public school parents was students (57 percent, Gallup Poll; 73 percent, SUNY – New Paltz).

The Gallup Poll's national totals indicate that newspapers were the prime source of information as identified by 52 percent of the respondents in 1988, up from 38 percent in 1973. It further indicates that students dropped to second place as a source of information in 1988, going from 43 percent in 1973 to 36 percent in 1988. Gallup points out that "since 1973, the percentage of adults in the U.S. with school-age children has dwindled from 39% to about 27%. This probably explains the lower percentage of the public that now depends on students as a source of information" (Gallup and Elam, 1988).

A concerted effort to reach out to your publics is necessary to assure that the image the public holds of your school(s) is positive and that, as needed, informed decisions are made. It is no longer acceptable to sit back and hope, or expect, that the message will be delivered. The messages to the community must be clear, consistent, and address the educational issues, plans, and ongoing activities designed to prepare both the students and the community for the twenty-first century. We can influence and shape the community's opinions and attitudes about schools and schooling by maintaining appropriate two-way communication with them.

PUBLIC RELATIONS — WHOSE JOB IS IT?

S C H O O L districts are particularly vulnerable to public opinion because they are often the largest industry in the community. They are the only government function over which the community can exercise its voice through the election of school board members and/or budget votes and referenda. The community consists of not only the parents of school-age children, but parents whose children are in non-public schools or are no longer in school, single adults and married adults who have no children, senior citizens, school district staff, and business and industry personnel who work and/or live in the community.

Districts must be responsive to the community and staff, and maintain open lines of two-way communication. The many successes of the district need to be shared. We need to celebrate education and build on the successes, rather than waiting to be torn down by critics and negative press.

Communities support schools only when they are familiar with the district, its goals, its programs, its successes, its needs, the direction in which it is headed, the planning efforts, and who is/was involved. Communities will support the district when they have confidence in it and understand what is going on. Information must be shared on a year-round basis, twelve months a year, not just prior to a budget vote or a bond referendum.

A "sound school public relations (program) must be *honest* in intent and execution, *intrinsic* in the school program, *continuous* in application, *positive* in approach, *comprehensive* in character, *sensitive* to the publics concerned, and *simple* in meaning and conception" (American Association of School Administrators, 1950). Left unto itself, good public relations will not happen. It takes time, it takes effort, it takes commitment!

Whose job is it to see to it that correct information is shared? that ample, accurate, meaningful facts are made available? that two-way communication takes place? It is not one person's job—it is everyone's job. Everyone associated with the operation of the school/district: board of education, superintendent of schools, cabinet level staff, central office staff, building principals, directors, department chairs, teachers, guidance counselors, library media specialists, nurses, secretaries, custodians and maintenance personnel, food service workers, school bus drivers, and crossing guards.

Community members—the external public—recognize that these individuals, often their friends and neighbors, are closely connected to the school system in one capacity or another. The community members look to these individuals for information and answers. They think that they have firsthand information and know what is going on in the district.

Board of Education

Court decisions, legislative acts, and state constitutions have defined education as a state function. State legislation created school boards that are considered to be the arms of the state government, endowed with broad powers to operate local school systems. School board members are officers of the state, and most of them do not get paid for their services or time spent on school district business.

In most states, school board members are elected by the constituencies of the school district—some as a result of non-partisan, non-political elections. In other states, candidates run on strict party lines. In some states, such as Connecticut, there is a minority rule that stipulates the number of members of the minority party that must have seats on the school board. The specific number of seats varies with the size of the board. At times a person of the minority party who has received fewer votes than a majority party candidate will be seated on the board because of the minority rule.

In other states, board members are appointed. A case in point is Fairfax County, Virginia, where the supervisor of each of the eight magisterial districts appoints a school board member. Two board members are appointed at-large. The school board appointee is generally of the same political persuasion as the supervisor. This does not mean, however, that the board member and the supervisor agree on all matters all the time. The school board members maintain their independence and integrity, take action, and present budgets to the supervisors as they see fit.

School board members are accountable to the public for the operation of the schools, including the instructional program and financial matters. School boards set policy, pass budgets, approve contracts, set tax rates, determine school boundaries, and decide when to close a school, when to build a school, and whether to approve the curriculum taught in the district. The board acts only when it is in legal session.

The manner in which the board conducts its business at board meetings influences public opinion. A board that, through its actions, respects its members, the superintendent, the school district personnel, and the public who come before it, is respected by the community. A board whose members have little respect for one another, the superintendent of schools, the district staff, or the public; or a board that engages in constant bickering, obviously has not done its "homework" prior to the meeting, does not listen to what is being said, cannot or will not give the rationale or reasons for its actions, is disrespected and suspect.

Headlines such as "Squabbles Abound at Board Meeting" and "Wappingers Board Members Squabble" (*Poughkeepsie Journal*, 1989) followed by a lead paragraph:

> Wappingers school board members yelled at each other about improper parliamentary procedures, disagreed about forming citizens advisory committees and accused each other of conducting "secret investigations" Tuesday night during a 3-1/2-hour meeting.

leave the community with an uneasy feeling about the leadership of the district. Board members can certainly disagree with one another, but they need to respect one another and conduct their business with dignity in a calm, rational manner. The chairman of the board must maintain decorum. The board chairman can always call for a temporary recess until tempers cool and reason prevails. It is far better to recess the meeting than to continue squabbling in public.

The surest way to develop and implement a public relations program is for the board to adopt a policy statement expressing the board's intent to communicate with the various publics. The responsibility for carrying out the board's policy does not rest with the board, except as the policy refers to them and their responsibilities as board members. The superintendent of schools, as the district's chief executive officer, is charged with implementing the board's policies. The superintendent of schools may issue regulations for policies as needed, the superintendent may delegate many of the responsibilities to other individuals; but – bottom line – the superintendent is responsible to the board.

The policy statement shown in Figure 2.1 entitled ''Public Relations,'' was adopted by the Board of Education of the City of Newburgh on April 27, 1982 and is reprinted here with permission.

The Danbury, Connecticut, Board of Education's policy statement on public relations is:

> The Board of Education recognizes that good public relations is essential to the development of public understanding and support of education.
>
> The Board of Education shall provide for a continuing program of public information.
>
> The Board of Education shall inform itself, through the best and most effective means, of public reaction to school programs and of the continuing educational needs of the community.

Other Danbury, Connecticut related board policies deal with topics such as communication with the public, participation by the public, public activities involving staff, students, or school facilities, and public complaints.

Many states have created regional service centers that provide services to local school districts in a designated service region. New York State's regional service centers are called ''Boards of Cooperative Educational Services,'' or BOCES. The need to maintain excellent public relations is multiplied in the regional service centers because the general public and tax base of each center covers a number of school districts/counties. Dr. Laura Fliegner, District Superintendent of the Ulster County BOCES, New York, works with a board policy entitled ''Public Information Program,'' which indicates the intent of the Ulster BOCES:

> The Board of Cooperative Educational Services schools also touch the lives of every person in the community, and every attempt shall be made to represent the people according to the best interest of their children. To this end, the Board shall attempt to:
>
> 1. keep themselves and the public informed regarding the policies, objectives, and successes or failures of the schools; and
> 2. provide the means for furnishing full and accurate information, favorable and unfavorable, together with interpretation and explanation of the schools' plans and programs.

PUBLIC RELATIONS

The success of the school system is dependent on the cooperation and participation of many people. The Board believes that the advancement of the school's efforts is fostered as the community and staff develops and maintains confidence in the school system. Such confidence can only be founded on an understanding and awareness of the Board's purposes, programs and facilities and Board knowledge of the public's attitude.

In support of this policy, publicity shall be given to the major changes or innovations which occur from time to time in curriculum, in teaching procedures, and in physical facilities. Publicity shall be balanced. All schools, all grades, all subject matter fields, and all types of activities shall be reported.

All publicity concerning a school and its program to be released through the news media must be cleared by the building principal. Individual photographs identifying a child may be released if they:

a. in no way reflect on the child's lack of ability;
b. are not derogatory in nature;
c. do not identify the child as a special education pupil; or
d. would not, in any way, cause a child embarrassment.

Copies of all news releases are to be forwarded to the Office of the Superintendent of Schools. The Office of the Superintendent will help interpret the school program to the public as accurately and effectively as possible.

Figure 2.1 Policy statement of the Board of Education of the City School District of the City of Newburgh, New York.

The Board of Education of the Topeka Public Schools, Topeka, Kansas, has the following policy statement:

The Board of Education recognizes that the public schools belong to the community and that support of the schools is dependent upon full knowledge, understanding, and participation of the staff and citizenry.

An active involvement and communications program shall be maintained with the community and with the staff and students of the District. The administrative, instructional, and operational staffs are charged with carrying out this policy as an integral part of their regular activities and responsibilities.

Board policy statements are usually followed up by the issuance of operational regulations and yearly goals. The progress made to achieve the yearly goals and compliance with key board policies are included in the annual report to the board.

Superintendent of Schools

In most districts the superintendent is employed by the board of education. There are some states/districts in which the superintendent runs for the position in the same manner as board members do. The superintendent is responsible for carrying out all board policies, board directives, federal and state mandates/directives, and all legal requirements. The superintendent is the educational leader of the community who, by virtue of training and experience, is able to advise the board and plan, initiate, manage, and execute the programs recommended by the staff that are needed by the students.

The superintendent is often the most visible person in the school district. The public is aware of the relations between the board and the superintendent; the newspapers invariably pick these items up. Poor relations between the board and the superintendent, as evidenced by the manner in which the superintendent is addressed at board meetings, referred to in conversation, and openly criticized, cause a lack of confidence and trust in the system, distress, and discord. Likewise, the manner in which the superintendent treats, and refers to, the board is quickly noticed and picked up.

It is essential that whenever there are negative feelings between the board and the superintendent, they be dealt with in the privacy of an executive session of the board, not in the public spotlight. Once aired, the matter cannot be withdrawn quickly. The public has a long memory and does not readily forget. In an atmosphere of conflict, school district employees begin to feel insecure and tensions mount. It is far better to treat the superintendent and the board with the respect due their respective positions. Problem areas, taken care of privately, will not adversely affect the district.

The superintendent of schools represents the school district to the community. The superintendent is expected to attend public functions; speak at these functions; participate in community affairs; be involved with, and on, the boards of such agencies as United Way, Boy Scout Council, Girl Scout Council, American Heart Association, and Junior Achievement. Appearances on television and radio programs, at school building functions such as spaghetti dinners, plays, sports events, concerts, and ceremonies, are expected, as are visits with staff members and community leaders. Work with parent-teacher associations, advisory groups, special interest and advocacy groups, and student groups, involves countless hours of time.

The need to meet and communicate with employees/associations, listen to complaints and grievances, respond to questions raised by the press, and maintain positive relations with the local politicians and business establishments calls for tact and diplomacy. These responsibilities must be carried out by the superintendent with great care and skill, while carefully balancing his/her prime responsibility as the educational leader of the district. Kindred notes that ''in reality, superintendents are cast by circumstances into the role of educational statesmen and must spend much of their time dealing with individuals and groups whose influence and power help to shape the quality of educational opportunity in the community'' (Kindred et al., 1984).

Cabinet Level Staff

The scope of the superintendent's responsibilities are such that he/she depends to a large extent on a select group of administrators who have specialized skills and to whom the superintendent can delegate the oversight of major divisions/programs within the district. By working as an administrative team, cabinet members bring their expertise to the group. Ideas, solutions, and operations are viewed from various vantage points.

There is no hard and fast rule as to the number of individuals that the superintendent works with or specific position descriptions for each. The size of the district, the goals and objectives that are to be achieved, and job expectations all influence the administrative structure. The willingness of the board to employ the recommended number of administrators is a key factor in determining the number of administrators employed by a district.

In a district of some 10,000 students, the superintendent's cabinet could well include an associate superintendent, assistant superintendent for elementary education, assistant superintendent for secondary education, assistant superintendent for pupil personnel services, director of finance and support services, director of personnel and employee relations, and an administrative assistant, one of whose major responsibilities is public relations.

Each individual would be responsible for a major program area(s) and have hundreds of employees that he/she is indirectly responsible for through the principals, supervisors, and directors reporting to him/her. Recognizing the importance of public relations in the day-to-day operations of the district, each of the cabinet level position descriptions should contain the following items.

- Involve community representatives in curriculum study and planning groups with staff.
- Cooperate with other administrative personnel, evaluate and recommend community resources of benefit to the instructional program.
- Work with community groups as needed, including parent groups, to discuss, inform, and clarify curriculum-related questions.
- Communicate effectively with parents and the community on matters relating to curriculum and student progress.
- Provide individual opportunities for parents to discuss curriculum matters.
- Cooperate with the district's public relations office in disseminating information of interest to the community.
- Provide information on the instructional services of the district to the board, community, and staff, as needed.
- Direct and participate in the development of interpretive and informational materials regarding student services and related needs for use in the school district and community.
- Develop an ongoing program and present information to the schools and general community regarding the district's goals and objectives.
- Serve as a resource for information relative to the district, its programs, and operations.

Public Relations Officer

There is a tremendous advantage to having an individual employed by the school district who is responsible for public relations. Decisions as to the feasibility of that position, whether it will be full-time or part-time, whether the position will be a reasonable combination of several responsibilities, depend on the expectations of the district and the job that it wants accomplished.

All too often public relations positions are not included in the staffing of the district because boards tend to shy away from the possibility of public criticism. However, once the district employs a person in that position, the board soon realizes how much more positive press is being received. The board will undoubtedly retain the position in the budget.

An inclusive position description for a full-time person holding the public relations or school/community relations position could read as below (adapted from an existing job description).

Job Description for Public Relations Officer

The primary function of the public relations officer is to develop and maintain informational communication supportive of the district's programs through various forms of media within the schools, the community, and with the press, television, and radio stations. Emphasis is on promoting good educational practices and community betterment, and overseeing all avenues of public relations. Skills must include the ability to be the voice of the district, to work with reporters, and to respond to parents' calls. The public relations officer is directly responsible to the superintendent.

Responsibilities include the following.

- Be sensitive to the needs of the district, knowledgeable of district status, and available when and where stories break. Know what is going on.
- Hold press briefings before and after board meetings.
- Write and mail press releases and photo releases to the media every week that are supportive of the district's program and interesting to the public.
- Contact media to secure television coverage and to generate newspaper feature stories in addition to weekly press and photo releases.
- Answer media requests for information. Exception: requests involving policy of a sensitive nature are referred to the appropriate administrator.
- Take the majority of photographs used for press releases. Respond to special requests within the district.
- Be responsible for attractive, interesting, and inviting public relations flyers and formats. Be timely with fact sheets, recruiting brochures.

- Secure special guests to add interest to events in the district and increase opportunities for favorable citizen reaction and publicity.
- Serve as the public relations contact person for other school districts.
- Work with community groups to develop strong school/community relations.
- Respond to citizens' and prospective residents' requests for information. Furnish general information on the district to incoming new residents via telephone, personal contacts, and correspondence.
- Maintain a file card mailing list for use for various occasions. Cross-index a list of former board members, supportive citizens, and key election workers.
- Maintain mailing lists and mail agenda sheets of upcoming board meetings to PTA presidents and citizens who have requested to be on the mailing list for agendas.
- Place board packets in the public library. Mail public board packets to parochial school principals.
- Make personal contacts with parochial school principals whenever possible to foster good relations.
- Assist in all aspects of a school tax levy/budget/referendum election campaign. Conduct campaigns that are meaningful and catchy.
- Attend community meetings, school meetings, and events to maintain close contact with the citizens, staff, and students.
- Coordinate special events such as the reception for retirees, recognition and awards events.
- Maintain the master calendar for the district.
- Maintain knowledge of the district's curriculum and instructional programs and report information meaningfully.
- Visit schools and solicit stories suitable for press coverage.
- Help schools and staff with special mailings to promote events.
- Plan activities with the principals for American Education Week.
- Maintain a public relations bulletin board in the administration building.
- Supply the superintendent with daily newspaper clippings of local school news and news of general education.
- Maintain clippings of district news for distribution to board members and key administrators.
- Handle crisis situations when the news media must be contacted quickly by telephone.

- Track down and stop rumors.
- Draft letters for the superintendent upon request.
- Provide in-service education on communications for the administrators and other staff members and counsel them regarding the public relations implications of various matters.
- Conduct in-service seminars for all secretaries who answer the telephone in the district as to tone of voice, cordiality, and how to take a message helpfully. These persons create good will or bad will.
- Prepare a budget annually for submission to the superintendent and fiscal officer.
- Meet periodically with the Communication Advisory Board and seek the assistance of its members in evaluating the effectiveness of the district's public relations program.
- Maintain contact with the National School Public Relations Association, its affiliates, and other school communications resources as a partial means of professional growth and development.
- Be responsible for mailing changes in board policies and regulations to the public library and other such local governmental agencies, as appropriate.
- Assume other tasks related to school/community relations as assigned by the superintendent or designee.
- Be able to type well, proofread closely, edit carefully, and catch errors before the materials leave the public relations office.
- Be versatile; keep several jobs going at once.

Central Office Staff

This category refers to employees in the central offices of the school district, individual schools, and school district field offices. Their positions may call for interaction with other employees and/or with community members. They may be in positions where they are routinely called upon to respond to questions that are asked of them. Some of the job titles in this category are: purchasing agent, accounts payable, accounts receivable, safety officer, records clerk, payroll clerk, school secretary, and attendance officer.

These employees need to be kept informed so that they have an understanding of what is happening within the district. All too often they are not informed, and learn what is going on from the newspapers or radio. These employees reach many people in the community and can serve as great public relations spokespersons; they can represent the best side of the district, speaking positively to an issue only when information is shared with them on a timely basis. A district cannot afford to have these employees feeling left out of the mainstream and virtually ignored.

Building Principals

The school principal's position is the most exciting, most rewarding one in the district, because schools are where the action takes place, where teaching and learning take place, and where the reputation of a district is built. The key individual who works with staff members to implement the board's policies and the superintendent's directives and regulations is the building principal.

The building principal is the person who has a direct line to the parents, students, and staff. The principal interprets policy, establishes rules and regulations, sets the tone for the building, and usually identifies a budget to accommodate the needs of the staff and students based on a vision he/she has for the school. The articulated vision of the principal serves as the guiding light that moves the building forward. The principal sets the tone for the building and its appearance; the format and frequency of communications to staff, students, and parents; the manner in which staff, students, and parents are treated; and the manner in which the telephone is answered.

A very interesting study was conducted by Dr. Leslie Brady, focusing on principals of effective schools and less than effective schools relative to their interaction with the community. As Brady states, ''The purpose of the study was to determine if principals of effective schools reported actions that were significantly different than the actions of principals of less than effective schools'' (Brady, 1989).

A questionnaire was sent to a selected sample of secondary school principals in Ohio (fifty principals) based on their reputations of being principals of effective schools or principals of less than effective schools. Responses were received from thirty-one principals from effective or good schools, and nineteen from less than effective or problem schools.

The principals were asked to which of four groups they owed their highest allegiance (Table 2.1):

Table 2.1. Amount of allegiance toward groups.

Group	Schools	
	Good	**Problem**
Other citizens (no child in your school)	3.04	2.56
Parents (with child in your school)	3.74	3.44
People in the system who provide support services for my work	3.37	3.19
People in the system with direct administrative authority over my position	3.67	3.75

Note: 4 = highest allegiance, 1 = little allegiance.
Source: Brady, L. 1989. "Principals in Good and Problem Secondary Schools in Ohio Report Interaction with the External Environment," reprinted and reformatted with permission from the author.

(1) Other citizens

(2) Parents

(3) People in the system who provided support services for my work

(4) People in the system with direct administrative authority over my position

Principals of effective (good) schools reported the highest allegiance to parents, while principals of less than effective (problem) schools reported the highest allegiance to people in the system with direct administrative authority over their positions. The study further indicated that effective principals, caught in the middle between administrative directives and the will of the people, will be more likely to side with the people.

The principals were asked to respond to a question that related to their preference for active participation or no participation from four groups (Table 2.2):

(1) Other citizens

(2) Parents

(3) People in the system who provided support services for my work

(4) People in the system with direct administrative authority over my position

Principals of effective (good) schools preferred active participation from parents, while principals of less than effective (problem) schools preferred active participation from the people in the system with direct

Table 2.2. Principals' preferences regarding level of participation from groups.

Group	Schools	
	Good	Problem
Other citizens (no child in your school)	3.52	3.06
Parents (with child in your school)	4.00	3.25
People in the system who provide support services for my work	3.89	3.63
People in the system with direct administrative authority over my position	3.67	3.81

Note: 4 = active participation, 1 = no participation.
Source: Brady, L. 1989. ''Principals in Good and Problem Secondary Schools in Ohio Report Interaction with the External Environment,'' reprinted and reformatted with permission from the author.

administrative authority over their positions. Principals of problem schools ranked active participation from the parent group as their third preferred category of the four categories to which they were asked to respond.

The study found that principals of effective schools were more active in the community, giving speeches or presentations, than were the principals of less than effective schools (Table 2.3).

Although there was one group, ''professional meetings,'' where the principals of less than effective schools gave more speeches or presentations than the principals of effective schools, principals of good schools took a more active stance in sharing the school story with the community.

Principals need to have information about community concerns. One question asked principals about their sources of information about community concerns (Table 2.4).

While principals from both good and problem schools relied on formal school advisory groups and informal groups, the principals from good schools relied heavily on volunteers in their schools as sources of information about the school and community concerns. Principals of the problem schools relied more heavily on beauticians, barbers, or other similar service people for their information than did principals of good schools.

The principals were asked the importance they placed on paying attention to various groups. Principals of good schools indicated a high importance to paying attention to parents, differing significantly from the principals of problem schools. This serves as a further indicator of the linkage between principals of effective schools and parents.

Table 2.3. Number of times principals gave speeches or presentations to groups.

	Schools	
Group	**Good**	**Problem**
Parents group	2.18	1.00
Ad hoc group	1.36	.63
Kiwanis, Lions, or other civic club	1.39	.81
Professional meeting (education related)	1.64	1.13
Women's service group	.82	.63
Community group	1.39	1.25
Professional meeting (not education related)	.86	.88

Note: 1 = one time or less, 4 = ten times or more.
Source: Brady, L. 1989. "Principals in Good and Problem Secondary Schools in Ohio Report Interaction with the External Environment," reprinted and reformatted with permission from the author.

The last question to be included here is the one asking principals if they tried to influence various segments of the community (Table 2.5).

Principals of effective schools were more active in trying to influence service clubs and industry than principals of less than effective schools, with the exception of banks and other fiscal agencies, where principals of less than effective schools tried a little harder. Effective principals took a more active position.

Brady summarizes by saying, "In conclusion, the findings of the research give substantial support to the idea that principals of effective schools interact with the community, and value the interaction. In terms of interaction with the community, principals of effective schools differ significantly from principals of less than effective schools" (Brady, 1989).

Table 2.4. Sources of information about the school.

	Schools	
Source	**Good**	**Problem**
Volunteers in your school	2.30	1.69
Informal groups (such as a coffee klatsch)	2.78	2.13
Formal school advisory groups	3.48	3.00
Beauticians, barbers, or other similar service people	1.33	1.63
People who live by the school	2.04	2.00

Note: 1 = not a source, 4 = important source.
Source: Brady, L. 1989. "Principals in Good and Problem Secondary Schools in Ohio Report Interaction with the External Environment," reprinted and reformatted with permission from the author.

Table 2.5. How much principals try to influence community members.

Community Groups	Schools	
	Good	Problem
Service clubs and fraternal organizations	2.33	1.50
Media (newspaper, radio, TV)	2.78	2.00
Business and industry	2.15	1.56
Recreational agencies	1.78	1.44
Local or county government (not including school board)	1.93	1.56
Colleges and universities	2.07	1.88
Chamber of commerce	1.59	1.44
Labor organizations	1.52	1.38
Churches and other religious groups	1.78	1.75
Banks and other fiscal agencies	1.37	1.38

Note: 4 = a great deal, 1 = little.
Source: Brady, L. 1989. "Principals in Good and Problem Secondary Schools in Ohio Report Interaction with the External Environment," reprinted and reformatted with permission from the author.

The key role that principals play in building the public's confidence cannot be overstated. They have the students in the schools, who are the prime source of information for their parents and the community. Inasmuch as attitudes are based largely on our own experiences and those of people we trust and love, we need to recognize that students' attitudes are important. When children speak poorly about a school and have unsatisfactory experiences at school, their parents, relatives, and friends will see the school in a similar light. Despite the fact that it may well have an outstanding program, support for the program will not be forthcoming.

By reaching out to the community and getting to know who they are, what their concerns are, and what they would like to see in the school, a principal is able to respond. The community needs to get to know the principal not only as the educational leader of the school, but as a person who understands them, gives them "straight" answers, and can be trusted. The principal needs to earn the respect of the community and take a proactive role in establishing meaningful communication between the school and the community, students, and staff. To do otherwise is to ask for a short-lived stay at the school.

There is no question that changes will be taking place in schools as a result of the many pressures to reform education. When changes need to be made, the principal who has been accepted by, and is in touch with, the community will accomplish the changes more easily, and with community support, than the principal who is not known and has not gained the confidence of the community. The days are gone when principals remain in the office most of the day "doing paperwork." Principals are out and about; they recognize the value of maintaining personal contact with the many publics served by the school.

Directors

A director usually has responsibility for a curriculum area or a specific operation. Another title for this type of position could well be supervisor or coordinator. It is a middle management position. Many times the directors have limited authority and decision-making power; they are the conveyors of information, directives, and the like.

Their ability to communicate up and down the line is crucial to their being effective, as is their ability and willingness to talk with community groups and staff about their program. A good way for the public to learn firsthand about the program is to hear the information from the professional. Community members can generally have their questions answered by a director because he/she is familiar with all aspects of his/her program. The directors or supervisors can gain tremendous support by going out to the community.

"Research has shown that school employees prefer to receive information from their supervisors directly rather than through the grapevine" (Palmer Gould, 1989). Directors must recognize this fact and identify communication strategies that will work best for them, e.g., formal and informal meetings; small, informal discussions; periodic written communications; inservice/staff development activities; and conferences. Supervisors should consider open forums, coffees, and teas as less formal means for sharing information and discussions.

Supervisors must not hesitate to accept an invitation to speak, as they know the program best. An invitation is a welcome opportunity to cultivate new supporters. When a vote is to be taken by the school board concerning a program, people who have become familiar with the program through these speeches can usually be counted on to support that program. Boards are swayed by numbers of people and the statements they make.

Department Chairs

Depending on the job description, the department chair may be full- or part-time, responsible for staff in one or more buildings or curriculum areas. Part-time department chairs are usually responsible for the curriculum in their own building.

As with directors, department chairs must share information with the teaching staff and must maintain good rapport with the staff and the administration. They may be asked to be the building's/district's chief speaker for their particular curriculum area; they may be charged with staff observations and supervision. Above all else, they need to know what is going on in their departments, what the strengths and weaknesses are, and must be able to effect changes as they see fit. They need to keep abreast of the literature in the field and be knowledgeable of what works and what does not.

Their activities are largely confined to dealing with members of the department, building and central office administrators, the students who are or will be taking courses, and, on occasion, the parents of the students. While recognizing the emphasis placed on their program, the department chair should not isolate himself/herself from the staff members in the other departments. It is imperative to reach out to the other departments to avoid isolating your department and creating a "we-they" situation. All departments are part of the school and are only as strong as the weakest link. Being a member of the team is important; they can help when support is needed.

Teachers

The teacher is the linking pin between the student, the home, and the school. Teachers are the people who make coming to school a joy or a disappointment. How they talk and listen to students and their parents, respond to questions, teach and challenge students, and care and understand students' problems, triggers a response. Students are delighted when teachers are knowledgeable, patient, caring, and have a sense of humor. Praise and a smile go a long way towards making students feel good about school. No child wants to come to school to be frustrated.

Teachers should communicate with parents early and often, instead of waiting until the student has gotten into trouble. The parents should be contacted early in the school year. A telephone call within the first few weeks of school by the teacher introducing himself/herself is sure to impress the parents. They will feel the care shown for their child and will offer support when they are called with a problem at a later date. This will open the door and extend a welcoming arm; parents appreciate that very much.

A child should know when he/she is doing well. A note to the child or the parent takes but a few minutes, and will be well received. Many teachers' notes are hung on refrigerator doors because the family is so proud to have received them and to know that the teacher has noticed their child.

Teachers are the first to see the children in the morning and the last to see them at the end of the day. It is important to greet them with a smile, and send them home feeling good about themselves. Teachers can make a child's day!

Guidance Counselors

The value of getting to know a student on a one-to-one basis is recognized by guidance counselors. Counselors schedule both large and small group meetings to inform students of such things as graduation requirements, the next year's program offerings, and the need to plan a course of study. They try to follow up these meetings with individual conferences with students, where they talk about the student's progress, likes, dislikes, future plans, and problems.

Counselors often talk with parents on the telephone and at conferences because many parents want to be involved in decisions that affect their children. However, no parent should be written off. A determined effort must be made to contact those parents who do not come. These no-show parents may not be familiar with the processes of the school, may be intimidated by the school, just don't know what to do once they get there, or may be too busy working to come to school. It is the counselor's responsibility to reach out and encourage them to come. Parents need to know that they are wanted and needed. An understanding counselor can lay the foundation for future meetings, telephone calls, and conversations. Once parents feel that they are welcome and are valued, they will feel much better about coming to school and will make every effort to get there when needed. They will be very positive about the school.

Recognizing the current drug and alcohol abuse problems in the schools, school districts have employed crisis intervention and drug and alcohol abuse counselors. Their hours usually extend far beyond the regular school day; these counselors are called on at all hours of the day and night. They interact with members of other community agencies while resolving problems. The positive public relations created as a result of the work of these counselors cannot be overstated.

Library Media Specialists

Students use the new open libraries in place at many schools far more frequently than they did previously, when they could only go to the library for half an hour during the class's scheduled weekly library period. How welcome they feel and whether or not they go depends largely on the attitude of the library media specialist. When the media specialist is more interested in working with students than shelving books and maintaining order, students flock to the library. They go there to work because they know that the librarian cares and is trying to help them, that the librarian is interested in what they are doing. Parents are told about their children's visits to the library and they see the books their children bring home to read. Where children are welcome, circulation is high, parents are pleased, and support for the library/media center is high. Many parents volunteer their time to help out in the library because they know that if they do so the librarian can do more with, and for, the children.

The library/media center is an excellent place to schedule meetings attended by community members. Strangers to the school generally walk out feeling that their tax money is working for them. Media centers generate good public relations.

Nurses

School nurses, nurse practitioners, and aides work with students by doing routine screenings, maintaining health records, and helping students when they are sick or hurt. They talk to parents and doctors as needed. The caring, understanding, and professional manner they use dealing with illness and emergencies is comforting to parents. The positive public relations created by them is difficult to measure. More often than not, parents are pressuring school districts to staff the school clinics with full-time nurses.

Secretaries

The first person that an individual talks to on the telephone or when visiting a school is the secretary who reflects the attitude of the building principal towards students, parents, staff, and visitors. When a principal wants to sit in the office behind a closed door and keep people at a distance, the secretary makes sure that this happens. On the other hand, when a principal welcomes people to the office, secretaries respond in like manner. Secretaries have been known to make a complete turnabout with the coming of a new principal. The chances are that if the secretary does not make the change, she/he will not keep the position very long.

A ready smile, kind voice, understanding, willingness to listen and lend a helping hand, should all be job prerequisites. They go beyond the technical skills that a secretary needs; they are the people skills that are needed in that position. Secretaries can make a caller feel comfortable and welcome. They can usually calm an angry person down and get to the heart of why a person has called or come to school. They need to balance professionalism and friendliness.

The reception area of the school office needs to reflect the school climate. It should not be a lounge area, but it should be maintained to reflect a business-like office environment that serves students.

Are the secretaries an element in a good public relations program? They most certainly are – they are in the front lines. An enthusiastic secretary who is upbeat about the school and its staff and students reflects most favorably on the school.

Custodians and Maintenance Personnel

Many times a visitor to the building will see a custodian or a maintenance person before seeing the school secretary.

Custodians are a very important part of the educational system. The basic reason for having school custodians is to ensure clean, safe, attractive, efficient, functioning facilities. If custodians execute their responsibilities faithfully, conscientiously and intelligently, the results will be most satisfying and rewarding. Students and their teachers will, as a result, gain the full advantage of the academic and technical facilities that our school systems offer; facilities where children can learn and teachers can teach, that encourage desired positive public relations. (ASBO, International, 1986)

When the school building is used after school hours by community groups, they deal with the custodians in order to gain access to the designated area in the building. The interaction between the custodian and the user needs to be friendly and positive. Community members remember how they are treated in the building.

Most custodians and maintenance workers live in the school district, influence their neighbors, and vote at election time. They should be treated with respect and informed of what is going on in the building/district. The administration should meet with them to let them know they are pleased with their work and to share information with them. It would be wise to place the head custodian on the agenda of a faculty meeting from time to time, and to recognize him/her as the vital member of the staff that he/she is.

Food Service Workers

This group of dedicated school district employees often takes on the role of surrogate parent in terms of the students' breakfasts (where they are available) and lunches. Despite the fact that they are the lowest of the paid support personnel, they work very hard, take tremendous pride in their work, and like nothing better than having the children eat the food they prepare (Educational Research Service, 1989).

Food service workers generally live in the vicinity of the school in which they work; much of the time they walk to work. They know the community, they are looked to as trusted sources of information about the school. They should not be ignored or taken for granted. Administrators should talk to them about problem areas, the direction that the district/school is heading, and the goals that have been set for the school; they should enlist their support, and tell them how much they mean to the school/district. Such efforts will be well rewarded.

School Bus Drivers

The job of the school bus drivers is not an easy one. They make two or three runs twice a day, bringing the children to and from school. Many times they take the kindergarten runs, field trips, and extracurricular activities. The bus drivers have direct charge over hundreds of students while they are driving the busses.

When problems occur on the bus, the drivers use an established procedure for reporting the problem/student to the school. There is nothing more frustrating to a bus driver than to have a complaint ignored. Administrators should take time and give the driver feedback as to what action was taken with reference to the complaints that were filed. Let the drivers know their efforts are appreciated. Consider planning a ''thank you'' coffee for them. They should not be taken for granted. They are key communicators in the community and have access to many citizens. It is important that they know that administrators recognize the job they do and support them.

Crossing Guards

Although they are generally on the city's payroll rather than on the school district's, crossing guards enable your students to cross dangerous intersections safely. In many cities they are political appointees serving at the whim of the mayor/supervisor and have ties into the political structure of the city.

They stand out in the streets for hours and cannot leave their duty stations; they are out on the cold days when it is freezing and on the hot days when the heat is oppressive. Offer them a cup of coffee on a cold winter day, or a cool drink on a hot day. Invite them to visit the school, have lunch, or attend a student performance. Build a positive relationship with these very special people.

Doing Our Job

> Public relations is the practice of social responsibility. It consists first of seeing that the right thing is done, seeing that our schools are indeed acting in the best interest of boys and girls and the community, that we are doing our job to the best of our ability. Public relations is based on action, on our performance. (Wherry, 1979)

The foregoing notwithstanding, the reality is that unless administrators take very specific actions to tell the community what is going on in the schools, parents and community members will continue to rely on the information they read in the newspapers or hear on the radio. They will continue to hear negative press.

With the issue of choice at the doorstep, administrators must take a proactive role and use public relations strategies to keep the communities involved and informed. The following chapters deal with specific hands-on practices that have worked and should serve administrators well.

Public relations is not based on one person's action, on one person's performance; it is based on the action and performance of everyone associated with the operation of the schools. Public relations is everyone's job!

CHAPTER 3

DEALING WITH OUR PUBLICS

I N talking about the publics that a school serves, we are essentially talking about two publics—the internal public and the external public. Are they different, and do we use different strategies to reach them? Yes, we do.

The Internal Public

Who Are They?

They are the students and staff of a school/district; the students who are in the buildings and the employees of the school district—professional and support staff, both in the school buildings and in the district offices.

Why Concern Yourself with Them?

Concern yourself with members of the internal public because they are the lifeblood of the school and because no good external public relations program can survive without a good internal program. A good internal two-way communication program is essential for the well-being of the school. When people are aware of what is going on and are involved, they very often make suggestions that have not been considered because they view situations from different vantage points. As they become more involved, they develop an allegiance and a loyalty to the organization, support the efforts under way, and are more productive.

As indicated in the survey reported earlier, students are a prime source of information for their parents. They can convey a message from a unique vantage point. If students feel good about their classes, do well, and understand what is going on, they will speak well of the school and respond positively to questions. On the other hand, if students are uninformed and do not know what is going on, their frustrations are vented at home and in the community. They raise obvious questions about the school and speak negatively about what is going on. It is then difficult for the family and friends to believe statements issued by the school that are in direct contrast to what they ''know'' is going on. Students' opinions influence not only their parents, but their relatives, friends, and adults in the community they contact.

Staff members often live in the school community and come into contact with relatives, friends, and neighbors. They are often the ones that are asked about the district because ''they work for the district, therefore they should know.'' Staff members who do not live in the district often go shopping in the district, join organizations in the community, and seek medical care in the vicinity of their work location. They, too, are always being asked questions.

There is a need to attract and retain quality staff members. If people feel left out and uninformed, they will have low morale and look to move to a district where they will, at least, know what is going on. Employees generally have a vested interest in the school district, and do not like to be the last to be informed about what is about to take place. They want to be knowledgeable and involved to the highest degree possible. The major effort to move to school-based management represents a clear illustration of the interest of the professional staff in becoming more involved in matters that relate to their job responsibilities. They want to be informed and involved in making decisions that affect them.

What Do They Want to Know?

Students want to know about the areas that directly affect them, such as:

- what the course requirements are
- the length of the school day, school year
- what the extracurricular program is like
- who the teachers are
- whether they can choose their own courses, their own teachers, their own schedule

- whether there is a discipline code in the building, and how it is enforced
- whether there is a guidance counselor
- who the administrators are, what they are like
- whether there are opportunities for student government

Employees of the district are interested in the success of the students, the financial well-being of the district, district/department budget, staffing and pupil/teacher ratios, goals and directions of the district, programs being implemented and planned, condition of the physical plant and facilities, union contracts (where applicable), salary schedules, benefits, retirement plans, and opportunities for advancement.

How Do We Communicate with Students?

Generally we do not communicate very well with students. All too often the students are not recognized as the key communication link they are with their parents and the community. If something happens at the school, students are usually among the last to find out what has occurred. They learn what they can by picking up information here and there. We do not take the time to establish mechanisms for sharing information with students. There is a need to establish lines of communication and make contact with the students, involving them in accordance with their age/grade.

Welcome the Students to School

It takes little effort to send a letter to the students in your building welcoming them back to school. A letter coming at the end of August is usually well received. The letter could tell the parents and students what has been going on during the course of the summer and the preparations that have been made for the opening of school. It could list dates and times for the first few days of school, school meetings that you would like the parents to know about, the names and telephone numbers of key staff members, and the like. Informing parents that you would be pleased to talk with them sets a very positive tone for the year.

The cost of the letter can be cut substantially from the first-class rate by using third-class bulk mail. In order to use the bulk third-class mail option, each mailing must consist of a minimum of 200 pieces, each weighing less than sixteen ounces, and contain a general message aimed at all who receive it, rather than a personal message aimed at a particular individual (United States Postal Service, 1988). The contents of the letter must not be individualized or personalized in any way; all letters must be identical. The only place where any personalization may take place is on the address label. By skillfully designing the label, limited personal information can be sent to the student. For example, if you want to give the students their room assignments, you can use the label.

In the letter you can say, ''Your homeroom number is the number located in the upper right hand corner of the address label. Please report to that room when you come to school on . . .'' The label could look like this:

```
┌---------------------------┐
│                       203 │
│ Lee Jones                 │
│ 123 East 45 Street        │
│ Anytown, USA  12345       │
└---------------------------┘
```

A bulk mail permit is required and can be obtained at a post office. This permit is good for twelve months (Figure 3.1). There are specific requirements for using, preparing, and packaging bulk mail (Figure 3.2). Bulk mail may not be dropped into collection boxes or left on a post office receiving dock. It must be deposited during operating hours at a bulk mail acceptance unit at the post office where your permit is held. Select the main post office in the city most convenient for your needs (United States Postal Service, 1988).

Payment for the mailing can be made by using precanceled stamps, permit imprint, or a postage meter (Figure 3.3). The cost for each piece of bulk mail depends on the presorting that you do: the basic presort, the five-digit presort, or the carrier route presort. The current rate for the bulk mail permit and the rates for the various categories of bulk mail are available at your post office. Ask for the ''Current Rates and Fees'' chart. An informal aid to third-class mailers, ''Creative Solutions for Your Business Needs, Third-Class Mail Preparation,'' is available at your post office. It is an easy guide to follow. Most postal clerks will be happy to help you decide how, when, and whether to use bulk mail.

Be Visible

Greet the students when they get off the busses in the morning, or when they walk into the building. Let them see you, talk to them, learn their names. Just a few new names each day will soon result in knowing

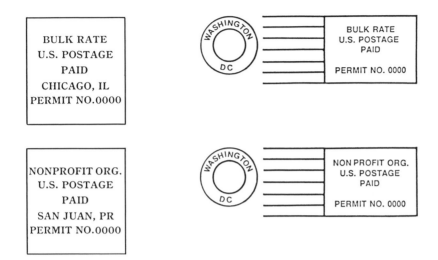

Figure 3.1 Permit imprint.

many of the students. It will surely impress them when they realize that you know who they are.

Exemplary Practice: There is a high school principal in Missouri who takes fifty of the picture Rolodex cards of the entering class home with him each week in the summertime in order to familiarize himself with the faces and names of the incoming students. He gets the cards from the sending school. By the end of the summer he has memorized the faces and names of the entering class. Needless to say, when he calls the students by name on the first day of school, the students just do not understand how he does it. He gains their respect immediately.

Be visible during passing time between classes; be in the school cafeteria; be out in the hall at the end of the day. Talk to the students and let them know that you are there for them and that you are approachable.

Drop in on Classes

Make it a point to drop in on the classes. One very effective way to do this is to drop in on all the classes during the first period of the first day back in school. Say something like, "Hello, welcome back. I want you to know that I am your principal and I am here if you want to talk with

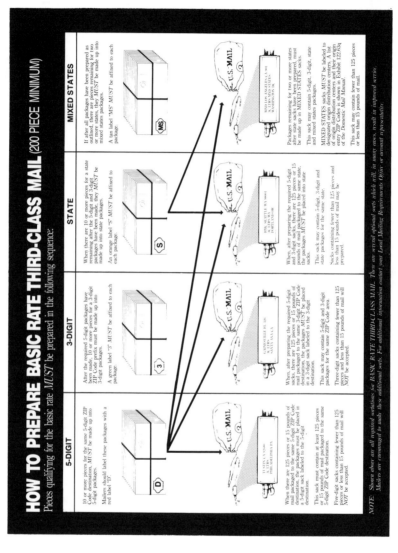

Figure 3.2

Each bulk rate mailing requires payment of postage.

METHODS OF PAYMENT

There are three methods of postage payment for your bulk mailing. They are:

1. Precanceled Stamps
2. Permit Imprint
3. Postage Meter

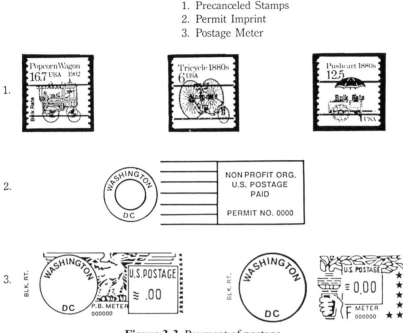

Figure 3.3 Payment of postage.

me. I will be back to visit your class, but right now I am going to welcome the other boys and girls back to school. Have a great school year!'' and move on to the next class. By not slowing down and not engaging in conversation, you should cover a fairly large school within the first hour of school, before the students change periods.

Have Lunch with the Students

Make it a point to have lunch with a small group of students in your office once a week. Consider asking students to sign up if they would like to eat with you. Then select a small group of some ten to twelve students and invite them. Keep the agenda open so that students can discuss a topic(s) that is troubling them. If you have the funds, buy their lunch. If not, you can ask them to bring a bag lunch or buy their lunch and bring it into your office/conference room. When the lunch is going on, do not let telephone calls or visitors interrupt the meeting. Keep it informal and be responsive to their questions.

Many parents have reported how surprised they were to see their children fussing with the selection of school clothes one morning. And when asked why they were getting dressed up, the students exhibited tremendous pride in saying, "I am having lunch with the principal today." You can easily have lunch with 450−500 students in your building during the course of the school year.

Maintain an Open Door Policy to Your Office

Keep an open door policy when you are in the office. Let students and staff see you working or talking with someone. If someone lingers and looks as if they want to talk to you, encourage them to come in and talk with you. Be pleasant and do not be annoyed that they are seeking you out. Consider it a compliment that the student or staff member wants to see you. Close the door only when the matter being discussed is serious and you cannot be disturbed.

Use the Intercom/Public Address System (PA)

Make a decision as to how and when you are going to use the intercom/PA. Do not get on it several times a day and say nothing. All too often the staff and students are tired of hearing the "same old thing" every morning. They tune it out and don't even listen when it comes on. Consideration needs to be given as to what the best time is to make announcements and who will make them. Most schools have students make the announcements in the morning, before classes begin, and they do not make them again that day.

Student Bulletin Boards

Schools have placed bulletin boards in areas that are readily accessible to students. Notices are put up that follow up on the morning announcements and serve as reminders. Future announcements are also identified. Items that come up during the day are also posted. Students soon learn to look at the bulletin boards on a routine basis.

Meet with the Student Government Association

Be available to attend meetings of the student government association in your building. Although they have a sponsor, they may want to discuss a matter with you directly. It may be that you have some information that you want to share with the student government association, or you may want to solicit their input on a matter. Know when they are meeting and make it a practice to be available.

Student Advisory Committees

You may be considering making a change and decide that you would like student input. This can be obtained by including a student representative on the committee or by forming a student advisory committee. The designation of the advisory committee members is often left to the students and their governance structures. If you are selecting the members, make certain that the advisory committee is representative of the student body. As in working with adults, give the committee a specific charge, timeline, and support needed for them to reach consensus on the matter.

Join in on the Activities of a Class

When walking around the building, drop in on classrooms. Join an academic activity or one of the labs. Make a small project that will not take too long to complete. Students in the class will be very impressed that the principal can actually do something; they will tell everyone who will listen. Visit the physical education classes and, if you feel comfortable, pick up a ball and shoot a basket or two.

Exemplary Practice: A junior high school principal was walking through the hall when a basketball came rolling into the hall from the gymnasium. She picked it up and walked into the gym with it. The students started chanting, ''Shoot, shoot, shoot!'' She went to the foul line and shot a basket, getting it in. The students said it was an accident and urged her to try again. Reluctantly the principal went to the foul line and shot again. She scored a second basket. When the students called for her to do it again, she did not and said, ''You have seen me shoot twice now, you know that I can.'' She was afraid that she would not be able to hit a third basket and wanted to quit while she was ahead. The next issue of the school newspaper carried the headline: "Principal Makes It Two for Two."

The good will and respect that the principal earned by shooting baskets was not anticipated when she started walking down the hall. Take advantage of every opportunity to interact with the students.

Student Discipline

Let the students know what the discipline code is in your building early in the year. Enforce the code in a fair, firm, and consistent manner. Students can understand a code, but have a problem when the administration is not consistent in enforcing it.

When Dr. Michael Altman, Principal of Clallam Bay School, Sekui, Washington, was the Assistant Principal at Wasilla High School in Wasilla, Alaska, he recognized the need for uniform, consistent guidelines for the school's extracurricular programs. He put together a comprehensive *Coach's/Sponsor's Handbook* that very clearly spells out the school's expectations and procedures relative to duties of the activities' sponsors, fund raising, out-of-district travel, and athletic rules. The Activity Code also spells out expectations for students. The students and their parents are asked to read the Activity Code and return the Activity Code Permission Slip for retention in the school files until the close of the activity (Figure 3.4).

Some districts have a document that details the student's rights and responsibilities. The document is distributed to the students at the beginning of each school year and discussed in either their social studies or English class during the first week of school. The students and their parents are asked to sign a slip indicating that they are aware of the contents of the document. This signed slip is placed in the student's file.

Resolve Disputes at the Lowest Possible Level

Resolve disputes at the lowest possible level so that the matter does not escalate. Do not feel that you, as the administrator, must be involved with everything. Many times the teachers themselves can resolve problems. Problems are kept to a minimum when there are clearly defined expectations and steps identified in handling violations. At Wasilla High School, Alaska, when a coach or sponsor has the team on

Revised 5-22-85

WASILLA HIGH SCHOOL ACTIVITY CODE

PERMISSION SLIP

PLEASE RETURN SIGNED CODE TO MAIN OFFICE

_____
ACTIVITY

_____   _____
Student's Signature   Parent or Guardian's Signature

_____   _____
Date   Date

Figure 3.4

47

the road and finds that a student has broken the controlled substance laws, and has been drinking or taking drugs, there is a set policy in place so that the coach can respond while affording the student his/her due process. All staff members have, and can refer to, a small card that reminds the coach or sponsor of what to do in case of substance abuse.

Exemplary Practice: Recognizing the need to resolve disputes at the lowest possible level and to maintain continuity in the application of the school's discipline code, the following procedure was used by Wasilla High School.

If the alleged violation is substance abuse, call the local police or the state troopers. This is important for a couple of reasons: (1) it is illegal for a student who is under the drinking age to consume alcohol, and (2) the use of drugs is also illegal. In notifying the police, the coach or administrator in a sense gives the problem away and does not "bring it back home" with him/her.

When a coach or sponsor brings a problem back home, it becomes the administration's problem to deal with. The student must be disciplined, all details must be rehashed, the other students are looking to see what discipline will be meted out, parents have to be apprised of the incident, coaches have to be disciplined for not following instructions, etc.! However, if a coach calls the local law enforcement agency, reports the incident and turns the problem over to them, it becomes very clean. If the police find out that the kid has been drinking or smoking dope they may arrest the student or write him/her a ticket or whatever they do in that situation. If, on the other hand, the student is found innocent by the local law enforcement authorities, then the issue is dead.

Suppose the student is found guilty by the local law enforcement agency, then what? The student is suspended from participating on the team for the remainder of the school year. The high school administration does not get a lot of complaints from the parents, the other students clearly see that the high school administration does not put up with that sort of thing and everyone sees that the high school administration enforces the rules of the district and the *Coaches and Sponsor's Handbook,* vis-a-vis the Student Activity Code, which all sign. (Altman, 1989)

Student Handbooks

Student handbooks are an excellent way to give routine information that is needed by all students and their parents. Information such as attendance policies, student conduct, smoking, grading and testing, promotion, extra- and cocurricular activities, field trips, bell schedules, identification cards, and lockers, can be published in a small brochure, or in a heavy-duty, coated pocket-folder that is printed with the school's mascot on the front cover and the remaining information on the other sides. Newburgh Free Academy (NFA), Newburgh, New York, a nationally recognized High School of Excellence, issues each student entering the school a student handbook which contains much of the information that is routinely shared with students and their parents. It is expected that the student will retain the handbook for the three years that they attend the school. The cover is laminated to give it additional durability. The table of contents is arranged by topic (Figure 3.5).

Class Discussions

There are times when school-related, non-curricular matters are raised during regular classroom instructional periods. Encourage the teachers to take the few minutes necessary to respond to student questions. If teachers do not have the necessary information, they may tell the student where the information can be obtained. If the topic under discussion is deemed important enough, a staff member who has greater expertise, or who is more intimately involved with the topic under discussion, can usually be asked to visit with the class the next time it meets. Whatever you decide to do, do not ignore a request for information.

How Do We Communicate with Staff?

Staff members are often among the last to be told what is going on in the district. Very often they learn about what is happening in the district or their own buildings when, or even after, it actually happens. Some administrators do not feel that it is necessary to inform or involve staff. But employees need to be involved, they need to know what is going on for many of the same reasons as students—they are key communication links to the parents and community, and they have a vested interest in their building and the district. Do not overlook the input they can offer. Recognize that they view situations from their particular vantage points and very often can offer suggestions that have not been considered. When employees are informed and have an opportunity to give input, they support the end result. To put it another way: when they help write it, they underwrite it.

TABLE OF CONTENTS

2

Figure 3.5

50

STUDENT ACTIVITIES

MISCELLANEOUS

NEWBURGH FREE ACADEMY

3

Reproduced from *The Newburgh Free Academy Student Handbook*, Newburgh, New York.

Figure 3.5 (continued)

Topeka Public Schools has a regulation whose subject is "Building-Level Communications." This regulation's purpose is "to define the basic communications program of each school." Among other areas that it covers, item III, D, "Communications with Staff," states "Each principal will communicate regularly with staff via bulletins, conferences, and staff meetings" (Figure 3.6).

Contract Service Employees

In addition to the cadre of employees traditionally found in a school building, there may be employees of a company that is operating a contract service for the district, such as food service or custodial/maintenance operations, working in your building. Do not ignore these people. They are interested in the building and district in which they work; they want to know what is going on. Recognize this and make every effort to share information with them. Coordinate with the representatives of the contract service company how the information is to be given to these employees to be certain that you are in compliance with the company's procedures. The sharing could take the form of a memorandum that presents the information, or one of their employees could be invited to attend one of your meetings. Yet another way to accomplish this is to attend one of their meetings and be given time to talk about the school/district and what is going on. Afford the employees an opportunity to ask questions. Listen to what they have to say. They will very often present ideas that are not forthcoming from the district employees. They will be appreciative of your coming to share information with them; you will have gained support from yet another group of employees.

Welcome Them Back Each Year

Staff members feel good when they receive a letter from the building principal and/or the superintendent of schools welcoming them back to the new school year. Just make certain that you do not use the same letter year after year.

Many districts invite all their employees to a district-wide meeting that is preceded by a continental breakfast. Although the format varies by district, the district-wide meeting is generally one in which the chairman of the school board, the superintendent of schools, and the union president all present inspirational messages. They are followed by a motivational speaker and small work sessions related to the district's

TOPEKA PUBLIC SCHOOLS	REGULATION NUMBER: 2525-8
SUBJECT: BUILDING-LEVEL COMMUNICATIONS	DATE OF ISSUE: 7/29/80
	REVISIONS: 2/9/83; 3/22/85; 10/24/86
	PREPARING OFFICE: COMMUNICATIONS DEPARTMENT

I. PURPOSE:

To define the basic communications program of each school.

II. PERSONNEL AFFECTED:

Building administrators and staffs.

III. Each school will maintain a planned communications program, including as a minimum the following as regular communications channels:

A. Conferences

Parent-teacher conferences will be held in all schools at the end of the first and third quarters. Grade cards will be used as a means of communicating student progress at the end of each quarter.

Individual conferences with parent(s) will be scheduled as needed.

B. Newsletters

Building administrators will send a newsletter to the parents of the students attending their school preferably at least once a month.

Information copies of the newsletter should be sent to the Communications Department and the General Directors of Elementary and Secondary Education.

C. Parent Organizations

Each school will maintain an active parent organization as an advisory support group to the school.

D. Communications with Staff

Each principal will communicate regularly with staff via bulletins, conferences, and staff meetings.

E. Communications with the Central Administration

Building administrators will keep the central administration informed of instructional and management developments in their schools, primarily through the General Directors of Elementary and Secondary Education.

Figure 3.6

yearly theme. Half a day is generally spent in these activities; the employees go back to their buildings in the afternoon.

Some districts realize that it may be more important for staff members to spend time in their own buildings preparing for the arrival of the students. In cases where no district-wide meeting of employees is held, and where there is a desire to deliver the same welcoming message of the superintendent of schools and/or chairman of the board, closed circuit television or videotaped messages are often used (Figure 3.7).

Many individual schools hold their own breakfast for their staff and invite the superintendent of schools, board members, union officials, and community leaders to attend their breakfast. Staff members feel that there is good support for the school when key administrators come and spend time with them. Recognizing that this could well place a strain on the invitees, it is necessary to set the date, and issue the invitations, well in advance of the actual date.

Be Visible

Just as visibility improves relations with students, it also improves relations with teachers and staff. Make it a point to get out of the office and visit the classrooms/schools as often as you can, and certainly do so early in the school year. There are superintendents of schools who make it a practice to personally visit each and every teacher in the district. They go into each teacher's room, shake the teacher's hand, and wish the teacher a good school year within the first few weeks of school. Building principals need to walk into the classrooms and show the teachers that they care. Visit with the staff over lunch; chat informally in a relaxed manner. Staff needs to get to know you as an individual rather than as an administrator. The human side of the school enterprise is very important to its success.

Be out in the halls at passing time. Stop and say hello to staff members on a casual basis. Get to know them and let them get to know you.

If you need to discuss a matter of importance, do not do it when there is not sufficient, uninterrupted time to spend on the matter. If it is urgent that you discuss a matter with a particular staff member, consider asking another staff member to take that person's class for a short time until the matter is taken care of. Do not walk into a room and have a conversation with the teacher while the class is coming in for the next period. You are not being fair to the staff member or to yourself. You are better off waiting until both parties can discuss the issue in a reasonable manner.

NEWBURGH
ENLARGED CITY SCHOOL DISTRICT

124 GRAND STREET   P. O. BOX 711   NEWBURGH, NEW YORK 12550   (914) 561-3232

Mr. Kenneth DeWitt - *Deputy Superintendent*
Mr. Alfred C. DiCesare - *Associate Superintendent*
Mr. Charles A. Winters - *Assistant Superintendent for Business*
Mr. Walter Millman - *Asst. Supt. for Instruction and Magnet Schools*
Ms. Donna L. Broyard - *Asst. to the Supt. Pupil Personnel Services*

Dr. Phillip E. Leahy — *Superintendent*

August 10, 1989

Dear Colleague:

As usual, the summer hiatus moves all too quickly and we are left with the words of the immortal Bard, "And summer's lease hath all too short a date."

Welcome back to another year filled with positive beginnings. Several of our schools are undergoing renovations and the addition to Gardnertown is underway. Our Magnet School Program is expanding with the addition of the Fostertown and Middle School Magnets, and the awarding of the approximately $1.4 million Federal grant.

Our orientation meeting will be held on Tuesday, September 5, 1989, at 8:00 a.m. at your individual building. The activities will be as follows:

8:00 - 8:30	Staff meets with Principal for coffee.
8:30 - 8:45	A taped welcome by Mr. Robert Roth, President of the Board, and Dr. Phillip E. Leahy, Superintendent of Schools.
8:45 - 11:55	Principal works with teachers.
12:00 - 1:00	---- Lunch ----
1:05 - 3:00	Classroom preparation and other tasks as assigned by your Principal.

All schools will be open on August 28 if you care to visit earlier. As usual, I will be in your building throughout the year to share ideas with you, but I also invite you to stop by the office at any time.

As always, I thank you for your cooperation and wish you a very rewarding year.

Sincerely,

Dr. Phillip E. Leahy
Superintendent of Schools

PEL/es

AN EQUAL OPPORTUNITY EMPLOYER

Figure 3.7

Keep your office door open and let staff see that you are there. Let them come in and say hello or ask you a quick question. Be in the outer office when staff are coming in to work. Greet them as if you are glad to see them; they deserve this. Consider having coffee available. The staff will gladly pay for the coffee if you cannot cover the cost.

Staff Handbook — District Level

Staff handbooks are written to address specific audiences and to accomplish specific purposes. One school district publishes a *Handbook of General Regulations and Practices* prepared by the Office of the Assistant Superintendent for Instructional Services. This handbook is given to each staff member with the understanding that, as the front cover states, "Each staff member is responsible for a knowledge of the information contained in this Handbook and is expected to observe any regulations stated herein. Questions should be referred to the building principal. The Handbook is to be retained in the classroom or office." The opening page of the handbook indicates that the handbook contains the "Regulations of the Board of Education and a compilation of the basic practices effecting the day to day operation of the schools. . . . Further information regarding these practices may be found in the Board of Education Policy Book in the Principal's Office or in the various directives from the State Education Department" (Newburgh City School District, 1982).

Staff members should not be frustrated because of day-to-day operational procedures. A ready reference such as this is an invaluable tool for the staff because they can find the answers to almost all of their questions. There should be a detailed index that facilitates the use of the handbook. As new or revised regulations or practices evolve, they should be issued and carry an identification number as to the section and page number. Topics covered in the handbook should include such items as absences, both employee and student; admission, placement and promotion of pupils; cafeteria charge accounts; certification of teachers; coffee breaks; deposit of monies; disaster preparedness; mandated subjects of instruction; homework; and opening exercises.

Staff Handbook — Building Level

Building principals usually put together their own staff handbooks, regardless of whether or not the district has one. These handbooks contain information that relates more directly to the building/program operation, and may contain a restatement of some of the more important board policies and district regulations. A typical table of contents could well include (not listed in priority order):

- statement by the principal or administrator
- philosophy – school and/or district
- names, addresses, and home telephone numbers of staff members in the building/program
- room assignments
- names, addresses, and telephone numbers of key central office staff and board members
- specialists, guidance counselors
- school calendar
- duty rosters – bus, lunchroom, bulletin boards, etc.
- conference days
- attendance – teacher and student
- arrival/dismissal procedures
- bell schedule
- fire drills
- faculty meetings – attendance, expectations
- staff development
- staff evaluation procedure
- map of the building
- safety plan for the building
- substitutes
- emergency school closings
- discipline policy – district and school
- homework policy – district and school
- dress policy – district and school
- lunchroom procedures
- assemblies
- grading, reporting to parents
- promotion/retention/acceleration procedures
- lesson plans
- student referral procedures
- cumulative record folders
- health and special needs of children
- supplies and equipment
- audio-visual equipment
- purchase orders – allocations

- school field trips
- forms
- visitors to the building
- confidentiality of records
- volunteers
- job descriptions

Staff Handbook — Program Area

Staff handbooks are often written by program directors where the personnel and program are housed in different buildings in the school district. There is a need to have common understandings and procedures regardless of the physical location of the program. Handbooks have been written in such areas as art, music, physical education, and special education. An example of a staff handbook written for a particular department is *Special Education Department Orientation Guide, 1989 – 1990 School Year.* It is an internal communications public relations handbook that was written because it was felt that:

> It is essential that the internal communication of the Special Education Department's practices and procedures be reviewed and reinforced on a yearly basis. If such communication is introduced at the beginning of the school year to new teachers, veteran teachers and all Sub-Committee members, then questions related to practices and procedures should be minimal. A yearly handbook/orientation guide is a fundamental tool which can be used to keep professional and non-professional staff abreast of changes in practices and procedures, as well as set expectations for how the Special Education Department should be operating in every school building. It is necessary to keep all professional and non-professional staff informed so that they can function better in their position. (Stanton-Cuevas, 1989)

It is advisable that the handbooks be loose-leaf editions so that changes/additions can be made as needed without requiring a major rewriting/reprinting. Do not take for granted that the staff knows what is in the handbook. Go over the important areas at a staff meeting early in the school year.

While the worth of the staff handbooks is recognized, there usually is a large group of employees who do not have a handbook and never get to see one. The support staff — the non-instructional staff — is generally the group that is by and large ignored in this area. Take the time to either draft a handbook for them, take appropriate portions from the building handbook, or plan a series of meetings at which time you can share the necessary information with them. By not addressing their needs, you are leaving a void in the communication chain.

Meetings

Meetings are valuable in that there can be an exchange of information and ideas if they are well planned and the timing controlled. Do not have a staff meeting just for the sake of having a meeting, or because it is Monday afternoon. Staff resent that; their time is valuable too. Call a meeting when that is the best vehicle to resolve an issue.

Do not call a general faculty meeting if the agenda involves certain people. Call a meeting of those people who are involved and can contribute to the meeting. Remember that as the number of participants goes down, efficiency usually increases. In planning the meeting, set specific outcomes for the meeting. Make certain that the group knows what the meeting is all about and has the available information they need in order to discuss the agenda item.

Structure the agenda so that it is meaningful and can be covered in a reasonable time. If there are items that you want to share, then do so. If an item is in print form, give it to the staff—do not read it to them. Some of the greatest resentment comes from having to sit and listen to an administrator read a notice that the employee has in his/her hand. If a discussion on the item is needed, hand out the printed material in advance of the meeting and ask the staff to come prepared to discuss the item at the next meeting.

In order to have a more productive meeting, send out the agenda and any support materials well in advance of the meeting. If specific assignments were made for participation at the meeting, contact the members and make certain that they understand what they are to do and that they are doing their homework.

Begin meetings on time, do not wait until the last person gets there. By delaying the start of the meeting, you are in essence punishing the people who arrived on time for the meeting and rewarding those individuals who were late. The staff will respect you for starting on time and the latecomers will realize that the time stated is, in fact, the time that the meeting will begin.

Do not let extraneous matters cloud the topic under discussion. Do not let any one individual monopolize the conversation or try to unduly pressure the others in the group. Do not allow side conversations to take place, because they tend to cause the meeting to break down. Recognize that humor relieves tension and can get the group back on track. Encourage some of the quieter participants to speak and contribute to the group. Try to reach consensus or a workable compromise when it is deemed in the best interest of all.

Take advantage of time available during the day for meetings. Most staffs have time during the course of the school day to use for planning purposes/prep time. Try to arrange for common planning time for the members of a team, grade level, or department. This facilitates their ability to meet on company time as opposed to meeting after school. This can be done through scheduling, be it with the "special teachers," or through the master schedule. Chapter 6, "Meetings and Conferences," contains additional information that will be helpful in planning and carrying out successful meetings.

Weekly Newsletters

In order to share information with your staff, consider issuing a weekly newsletter to them. One principal issued a newsletter called *Friday Flash* every Friday in order to share dates and information that the principal felt the staff needed to know. The faculty looked for the newsletter every week because they knew it had information that was meaningful to them. Using this means of communication eliminated the need for many faculty meetings. Additionally, the staff had a written record of notices and deadlines.

Staff Mailboxes and Bulletin Board

In all too many of the older schools, the faculty mailboxes and the staff bulletin boards are the first things that a visitor to the school office sees. The mailboxes and bulletin boards are for staff use. Consider moving them to a place less visible to the public. Monitor the notices on the bulletin board and have outdated items routinely removed. Identify areas on the bulletin board where you will put personnel items, district policies and regulations, etc. Encourage staff to use the bulletin board. Staff will then find the contents to be meaningful, be able to recognize the new items, and not be bogged down by having to wade through the old, outdated ones.

Recognize Accomplishments

Do not take people for granted. Give full credit to staff members for their personal accomplishments and those of their students. Send them a congratulatory note, with a copy to the superintendent of schools and their personnel file. Recognize them in their own buildings, before their peer groups, and at board meetings. If the accomplishment is outstanding, or the program is exceptional, consider asking the superintendent if you could have the teacher present it at the next board meeting.

When board meetings start out with program-related accomplishments, you usually end up with a positive meeting. The tone is set for the evening. Bring the winning teams, such as debate, athletics, math, and their coaches to the board meeting. Introduce them to the board and the public. Everyone feels good, and sometimes the newspapers will pick up the story.

Send a "glad note" to students and staff. Just a few words on a card will go a long way towards telling them that you know what they have accomplished and that you are pleased (Figure 3.8).

Impact Statement

Consider using an "impact statement" (Figure 3.9). This is a form on which staff members can give their comments and recommendations for additions, deletions, or changes pertaining to a particular item being addressed. Soliciting input and encouraging staff members to comment on a proposed change, or board policy, before it is in final form, gives the administration an opportunity to consider staff concerns and suggestions. It is anticipated that viable suggestions will be incorporated as the final document is being drafted.

Exemplary Practice: One superintendent of schools used this form in order to obtain staff reaction to proposed board policies and the corresponding implementing regulations. Staff could identify themselves or remain anonymous. It was helpful when individuals listed their names because they could then be contacted for clarification if needed. Where the name was listed, the superintendent responded to the staff member, relating what was done as a result of the comments made. In order to focus the comments, the impact statement asks the staff to consider certain items when commenting on the proposal (bottom of the form). This vehicle proved to be very effective; staff

Figure 3.8

were alerted to the proposed additions/changes to board policies and district practices, and staff had an opportunity to make comments, thus influencing the policies themselves.

Principal's Advisory Council

Principals need feedback from their staff. This is often difficult to obtain. Forming a Principal's Advisory Council (PAC) is one way to systematically obtain feedback from staff. The representatives should be elected by the faculty themselves. The council can consist of one member from each grade level, each department, or from the school, depending on the size and configuration of the school. This group is then asked to bring questions, comments, concerns, and suggestions to the meetings of the PAC. The meetings are generally non-threatening and do air some of the grievances troubling the staff.

Superintendent's Advisory Council

Operating in a manner similar to the Principal's Advisory Council, the Superintendent's Advisory Council (SAC) consists of elected members of each school in the district. They bring matters to the attention of

```
┌─────────────────────────────────────────────────────────────────────┐
│                        IMPACT STATEMENT                             │
│                                                                     │
│  Subject _____    Date _____  │
│                                                                     │
│  Reactor _____    Location _____      │
│                                                                     │
│  Comments: (use other side if needed)                               │
│                                                                     │
│                                                                     │
│                                                                     │
│                                                                     │
│                                                                     │
│                                                                     │
│                                                                     │
│                                                                     │
│                                                                     │
│                                                                     │
│                                                                     │
│  Please consider the following when commenting on the proposal:     │
│                                                                     │
│  -  The relationship of the proposed action to existing educational │
│     plans, policies and controls for their area of responsibility   │
│  -  The probable impact of the proposed action on the unit commenting│
│  -  Alternatives to the proposed action                             │
│  -  Any probable adverse educational effects which cannot be avoided │
│  -  The relationship between the local short-term effects on the     │
│     educational program and the maintenance and enhancement of long- │
│     term productivity                                               │
│  -  Any irreversible and/or irretrievable commitments of resources  │
│     that would be involved with the proposed action                 │
│  -  An indication of what other interests and considerations of the │
│     district or state policies are thought to offset the adverse    │
│     educational effects of the proposed action.                     │
└─────────────────────────────────────────────────────────────────────┘
```

Figure 3.9

the superintendent and solicit explanations for areas of concern. Where districts have Principal's Advisory Councils as viable groups, the minutes of each PAC are forwarded to the superintendent. Those items that will be brought up at the Superintendent's Advisory Council are starred. The superintendent then has a fair idea as to the items that are going to be raised. The superintendent can bring the necessary information to the SAC meeting and avoid the delay of getting back to the staff with the answers. This is an excellent means of getting two-way communication going. It should be noted that some unions do not like the SAC because they say that it preempts the union's role. On the other hand, there are many union contracts that require the establishment of a Superintendent's Advisory Council.

Have Lunch with the Staff

Join the staff for lunch in the faculty lunchroom, or invite them in to join you for lunch in your office. Engage in informal talk, not necessarily school related. Give yourself the opportunity to get to know your staff on an informal basis, and let the staff get to know you on the same basis.

New Staff Orientation

Recognize that it is important for new staff members to feel that they are part of the staff. Invite them to come and visit you during the course of the summer, even before they are formally on the payroll. This will give them an opportunity to get to know you and the building. Have coffee ready, and take them to lunch if it is appropriate.

Encourage the district to schedule an orientation day for all new staff members before the regular staff members return. In some districts there is money set aside to pay the new teachers for this day. In other districts, the new staff members are required to put in this additional day. Schedule the orientation even if you cannot pay the new staff members; invite them to come on their own. They generally will.

Plan the visit so that it is meaningful and productive. Starting with a continental breakfast sets a good tone. Everyone feels relaxed with food in their hands. Invite some of the board members, district personnel, building principals, and union representatives. Decide the topic that each of the speakers will cover in advance; make certain that you limit the time they have to speak. Make certain that you include an overview of the community including its history, the goals and objectives of the district, and information on personnel procedures in the district. Give the new employees an opportunity to ask questions.

Arrange for a narrated bus drive through the community so that new staff members can get a feel for the community, its tradition, housing, commercial areas, and culture. Have lunch ready when they return from the bus trip. Following lunch, invite them to go to their individual buildings with their principals so that they can look around and become familiar with the facility, rooms, materials, and supplies. Assign a ''buddy'' to them when the staff returns so that the new teacher will have a friend in the building.

Halftime Meeting

All too often new staff members are forgotten once the school year is under way. One way for the central administration to let them know that they are cared for is to have an informal meeting after the first semester is over—a halftime meeting. The purpose of the meeting would be to talk with them informally and find out how everything is going, determine whether or not there is anything that needs to be done, and listen to their suggestions. This is also a good time to tell them how pleased the district is with them and how much they mean to the district. If retention of staff is a problem, meetings such as this could go a long way in letting them know that you care for them.

Substitute Teachers

Do not overlook the need to maintain lines of communication between the substitutes in your building and your staff. They come and go and are free to select the school(s) they will/will not work in. Your building will function much better if you have a group of substitutes that are willing to work there.

Invite last year's substitutes, and individuals who indicated that they were interested in subbing, for coffee before school opens. Have all the administrators there so that the substitutes can meet them and get to know them. Share the school's philosophy with them—tell them what you are trying to accomplish, your goals, and your strengths and weaknesses. Take them on a tour of the building so that they can get a feel for it.

Prepare a substitute handbook for them that includes policies and regulations that you feel they may need to know, facts about enrollment, the schedule of classes, duty assignments, the instructional program, a map of the building, and the procedures to follow when reporting to the building. Inform them that there will be a substitute folder for them when they get to school, which will contain lesson plans, the seating chart, identification of the books and materials that the teacher is using, location of the roll book, and the names of dependable student leaders in each class.

When substitutes come to work at your building, do not simply give them the room number and let them go. Have someone assigned to show the substitutes to their rooms and remain there until the substitutes have located the information they need to teach that day and are set for the day. During the course of the day, drop in to see how the substitute is doing and ask if any help is needed. Do not ignore them! Many substitutes never return to a building because they feel that nobody cares how and what they do. Remember that the substitute teachers are usually members of the community and gain impressions of the building that they take with them back into the community.

Student Teachers

Student teachers, coming into your building as they do for a short period of time, gain impressions that last. They are quick to pick up staff attitudes, whether good or bad. Make certain that you place them with teachers that model good teaching behaviors. When the student teachers come to your building, take the time to orient them to the school, its policies, and procedures. They need to know what is expected of them, and where they can get the support they need as they go through their experiences. Invite them to staff meetings, PTA meetings, and other school functions. Make them members of your staff. Urge them to notify their hometown newspaper that they are at the school. It is good for the student teacher and it is good for the school. Positive press never hurts anyone.

The External Public

Who Are They?

The external public includes the members of the community who can, in one way or another, support the school district. They are parents of students in public and private schools; preschool parents; single adults;

married couples with no children, either couples whose children are beyond school age (empty nesters), or young marrieds who have no children as yet (both are working); senior citizens; individuals who own businesses in the school district; and the people who come into the community to work. They are the crossing guards who stand outside the school building every day that it is open and know who goes in, how long the individual stays in the building, and who leaves the building. They are the barbers, beauticians, gas station attendants, and store clerks who get to listen to many people talk about a variety of community matters, including all too often the schools.

They are the local government officials, members of civic associations, advisory council members, taxpayers' alliance members, fund-raising leaders, and members of ethnic organizations. We are also talking about the key communicators in the school district; the individuals who are the power people behind the scenes, the opinion leaders, and the people who influence the directions and actions of the various organizations. The key communicators can get the message out very quickly; they are usually the power brokers.

Why Concern Yourself with Them?

Members of the external public are the people who go to the polls and vote for/against board members, tax levies, referenda, and school budgets. They are the taxpayers in the community, the people who use the services that the community has to offer. They have the ultimate power at the polls and usually make certain that their representatives on the board know how they stand on issues. A school district is severely hampered if there is a lack of understanding on the part of the external public.

What Do They Want to Know?

These people want to know how the students in their district are doing. Specifically:

- Are they learning?
- How does the district measure up to neighboring districts?
- How are their test scores on standardized state and national exams?
- Do the students enter into competition in the arts? in the sciences?

- Are the students attending classes?
- What is the dropout rate?
- What percent of the graduates are going on to higher education and to which colleges?
- Are the students not going to higher education prepared to enter the work force?
- Do they have minimum competencies to hold jobs?
- What scholarships are the students receiving?
- What extracurricular programs are offered?
- What are the athletic results/achievements?
- Are they motivated?

They want to know what the school climate is like:

- Are drugs prevalent in school?
- Are substance abuse programs available?
- What are the suspension rates?
- What is discipline like in the schools?
- Are the schools safe?
- What is the crime rate in the schools?
- Do the schools welcome visitors?
- Do they have an open or closed campus?

They want to know how competent the staff is:

- What are the credentials of the teaching staff?
- Are teachers evaluated? How often?
- Are teachers ever released because they are not competent?
- What support is given to teachers?
- What are the age levels of the teaching staff?
- Does the district employ guidance counselors at all levels?
- Does the district give staff recognition awards?
- Are they having trouble getting substitutes?

They want to know about the academic program:

- Is the district continually trying to improve the curriculum? How?
- Do they have innovative or special programs?
- Are computers available to students?
- Do they have a gifted and talented program?
- How prevalent are study halls?

- What percent of the students are in special education? Are they located in their home schools?
- How large are the schools?
- What is the class size?
- What is the student/teacher ratio?

They are interested in other areas as well:

- What is the racial breakdown in the schools?
- What are racial relations like in the schools?
- Do students attend their neighborhood schools, or are they bussed to other schools?
- How long do they spend on the bus?
- Does the school have a hot lunch program?
- What are the conditions and age of the physical plants?
- Is there any type of child care available—before or after-school care?
- Who can be called with questions?
- How does the board operate?

Dr. Robbie M. Kendall, the director of the Center of Excellence in Early Childhood Education at Winthrop College in Rock Hill, South Carolina, indicates that "parents with exceptional children must make certain that public relations programs ensure that the public is well informed of the needs and problems associated with the care and education of handicapped children" (Kendall, 1989). She goes on to say that good public relations can be a "powerful force in assisting parents of special needs and handicapped (exceptional) children. Effective PR can enhance special programs; supportive services; improve the children's educational opportunities; and promote positive public attitudes about the handicapped within the community." Parents have a vested interest in the information shared by school districts.

What community members see for themselves all too often is vandalism that has taken place in the schools, graffiti on the buildings, students hanging around outside the buildings, dirty buildings at election time, and assume that there is a general lack of control when they see students hanging out of the windows on the busses.

They do see some positive things from time to time—they go to the games and know how the teams are doing, go to performances at the upper level schools, and occasionally see posters about programs. Some serve on advisory committees and get information about the schools;

they see for themselves when they go to open house, have lunch with their children, and volunteer in the schools. They also talk with employees and neighbors and know what they tell them.

But, bottom line, they want to know whether or not their tax dollars are spent effectively. Are they getting their money's worth? Are their dollars being targeted to the district's objectives?

How Do We Communicate with the External Public?

By and large, members of the external public think that they are not getting their money's worth, that schools are spending too much and that there is no accountability and no discipline in the schools. They get their information largely from the media. They know the results of polls, reports, and surveys, and they hear about problems in the schools. They know when the first day of school is because there is always a picture in the paper of the children getting off a bus. Often they read of who made the honor roll (even if it is printed two months later), some few interesting programs that are being offered in the schools, that taxes are going up, and that there is a need to pay teachers more money.

Communicate on a Regular Basis

Decide on a plan for releasing information to the community, and let them know how and when to expect the information. Make certain that there is information being released on a continuous basis, and not only when their vote is needed to pass a bond issue or pass a budget. Use the various means (channels) available to you (see Chapter 10).

Newsletters

Release a newsletter on a regular basis—monthly, bimonthly, or quarterly, as it fits in with your overall operation. Set a time that the external public can expect to receive it. If it is a monthly newsletter, make a commitment to release it on a specific day each month—perhaps the first day of the month or the last day. Decide what the newsletter will contain and make certain that you issue it as planned and give the public the information that they need/want to know. Be timely, do not give them information that has already appeared in the press. If there are items that they need to know about that will take place in the near future, put those in the newsletter.

Decide on a distinctive masthead so that when the parents glance at the piece of paper, they will recognize that it is your newsletter. You may want to use a specific color of paper for the newsletter to further assist in its identification (Figure 3.10).

Conferences

Be available to meet with members of the public in small/large groups in order to discuss issues and areas of concern with them. Do not ignore a request for information. If individuals have questions that can be addressed at your level, do so. Try to take care of questions at the lowest possible level and resolve any concerns so that their escalation is controlled. People feel satisfied when they know that someone cares enough to talk with and listen to them.

Community Meetings

Attend community meetings in order to ascertain the pulse of the community, i.e., what they are thinking and questioning. When invited, speak at the meetings and functions, and celebrate the good. Tell the community where your school/district is, where it is going, and how it intends to get there. Talk about the staff, the graduates, and the successes of the various academic and athletic teams. Talk about the programs that are offered. Allow questions to be asked; invite comments and suggestions. Being open and aboveboard instills a level of confidence in people that is difficult to dispel. Enabling the public to relate a person to an institution personalizes the institution.

Visit Churches and Synagogues

Ask the clergy of the local churches and synagogues if you can be invited to address the congregation when education as a topic is being addressed. Many times churches and synagogues will host an Education Day in conjunction with American Education Week. That is a good time to address the congregation and respond to questions.

Radio and Television Shows

Agree to be a guest on the local radio talk show or the local television station. If a particular topic is being addressed, do your homework and come prepared to discuss all aspects of the topic. If there is no predetermined agenda, acquaint yourself with the hot topics of the day and the

THE COMMUNICATOR

Newsletter of the Pine Bush High School

Home — *of the Bushmen*

Pine Bush Central School District   Pine Bush, New York   March, 1990

Dear Parents,

By the time this newsletter arrives home, we will be well past the middle of the third marking period with only about fifteen weeks left to our school year. These last fifteen weeks are critical--the course curricula are completed, review for final examinations takes place and, of course, Regents examinations and school examinations are administered at the end of the school year. In addition, many activities take place during these last fifteen weeks, such as Pride Week, Honor Society Induction Ceremony, Senior Awards Banquet, Athletic Awards Banquets, Graduation Party, and Graduation itself. Your attendance at these functions is highly encouraged.

Please read the contents of this newsletter so that you are better informed about all that will be happening in school. If I or my staff can be of any help to you regarding the end of the school year activities or testing, please feel free to contact the high school.

Sincerely,

Kenneth R. Sherman

Kenneth R. Sherman
High School Principal

Messages From the Principal's Desk

Graduation Party

A committee of parents has been formed to begin preparation for the class of 1990's graduation party, which will be held on the night of June 23. I urge the parents of seniors to volunteer to work to organize this party for their children. Since this party is funded totally by donations, I also ask that the parents of seniors donate $20 towards the party as soon as possible. Checks can be made out to the Pine Bush Graduation Party and mailed to me at the high school. Your efforts on behalf of the graduates will insure a safe, alcohol-free graduation party. This year's party chairperson is Mrs. Karen Pehek. If you wish to volunteer your help, please call her at 692-2501.

Mission Statement

On page three of this newsletter you will find the Mission Statement of Pine Bush High School. This is a very important statement for our school community. I hope you take the time to read it because your input and help are needed if we are to achieve our mission. Our ultimate goal is to insure

(continued on page 2)

Reproduced from *The Communicator*, newsletter of the Pine Bush High School, Pine Bush, New York.

Figure 3.10

rumors that are circulating in the school district. You may also want to identify some very positive facts/programs/occurrences that you would like to weave into the dialogue during the course of being on the air. Remember that the radio broadcasts only the audio portion of the interview, while the television broadcasts both the audio and the video portions of the interview.

Senior Citizens

Issue ''gold cards'' to senior citizens that enable them to attend dress rehearsals of plays, band concerts, games, and the like. If you are concerned about the tremendous work in distributing them, contact your local Agency for the Aging. They will help you get the information you need and distribute the cards for you. Issue new cards each year. These gold cards will improve relations with senior citizens – an important bloc of voters, who often feel little connection to schools because their children have graduated. It will also help student morale by increasing the size of crowds at activities.

Realtors

Issue information sheets about the school/district to the realtors so that they will have information to respond to the questions that newcomers to the community generally ask. Individuals who are in the process of relocating, or buying a house, generally contact a realtor in order to get assistance. Unless the realtor has information to the contrary, he/she relies on the information that is found in the newspapers.

If the realtors have an association, ask to be invited in order to share information with them about the school/district and to respond to any questions that they may have. Prepare a fact sheet that you leave with them when you are done. Often they will take the fact sheet and give it to clients asking about the district.

Along the same lines, prepare a tri-fold information sheet about the various schools and programs that can fit into a #10 envelope. Give them to the realtors for use with potential home buyers and mail them out to individuals as they call or stop by for information (Figure 3.11).

Public Libraries, Banks, Utilities, Government Offices

Place copies of the information prepared by the school/district in the public libraries, banks, utility offices, mayor's and local officials'

WELCOME!

Dear Students & Parents,

We look forward to a great school year and hope that you are well rested and excited about your return to school. This brochure has been prepared to provide an overview of the services offered at Pine Bush Central High School. We invite your continuing involvement in the guidance, counseling and support services provided.

Sincerely,
RICHARD J. REICH
Director of Guidance

GUIDANCE SERVICES

There are many guidance services available to students, parents, and staff at Pine Bush Central High School. The following list provides an overview of these services:

□ High School Course Planning
□ Peer Leadership Activities
□ Monthly Guidance Newsletters
□ Computer Assisted Career & Educational Guidance
□ Testing & Testing Information: SAT, ACH, PSAT, ACT, ASVAB, Cognitive Abilities Test, Advanced Placement Tests
□ SAT/PSAT Preparation Course
□ College Admissions information:
  - Access to a data base of over 3,500 colleges
  - College visitation program
  - College Night
  - College representative visits
□ Career Phone Resource Program with Chamber of Commerce
□ Financial Aid & Scholarship Information
□ Financial Aid Session
□ College Credit Program

□ Student Registration & Record Requests
□ Career & Educational Trips
□ Orientation Programs

COUNSELING SERVICES

The following list includes the range of counseling services offered:

□ Personal Counseling:
  Support staff provide supportive counseling to students experiencing the normal range of problems confronting teens
□ Group Counseling
□ Career Counseling
□ College Counseling
□ Academic Counseling

SUPPORT SERVICES

Guidance and counseling is only one component of the support service network offered at the high school. Additional support services are listed below:

□ Eligibility Committee
□ Teacher Advisorship Program
□ Information & Referral Services for Substance and Alcohol Abuse
□ SADD Chapter
□ Psychological Testing and Evaluation
□ PTA Programs
□ Peer Leadership Retreats
□ Parent-Teacher Conferences
□ Special Education Services
□ Referral Services
□ Careline Program
□ Child Study Team
□ Teen Outreach Program
□ Report Card Pride Week with Chamber of Commerce
□ Drug Free Graduation Party

ANNUAL CALENDAR

August
Course Adjustments
Freshmen and new student orientation program and building tour

September
Course Adjustments
Senior interviews
College admissions counselors visitations begin
PBHS Open House

October
PSAT testing at PBHS
PTA Program: Homework Without Tears
Peer Support Retreat

November
SAT & Achievement testing at PBHS
College Night and Financial Aid Session at PBHS

December
College applications due to Guidance Office

January
SAT Prep Course Information Meeting
Orange-Ulster Vocational Technical Center assembly and visitation program (Sophomores)
SAT Prep Course begins (12 Saturdays)
High School Planning Meeting for grade 8 parents
Cognitive Abilities Test (Sophomores)
PTA Program: Stress Management
ASVAB testing at PBHS

January - February
Individual planning interviews for course selection

March
Student scheduling continues
PTA Program: Communicating With Your Child

Figure 3.11

Reproduced from *A Guide to Guidance Counseling, and Support Services*, Pine Bush High School, Pine Bush, New York.

offices, in order to make the information accessible. Include information that will enable people to have their questions answered about the school district: where it is, where it is going, and how and when it expects to get there. Include the latest facts and figures.

Volunteers

Encourage volunteers to work in the schools. Gains can be anticipated as a result of successful experiences: the volunteer derives a sense of accomplishment; the student has the opportunity to learn from a different source and gain additional knowledge; the district does not have to employ a staff member to give the students this additional support; and lastly, the volunteer will undoubtedly speak in positive terms about the school and be a prime source of positive public relations.

Open House – Visitors

In addition to back-to-school night, schedule an open house several times a year during the time that school is in session. Encourage visitors to come to school; have lunch, if they can; and learn what is going on in the school. Invite them in to see such things as science fair competition and big book displays that were made by the students. The community will be impressed with the tremendous job being done.

Annual Report

Prepare an annual report to the board and the community. Identify the goals and objectives that were set at the beginning of the year and indicate the progress the district has made in reaching these goals. Distribute copies of the annual report to the administrators, community leaders, and PTA boards. Make them available in each school district building and the public library.

District Calendar

Prepare a district calendar for the school year. List all the important dates that will be taking place. Include such items as days that school is in session, school holidays, PTA meetings, midpoint and end of marking periods, and concerts. Distribution is made in accordance with the plan that the district/school has developed.

The Public Needs Information

The 1988 Gallup Poll indicates that the percent of adults with children in school has dwindled from 39 percent in 1973 to 27 percent in 1988, and that newspapers are the prime source of information for most people. It is incumbent on schools/districts to plan and implement a public relations program that is open, honest, accurate, and clear. There is a need to reach out to the community at large.

In his address to the staff on the first day of the new school year, Terrence L. Olivo, Superintendent of Schools of the Monroe-Woodbury Central School District, talked about a need common to most districts when he said:

> There is a great deal that is right with education—especially in Monroe-Woodbury—but good education is expensive. Taxes are increasing at all levels and with those increases come increasing public attention and concern. It took two votes this past spring to get our current budget which carries one of the lowest tax increases in the county, in most cases by a factor of 2 to 3 times lower.

> If we are to continue to enjoy the support of the voters it is no longer enough to *be* among the best—we must constantly explain to the community how and why we are an exceptional district.

> To tell the community, our customers, that we are the best, we intend to do whatever is necessary to remain the best. And most important of all, to do what is best for kids. No one can or will ask more.

CHAPTER 4

ESTABLISHING TRUST
AND CONFIDENCE

CONFIDENCE! THE WORD ITSELF CAN
INSPIRE. CONFIDENCE IS TRUST.
CONFIDENCE IS ASSURANCE. CONFIDENCE
IS BELIEF IN SELF . . . A BELIEF IN OTHERS
. . . A BELIEF IN OUR INSTITUTIONS.

American Association of School Administrators
Building Public Confidence in Our Schools

C O N F I D E N C E has also been defined as a ''belief in, faith in, pride in, loyalty to, understanding of, and willingness to support and defend a school or school system.'' This definition is contained in the findings of a Phi Delta Kappa commission asked to identify districts and schools that enjoyed a high level of public confidence, and to determine the reasons for it. The commission's findings were published in 1988 in a book, *Handbook for Developing Public Confidence in Schools*, written by Wayson and Achilles, et al. In reviewing the book, Arthur W. Steller (1989) stated that ''As one would expect, the highest-ranking factor contributing to public confidence is 'the perception that teachers care for students, for learning, and for the school.' Ranked second is 'the perception that the principal cares about students.' School employees and children generally influence public perceptions more than other sources.''

Members of the public want to trust and have confidence in their schools, but they need information and contact in order to do so. In today's climate of information overload, there is relatively little that is communicated that is positive or informational about local schools. Results of studies and national and state reports are issued. They do not, however, give local school communities information that applies to their local schools. School communities in all too many instances have little or no information on which to make informed judgments. It is difficult for them to have confidence in, or to trust, their schools.

In the introduction to a series of articles dealing with school public relations published in the National Association of Secondary School Principals' publication, the *Bulletin* (1979), John W. Wherry, Executive

Director of the National School Public Relations Association (NSPRA), indicated that "four basic reasons for the lack of public confidence [in] education" were identified by NSPRA's Task Force on Building Public Confidence as:

(1) Negative personal experience with their schools
(2) Public feeling that schools are not doing a good job teaching the basic skills they have come to expect from schools
(3) The poor and ineffective job that has been and is being done to keep the public informed about education
(4) A decreasing feeling of public responsibility for their schools

These findings reinforce the need for us to make a commitment to sharpen our communication skills and share the information we have with the public. They need to learn about the schools from school people; from the individuals they should be turning to and trusting.

The audience/reader generally wants to know:

• What is this all about? Get to the point. If members of the audience have to wait too long to find out what is being discussed, they stop reading or lose interest.
• Exactly what is being proposed? If audience members are supposed to understand and accept a concept, they will generally listen more carefully. Unless the topic is covered specifically, and people know what is being proposed, they will leave feeling that the discussion was nothing more than a waste of time and that nothing was decided.
• Why is it needed? By whom? People need to believe what is being proposed.

Two-Way Communication

In all forms of communication there is a sender who is delivering a message to a receiver using a specific medium. The expectation is that the message will be received and will convey the intended meaning. There are, however, potential barriers—such as a lack of understanding of the terms being used, past experiences, and value systems—that tend to interfere with the clear transmission of the message. You need feedback, both verbal and non-verbal, to be certain that the message has been received as intended. You receive verbal feedback by listening to what people say, how they say it, which words they use, the rate of speech they use, as well as the pitch of their voices. Non-verbal feedback is readily detectable by watching the physical expressions of people as they receive the message.

"Effective communication is a two-way process—an exchange of thoughts between a sender and a receiver. Each party's participation in this process is based on personal perceptions that stem from past experiences, values, needs, and feelings" (Bingaman, 1985). Many times the mere status of an individual (psychological size) will preclude two-way communication in the workplace. Manning and Curtis (1988) identified factors that impede two-way communication. Among these factors are when one individual possesses:

- high status position
- power to evaluate performance
- power to hire, fire, and assign work
- power to dispense and withhold rewards
- use of sarcasm and ridicule
- formal, distant manner
- cruel and punishing remarks
- know-it-all, superior attitude
- ability to talk fluently
- imposing physical appearance
- tendency to interrupt
- expensive or privileged clothing
- power over life and freedom
- high social standing
- material wealth
- badges of status—large office, special dining room, automobile, parking privileges

You need to make certain that two-way communication exists throughout the organization; that subordinates know that their ideas are important, respected, and heard. Not only do subordinates need to know that their ideas are welcome and that the administration is hearing their ideas and opinions, they need to be informed as to the action taken/not taken in response to the suggestion(s). This can be readily accomplished by clearly articulating that management is interested in receiving input, both in support of and in opposition to an idea; by removing the barriers to communication that exist, such as inaccessibility; and by establishing vehicles by which ideas and suggestions are solicited and feedback received. One of the prime advantages of having two-way communication is that different perspectives on a particular subject can be identified and dealt with as appropriate, thus avoiding possible areas of conflict.

Each situation lends itself to the use of different strategies. Use those that you feel most comfortable with and the ones that fit the situation. Make a concerted effort to assure that two-way communication does take place and that you are getting the feedback that you need.

Messages must be well thought out. If the message is vague in your mind, it will undoubtedly be vague when it is received. Use clearly defined words that convey the intended meaning. If you find that the message is not being received as intended, address the matter again so that you can achieve your desired end. An obstacle may be that the message is poorly stated or defined; the words used may mean different things to different people; the background of the receiver may not have been taken into account, or may have been inaccurately perceived; or there may be an assumption that there is only one correct point of view on the matter.

Poorly communicated messages often result in confusion, defensiveness, a lack of confidence, and a feeling of distrust. Leland Brown (1961) identified a checklist for communicators which you may want to use to guide you when you communicate (see Figure 4.1).

Using the checklist in Figure 4.1, you can make accommodations and changes as needed to assure that your message is received as intended and that the public receives the information it needs to have confidence and trust in what you say.

People should feel that you are sincere, honest, and trustworthy based on the actions taken and statements made over a period of time. Involve people by sharing information with them, asking them for their reaction/suggestions to proposed actions before the action is taken, responding to their suggestions, and thanking them for their interest and participation. Value the varied opinions of individuals, respect them, and be responsive. It is only when people know who you are, what you stand for, and feel comfortable in how you react/respond to issues that they begin to trust you and have confidence in you.

Speaking

Speaking is the most commonly used method of communicating; we communicate by voice from the minute we enter the world — we cry.

Beginning considerations
1. Why am I communicating?
2. For whom is my material presented?
3. Have I gotten off to a flying start?
4. What is the core idea I want to get across?
5. What will the audience do with what I say?

Development of message
1. Is the message well organized?
2. Are the ideas in logical order?
3. Can my audience follow step by step?
4. Is each idea pertinent? clearly developed?
5. Do important points stand out?
6. Have I used concrete examples wherever I could?

Wording and phrasing of ideas
1. Have I used familiar terms?
2. Have I omitted non-essential technical terminology?
3. Have I avoided hackneyed words and expressions?
4. Did I use specific words?
5. Did I adapt my language to the level and interest of the audience?

Stylistic considerations
1. Have I paced the material for the audience?
2. Are sentences clear and easily grasped?
3. Have I used questions and answers effectively?
4. Does my message have a warm, friendly quality?
5. Does it read like conversation?
6. Does it talk about the problem in terms of people?

Closing considerations
1. Have I summarized main points briefly and in the right places?
2. Does the communication accomplish its intended purposes?

Figure 4.1 Checklist for communicators.

Before you say anything, think carefully about what you want to say, what results you expect as a result of speaking, to whom you are speaking, and the way you will speak. Decide whether or not you want to inform, to persuade, or to entertain.

If you intend to inform the audience, try not to lecture. Depending on the information to be presented, and the audience, a lecture can be deadly; it is a one-sided presentation. A briefing or an orientation may be a more desirable format, as these are less formal, designed to share information and to respond to questions. They are not as one-sided as a lecture.

If you would like to persuade the audience, much as a salesperson does, you want to influence the listeners to change their thinking or behavior. You need to be able to share specific information and invite, and respond to, questions that may be raised by the audience. Small group settings are more desirable because people will ask questions in a small group setting more readily than in a large group setting.

If you are speaking to entertain, then make certain that you do in fact entertain. Personality, witty language, a flair for drama, the use of anecdotes, and humor all add to producing an enjoyable experience. You can be bright, sharp, knowledgeable, and still be entertaining.

In preparing your remarks, select your words carefully so that the meaning you intend to convey is understood. It takes great skill to be able to put what you want to say into words that your listeners will readily understand. Know who your audience is, and recognize that the listeners' interpretations are influenced by past experiences, their personal value systems, education, and needs.

Select from a variety of strategies and techniques that will help you get the message across. Use anecdotes and illustrations that support and clarify your points. If you have specific references and/or comparisons, make them so that the audience can establish a link to what they already know and understand. Use quotations and testimony of people the audience can relate to insofar as it supports the points you are trying to make. Statistics help, but make sure that they are readily understood and give the impact you want. Do not ramble on with statistics that are meaningless to the listener. Use graphic visual aids to present data, since these are more easily understood than words.

Do not simply take a written text and present it. Convert the text to reflect a conversation. Use personal pronouns and contractions. Eliminate lengthy, convoluted phrases. Keep sentences short and to the point, averaging about twenty words in length. Interject humor, illustrations, and anecdotes. The ease with which a person can listen is very important. In commenting on President John Kennedy's speech preparation, Sorensen (1965) said:

> Our chief criterion was always audience comprehension and comfort, and this meant: (1) short speeches, short clauses, and short words, wherever possible; (2) a series of points or propositions in numbered or logical sequence, wherever appropriate; and (3) the construction of sentences, phrases, and paragraphs in such a manner as to simplify, clarify, and emphasize.

Talk about an issue or problem as you see it. At all times be calm, be patient, give honest feedback to questions raised, and maintain self-control. You control the volume of your voice, the rate at which you speak, and generally the forum in which you speak. Everyone has a right to his/her opinion. Respect it, even though it may differ from yours. If you still want to change the person's opinions, go back and attack the problem from a different angle. Do not repeat the same ideas in the same way. Be creative, caring, and understanding. Do not undermine or belittle your listeners. Attack problems, not people, in order to depersonalize the issue.

In speaking, use the cardinal rule:

> Tell them what you want to say.
> Tell them.
> Tell them what you said.

Reinforce your message by restating your key points to assure that they are understood.

Telephone Use

The telephone is often the first contact that a person has with your school/office. The manner in which it is answered and the attention given to the request of the caller leaves an indelible impression.

Do not let the phones go unattended, and do not take them off the hook! Impress on the people in your building/department who answer the telephones that you would like the calls answered as promptly as possible, but no later than the third ring. Ask them to respond enthusiastically and with a pleasant tone of voice.

Ask them to answer the telephone and identify not only the name of the school or department, but to give their names as well. A response, "Good morning, this is Lori Schmidt in Guidance, may I help you?" is far better than "Hello" or "Extension 124." What you want them to do is to let callers know whom they reached.

Ask your people to be interested in the caller, to offer assistance and listen carefully to any requests the caller may have. By being pleasant, polite, and getting the message the first time, you will eliminate the problem of having frustrated callers make unnecessary callbacks. If a response is needed, respond promptly with informative answers and explanations.

Keep a telephone call pad near each phone. Confirm the spelling of the caller's name, telephone number, student's name, or the company worked for. Make certain that the date and time of the call are recorded on the message slip, as is the name of the person receiving the call. A coworker may have a question about the call and, knowing who took the call, would be able to talk to that person.

Repeat the message to the caller, to be certain that you have the correct information. If you are taking the message for someone who is out, explain that the person is unavailable at this time, state the reason for the absence, and tell the caller when he/she may expect to hear from the person.

Make arrangements to have someone answer your telephone whenever you will be away from your desk. This can easily be done if you have a call forwarding feature as part of your telephone system. Make your callbacks as promptly as you can upon your return. A rule of thumb is that you return the calls in the order received, but if certain calls have priority, then obviously return those first, and get back to the others just as soon as you can. If you find that your time is severely constrained, you may decide to set aside a time during the day during which you return all your calls. Advise the people taking the messages so that the callers can be told when to expect your return call.

When using the telephone, speak clearly because the party on the other end relies only on your voice; there are no non-verbal clues with which to interpret the meaning of your comments. Speak at a moderate rate of speed and avoid educationese. If you use a telephone answering machine to record your calls when you are not in the office, extend the same courtesies to your callers as you would if they left a message with another person; follow through and call back promptly.

When you place a call, make certain that you have uninterrupted time to talk. Place your own telephone calls. Plan your calls and have the information you need at hand along with a pad on which to take notes. In preparing for the call, you may find it helpful to prepare a list of questions/items that you need to cover. Then, even if the conversation should stray, you do know what it is that you wanted to cover. The list avoids having to make follow-up calls because you forgot something.

When making the call, identify yourself and your school/department. Do not expect the person receiving your call to instantly recognize your voice. It is difficult to place a voice by a mere "Hello." In placing the call to a person you know, begin with, "Hello, Bob, this is Lori." Use complete names and your school or department if you do not know the person or are not on a first name basis.

Remember that people judge you not only by what you say, but by the way in which you say it.

Listening

Although we spend most of our time listening, this is an area in which we receive virtually no training. In school we are taught to read, write, and speak, but rarely to listen. As stated earlier, "Effective communication is a two-way process—an exchange of thoughts between a sender and a receiver" (Bingaman, 1985). The message should be received as intended. The ability to listen becomes very important when you realize that most messages are spoken.

The rate of speech used affects the audience. The rate of speech of an individual addressing a group is generally 100 to 125 words a minute. The average person can process words at the rate of 500 words per minute. When you speak at 125 words per minute, members of your audience have spare time while they listen to you talk—spare time for their minds to wander, to daydream, or to think of any number of other things. Speak at a more normal (conversational) rate of speech when addressing an audience. Pretend that you are speaking to only one person, and use that rate of speech with the group. You will be making it easier for your audience to follow and listen to you.

When another person is speaking, engage in active listening by exhibiting a genuine interest in what he/she has to say, maintaining eye contact, being understanding, asking clarifying questions, and thereby making people feel free to communicate with you and to share ideas and thoughts. Try to draw people out; it is important not to dominate the conversation.

Often we are tempted to interrupt; exercise self-control. Listen, because that is often the only way you will find out what the others are thinking. Make certain that you are perceiving a speaker's meaning as he or she intended. A good way to do this is by mirroring back what the person has just said to you. This can be done by statements such as, "What I think I heard you say is . . ." The person can then affirm or restate/correct his/her thoughts.

Do not hurry a conversation. Take the time needed to take care of the matter at hand. All too often we tend to try to settle a matter in the shortest possible time. Give the person the uninterrupted time needed to hear what he/she has to say and to respond in a meaningful manner. Concentrate on what the individual has to say. Listen sympathetically, look at the speaker, give him/her your undivided attention, take notes as necessary, and respond non-verbally with a nod, a hand motion, a facial expression, and the like, as appropriate.

Non-Verbal Communication

Positive and negative feelings and attitudes are communicated consciously or unconsciously by non-verbal means. "Listen and hear" with your eyes. We receive cues, not facts, that relate to the message being delivered. Manning and Curtis (1988) show that meaning is communicated 55 percent by body, 38 percent by voice, and 7 percent by words. According to these studies, non-verbal communication accounts for fully 93 percent of the communication process. Do not ignore these non-verbal responses — interpret and react to them. Some of the most common sources of non-verbal communication are as follows.

- *Facial expressions* include frowning, smiling, anger, displeasure, happiness, amazement, pursing the lips, biting the lips, and raising the eyebrows.
- *Eye contact* can be made by maintaining steady eye contact, avoidance of direct eye contact, glancing, narrowing or opening of the eyes.
- *Hand and arm gestures* include waving your arms, holding your arms at your side, folding your arms, keeping your hands in your pockets, jingling coins in your pocket, fidgeting, doodling, pointing fingers, making a fist, pounding your fist on a surface, and placing your hands on your hips.
- *Body posture* may be limp, rigid, relaxed, sitting on the edge of

the seat, or slouching—indicating bored indifference. You may find that you are speaking to someone who is looking at his/her watch every few minutes to check the time. Although nothing has been said, you begin to feel uncomfortable; you realize that something is wrong. You may decide to bring the conversation to a close for the time being, or ask the person whether or not it would be more desirable to pick up the meeting at another time.

- The *appearance* of an individual is important in conveying a message. Consider the audience that you are addressing and the message that you want to deliver. Your appearance establishes a mindset for the audience before you begin to speak. Make certain that you are dressed in business attire and avoid trendy, flashy clothes adorned with extravagant jewelry that detracts from the message that you want to convey. Hairstyles, shoes, color, and makeup should enhance your appearance rather than detract from the image that you want to convey. Represent your school/district in the best possible light so that your message can be considered credible. Extremes tend to turn people off.
- The *distance* separating people has an affect on the interaction between the speaker and the listener/group. "Personal space" has been interpreted as distances ranging from eighteen inches to four feet, "social space" from four to eight feet, and "public space" from eight feet outward (Manning and Curtis, 1988). The positioning of furniture in an office and the configuration of a meeting room generally dictate the distance between the speaker and the audience. It has been stated that "those with more status 'control' space and those with less respect it" (Huseman, 1976).

Verbal and non-verbal messages need to be consistent in order to avoid sending confusing signals. It is confusing to hear one thing being said in the spoken word and another message received through non-verbal communication clues.

Know what it is that you want the audience to remember after you get done speaking. Be enthusiastic and confident as you deliver the message, vary your rate of speech so that it is more interesting, smile at your audience, and look at the audience as you speak so that you can gauge whether or not you need to alter, or further expand on your remarks. Use non-verbal communication techniques, such as hand movements, to support your words. Do not just mouth words, make them come alive as you say them.

Be mindful of the non-verbal communication techniques that you use. Do not exaggerate movements unless you are certain that they will support your message. If in doubt, consider videotaping a practice session so that you can get a better perspective on how you are seen by an audience. Avoid pacing while speaking. This is very distracting to an audience. Stand on your own two feet and do not lean on the podium for support. All of your non-verbal actions should support your verbal message and engender confidence and support for you and your message.

Writing

Although many of the same principles for effective speaking apply to effective writing as well, there are differences between oral and written communication—differences that induce you to use one form over the other. Huseman (1976) indicates that:

> One of the most significant differences between face-to-face and written communication is that the immediate feedback present in the former is absent in the latter. An effective oral communicator is cognizant of the feedback he receives and adapts his subsequent communicative efforts based on it. Since a writer is limited to feedback on a delayed basis, he is unable to do that immediately but must wait some time before being able to measure his effectiveness. . . .

> Another important difference is that the written message has a permanency missing in oral communication. If the message is lengthy or highly technical, or if there are legal or contractual considerations involved, it is advisable to write it. Tape recorders and the more surreptitious recording devices have increased the permanency of the spoken word but have not bequeathed it with the credibility of writing.

The effective writer recognizes these constraints and uses the communication method best suited to the task at hand. Before deciding to write, identify your purpose—what is it that you want to accomplish? Define the target audience that you need to reach, and what you would like them to do as a result of your message. Determine the format of the communication that will best serve your purpose.

Douglas Mealy (1984) identifies a number of reasons for communicating in writing. They have been modified for application to education.

(1) *Clarity*—Written documents can clarify the sender's message if they are well written. The object of writing is not merely to write to be

understood, but also to write so that you cannot possibly be misunderstood.

(2) *Documentation*—Written documents can serve as control or monitoring devices. A file of letters can become an audit trail so that you can trace the progress of an issue or project. If an individual cannot serve in his/her current capacity, or leaves the district, there is a record of what has been done to that point in time; a new person can pick up the pieces quickly and efficiently.

(3) *Accountability*—Written communications can identify the specific responsibilities of participants and can provide a statement of deadlines so the administrator knows who should be contacted if something goes wrong.

(4) *Distribution*—Written communications are sometimes the only way you can inform team members/staff of progress or new developments. Team members/staff may be unavailable for meetings, making written communications the only effective means of keeping everyone informed.

(5) *Written history*—Written communications provide a written history of what was done, the problems encountered, and the solutions reached; they provide an institutional memory, which prevents the current group from repeating some of the mistakes the original group may have made, or which may afford some guidelines to follow.

When you write, consider the audience that you are addressing. Determine their level of sophistication relative to the topic that you are writing about: How much do they know about the topic? How involved have they been? How much detail do you have to go into in order for them to know what you are talking about? What words can you use?

Be direct and get to the heart of the matter, cutting out unnecessary words. Use words that clearly convey your thoughts. Use small words where you can; do not try to use large words to impress people. Remember that your audience wants to understand what you are saying, so make it easy for them. Address them at a level and in a manner that they will feel most comfortable.

Consider following the Clear River Test (Morris, 1980) as you write. This test suggests guides to follow for business and government writing:

- 25 words per sentence
- 12 words per punctuated pause
- 75 words per paragraph
- 150 syllables per hundred words

On the average, most magazines and newspapers do not exceed these numbers, and many articles are written at lower levels. You may wish to use the test as you review what you have written, in order to be certain that you are not placing obstacles in the way of your readers. All too often educators have a tendency to be heavy-handed when they write. Try not to exceed the comfort levels that these numbers represent.

In deciding how to communicate, you can select from a number of communication strategies. You may decide to send a personal letter, a newsletter, a memorandum, or a report, depending on the result that you want to achieve.

Write to express, not to impress.

Letters and Memos

Letters and memos can serve as very effective public relations tools. Next to being there, your letters speak for you. Recognize that they represent you, in your absence; make certain that they reflect favorably on you and your institution. The form, clarity, and appearance leave a lasting impression on the reader.

Despite the fact that you may be using a computer to write letters to members of a group, personalize them so that the receiver feels that you are writing to him/her as an individual. Make certain that the contents address the issue directly. Letters can be used where the intent is to invite the receiver to a meeting or public event, solicit a donation, or give support to a proposal. At times you may wish to send letters in order to give the readers an update on what is happening at the school/district. If at all possible, sign the personalized letters yourself. People appreciate receiving a signed letter as opposed to receiving one that has been signed by a signature stamp.

Brownell (1955) presented simplified rules (known as Morris's Five Rules for Letter Writing) for use in writing letters. They are:

(1) *Adopt a "you" attitude.* Write in terms of your reader's wishes and needs.

(2) *Be courteous.* Tact and graciousness pay off—even in letters.

(3) *Be sincere.* Answer without evasion or alibis. Say nothing that can not be backed by facts. Say nothing that can be misconstrued.

(4) *Be enthusiastic.* Do not sound like a page from last year's almanac. Do not sound as though you are in a hurry or doing your reader a favor by answering.

(5) *Be natural.* You would not tell a man, "Please be advised . . ."
Why write it? Stereotyped language is a bore and seldom brings
results. Pretend you are reading your letters aloud to your cor-
respondent.

Memos are generally used internally in order to address a specific item
in an expedient manner. Memos are traditionally short, concise, and to
the point. They are less formal than a letter. A memo can be addressed
to a specific person or to a group. A memo can be posted on a bulletin
board and not have its meaning changed. The message it delivers will
dictate its distribution.

Consider adopting a masthead or set aside one color paper for your
memos (Figure 4.2). These signal the receiver that it is a memo from
you. Using catchy Action Stationery from time to time captures the
attention of your readers and prepares them for your message by the very
nature of the design you select (Figures 4.3 and 4.4).

Reports

From time to time it is necessary to issue a report following an
investigation in order to describe the status of a program, to provide the
necessary supportive facts prior to a decision being made, or to update
a prior report. Among the many reports written in a school district are
the superintendent's annual report; committee/task force reports on
topics such as attendance and dropouts, results of the district's testing
program, student discipline referrals, and enrollment projections; and
comprehensive school assessment reports.

If a report or proposal is longer than four pages, it would be very
helpful if you included a one-page summary. Often administrators and
board members have too much to read, and are overwhelmed by items
demanding their attention. The one page summary should identify:

- the topic being covered
- the purpose of the report/proposal
- the key facts, findings, and recommendations
- the benefits to be derived if the recommendations are followed

Append the full report to the summary. Individuals who have neither
the time nor the inclination to read the full report will appreciate the
summary.

Look at the report(s) you prepare as an example of your best work. It

NEWBURGH CITY SCHOOL DISTRICT
SUPERINTENDENT OF SCHOOLS

P E L

DR. PHILLIP E. LEAHY

Figure 4.2

92

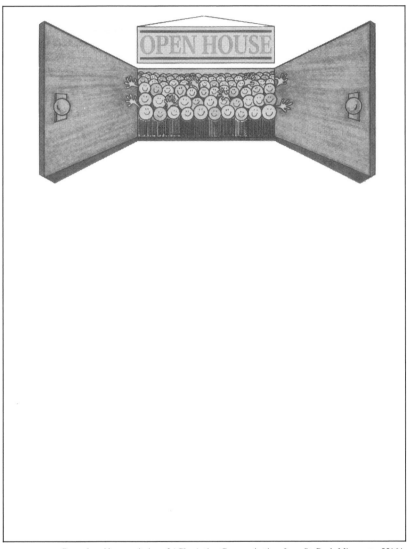

Figure 4.3

Reproduced by permission of ACI — Action Communication, Inc., St. Paul, Minnesota, 55164.

Figure 4.4

is going to be read by a number of people and can serve as a public relations tool for you. Often, the format can make or break a report. By carefully structuring the report into a meaningful sequence of ideas that flow from one to the other, you provide readers with a format they can easily follow. The summary of the report should reflect the sequence of the report. Do not throw a report together just to get it done. You generally put a great deal of effort into getting the material together; present it so that it reflects your efforts and knowledge.

Use the technology that is available to produce a clean, well-typed report. Use the styling features of your typewriter, word processor, or computer—underline where appropriate, use bold type and italics, and introduce graphics. Change the type font if it will add emphasis. Prepare a cover sheet and a table of contents. An appendix is appropriate if you have material that would be useful but which does not belong in the report proper. Consider color-coding sections of the report by using different colored paper.

Consider binding the report so that it reflects your style. You may want to use a traditional folder, a double pocket folder, a notebook, an Acco fastener cover, or grip strip spines with clear plastic sheets that cover the report. Consider using a plastic spiral binding where you can select the color of the spiral and the report covers. You can also use a relatively new desktop binding process by Velobind, which is relatively inexpensive and very effective and distinctive. Using a simple punch, a plastic strip, and cover sheets of your color choice, you can bind a report that has a professional look. Velobind claims that its ''plastic strip technology is the only process in the world able to meet virtually any requirement for fastening sheets of paper together.''

Above all, be yourself. Develop a style that you feel comfortable with and which suits your personality. You need to come across well in whichever communication strategy you decide to use.

Communication Breakdowns

Communication breakdowns occur when communication ceases. At times we think that we have communicated when information is given. Many times the message is never received because it never gets delivered. Mail gets lost and does not reach the addressee; telephone messages are lost. The sender of the message usually does not know that the message was never received unless he/she follows up on the non-response. We forget that communication needs to be two-way.

Up to 80 percent of a person's time is spent communicating, yet as much as 50 percent of the information is not interpreted correctly. We forget to pay attention to what others are saying. At times we distort the intent of the message because of our own experiences and value systems. Sometimes the sender does not communicate the true message because it is not pleasant to do so. An example of this is an individual's personnel evaluation, where a true evaluation would be negative and unpleasant. The superintendent decides instead to send a modified evaluation.

Breakdowns occur as a result of conflicting personalities, misunderstandings of words used, murky intent, and ineffective approach. They may occur as a result of an unwillingness to accept what the other person is saying, coupled with an unwillingness to continue to attempt to resolve the issue. All too often, we do not really listen, and when we do, we tend to listen for what we want to hear.

Try to resolve the breakdown by coming together in an open, honest effort to communicate. Do not attack individuals, and do not harbor ill feelings. Remember that what you want to do is resolve the problem — you do not need to "win." Many times, setting aside hostilities, and recognizing the vantage point and position of the other individual(s), will produce surprisingly effective results. Remember that mistrust is the greatest enemy of effective communication in any forum — whether it be in the international political arena or in the local public school system. By fostering an atmosphere of honesty, accountability, and caring from the very beginning, you can immediately clear away your school's greatest barrier to progress and to good public relations.

CHAPTER 5

INVOLVING THE PUBLICS

"... THE SCHOOL IS A PART OF THE
COMMUNITY AND MUST KEEP IN TOUCH
WITH IT CONSTANTLY."

Adolph Unruh and Robert A. Willier
Public Relations for Schools

F E W communities are homogeneous in composition today. In every community are families in transit, with varied cultural, racial, ethnic, and socioeconomic backgrounds. As school administrators, we have a responsibility to work with our communities and to involve the public in as many ways as possible. We need to make certain that members of the public, regardless of their cultural heritage, understand the mission and goals of the school so that they can support us not only at the polls, but within their respective ethnic groups.

Although students move in and out of schools for any number of reasons, you can readily determine the mobility of your school community by reviewing student transfers. Work/economic-related concerns are among the most prevalent reasons. Varied lifestyles, family composition, and availability of child care are often cited as reasons that cause families to move in and out of communities. Communicating with families in transit is difficult because their prime concern may not always be the education of their children; they have concerns that they view as far more basic to their survival. Involving them in our schools is infinitely more difficult.

Single-Focus Groups

Community members possess feelings, attitudes, personal values, and needs generated largely by their personal circumstances and educational and work-related experiences. Despite their many differences, there are times when members of the community have the same goals and objec-

97

tives. They want the same thing to happen regardless of their racial, ethnic, or socioeconomic status. On a single issue they may come together because they share a particular value. They often form groups with a single focus – allegiances to a single issue. They work together to see the objectives to fruition, then they disband and perhaps never work together again.

Single-focus groups will form for issues such as a proposed redistricting of a school's boundaries, the closing of a school, elimination of extracurricular programs, or a large increase in taxes. Once proposals such as these are known or talked about, groups will form on both sides of the issue.

> We generally do not consider groups with more than about twenty members as *small* groups. The reason for this is that the frequent, *face-to-face interaction* and *mutual influence* that is characteristic of small groups is much less likely to occur when there are more than about twenty people involved. . . . They meet on a more-or-less regular basis, usually in the same location, and while individual members of the group may come and go, the group itself endures . . . . The members of these small groups show a commonality of purpose . . . expressed in terms of goals upon which there is mutual agreement. (Mitchell and Larson, 1987)

Booster Clubs

Booster clubs are examples of groups who come together for one purpose. Most high schools have booster clubs for sports and music/band. The membership of the booster club is comprised of parents, interested community members, business establishments, and former students. They support the activities of the group by volunteering their time, and they are involved in money-raising efforts – donating their own money, and lending personal support by their presence at the games/musicals. They are generally the most vocal supporters of their activity before the school board and in the community.

Audience

An individual's opinions or attitude will be influenced by the group to which he/she belongs. An individual, as a member of a group that comes together to hear about a specific incident or to discuss a topic, is usually a member of an audience. An audience is addressed in order to share information and to obtain as much personal and group commitment as possible.

Large Groups, Crowds, Mobs

Large groups, or crowds, often come together as a result of an accident — e.g., a building collapse, an earthquake, a fire. The interaction between the members is minimal; their involvement is limited. They are interested, and tend to be spectators. This is in contrast to participants, such as emergency workers, volunteers, city/county personnel, medics, and the like who are actively participating in the rescue efforts or in containing further damage.

Other large groups, or crowds, come together to accomplish a particular purpose. The intensity of the feelings of a group can often transform a group into an uncontrolled mob as a result of the activities and/or interactions at a meeting. People at a ball game or a political rally are part of a crowd; they share the same identification and affiliation with the political party or team. They share a common purpose. Their focus at the time of the meeting is narrow — to support their party or team. These groups at times become mobs when their activities turn violent or spiral out of control. We have seen rallies and ball games become unruly mob scenes resulting in casualties and extensive damage to the physical facilities.

Community Groups

In every community there are social groups that come together because of ethnic, racial, or family ties. You need to recognize the existence and strengths of these groups, and utilize their strengths to support your position. Their needs must be addressed.

Churches and synagogues, business and civic groups, political and fraternal organizations, labor organizations, and service clubs are groups to which people belong. They can swing public sentiment and command large blocks of votes. Among the many groups present in most communities are organizations such as: Chamber of Commerce, Board of Realtors, Exchange Club, Jaycees, Kiwanis, Knights of Columbus, Lions, League of Women Voters, and senior citizen groups. They can be the source of support for, or against, an issue.

Identify the many diverse groups in your school community. Make contact and establish a relationship with them. Know where the community groups stand; be aware of their sentiments. Put them on your mailing list and provide them with information so that they will be apprised of what is going on in your school/district on a continuing basis. Do not approach them only when you need their support. Establish a relationship long before you want their support.

Offer to speak to the groups. Share information with them and talk about what you know best—education. Be the authority, the source of information, on education. A far better understanding of controversial issues is possible when information has been shared on a continuing basis and a prior relationship has been established. Unruh and Willier (1974) remark that "without facts, information, and understanding, people will be likely to act emotionally about an issue, almost instinctively if they sense that their values and even their prejudices are under attack. Under such conditions, a plea for school support will not be very successful."

Listen to groups representing both sides of an issue. Do not ignore a group that is opposed to your proposal. Talk with them, meet with them, work with them. Try to influence their opinions by giving them facts and figures to support your position while still respecting their positions. Try to put an end to rumors by first being informed of the rumors, and second, by providing information that should put an end to the rumors.

Key Communicators

Find out who the leaders are in the group/community, both formal and informal. These are the individuals who are respected and can usually get the word out to their groups. They are those members of your community who are looked up to and trusted by community members. They may be members of organizations, or they may be unaffiliated. They may be crossing guards, barbers, beauticians, gas station attendants, or bakers. They are sincere people who want to be involved and who care about the schools. They have contact with members of the school community and are listened to and respected. They can spread the word quickly because they have the wherewithal to contact their groups through their networks. Very often key communicators are seen as having greater credibility than school district employees because district employees are seen as having a vested interest.

If a rumor is circulating in the community, the chances are that the key communicators are aware of it because rumors and ideas are "bounced off" them for verification and/or amplification. You need to know what is going on in the community; you need to know the pulse of your community. The people best able to give you this information are the key communicators. Having this information enables you to take appropriate action.

How do you enlist the key communicators? First find out the groups that are present in your community. Read the local newspaper(s). Talk to members of the community; talk to members of the staff. They can tell you the people who play key roles in shaping public opinion in the community. Some of the key communicators are the silent, behind-the-scenes people in the community – the power brokers. They may be found working with charitable, political, social, and/or ethnic groups. They may be members of the Parent Teacher Association (PTA) or the business community. Whoever they are, once the word is out that you want to get to know them and talk with them, you will generally find out who they are. People will come to you and tell you who they are. Ask the staff members and administrators to identify people who they think could function as key communicators.

You need to establish two-way communication with these individuals so that they can share information, rumors, and concerns with you, and you can share information with them. You need to make them privy to what you are doing, what your school plans are, and the progress you are making. They need to have information in order to maintain their credibility with their constituents.

Invite them to have coffee with you and let them know the role you see for key communicators. Emphasize that you would like to have open two-way communication with them. Ask them to call you if they hear of any rumors, problems, or questions that need to be answered. Tell them that you will give them answers to these questions and track down the rumors and get back to them. Tell them that you will also give them information as to what the district is doing so that they can pass it along to members of their groups.

Establish a mailing list and make certain that the key communicators are sent information on a continuing basis. Send them copies of the press releases, abstracts of reports that the district has prepared, summaries of the board meetings, abstracts of the budget, information/fact sheets, and good news about the district staff and students. Send them information so that they can be a source of information.

Exemplary Practice: One woman was appointed as the superintendent of schools of a major midwestern city. She was the first woman superintendent in the state and knew absolutely no one in the community. She knew that she had to have input from the community; she had to know where the community stood on a variety of issues — what their aspirations were for the students, and of prime importance, why two tax levies had failed. She decided to find out who the key communicators were — the power brokers, the people who were trusted by the various segments of the community.

She solicited names from staff members, board members, and city officials. At the end of each day she went home with a list of names and called a minimum of three people. These people were key people in the community. She introduced herself, started a conversation, and asked their opinions about the school district. She made appointments to meet with many of them and members of their respective groups. Within a very short period of time she learned many things that would have taken months to find out otherwise.

Many of the concerns raised proved to be legitimate. She took actions that she deemed appropriate and continued to reach out to the staff and community to open the channels of communication and change community attitudes. While a fifty-five cent increase in the tax levy (requiring a two-thirds vote) failed twice before she came to the district, an eighty-eight cent levy passed nine months after her arrival. And that in the wake of Proposition 13 in California!

This superintendent felt that a lot of hard work by many people resulted in the change in community attitudes, but a key factor in the process was the outreach efforts to the community through key communicators. Having an honest, open manner; listening to the concerns of constituents; taking action where appropriate; and sharing information, all contributed to the success enjoyed by the district.

This strategy can work for every administrator in a school/district. View key communicators as tremendous resources. Nurture them, do not ignore them.

Advisory Groups/Councils

Advisory groups, citizen committees, and task forces are not new to education. National advisory committees were in operation as early as the year 1900, dealing with such areas as teacher certification, juvenile delinquency, and school examinations (Stauffer, 1957).

Schools and districts have citizen advisory groups/boards because they are mandated by the funding source. Chapter I advisory committees, Head Start advisory committees, vocational education advisory boards, and career education advisory boards are some examples. These advisory groups deal with specific programs; their memberships consist of members of the community and the staff who have expertise to lend to the group. The members give added insights to the district as a result of their participation and thereby strengthen the program.

Schools/districts/school boards form advisory groups in order to deal with a specific topic. There are two types of advisory committees: those appointed to serve by an administrator or school board, often called school-sponsored committees; and those organized by the citizens themselves, often called citizen-sponsored committees. School-sponsored committees are often viewed with suspicion as committees ''stacked'' by the district that will support the district's position.

In selecting members of an advisory committee, include people who are representative of the community at large, and reflective of your school/district. You need to make certain that you appoint individuals to represent the underrepresented groups on an advisory committee. Many times organizations such as the teachers' union are asked to submit the names of individuals they would like to serve as their representatives on advisory committees. Selecting individuals from a list such as this takes the onus off the school/district and is viewed with less suspicion than merely appointing members. Many times advisory group members come from the ranks of the PTA/PTO/PTSO (Parent Teacher Association, Parent Teacher Organization, Parent Teacher Student Organization). In larger school districts there may be a district-wide PTA/PTO/PTSO that usually has representation from each school in the district.

Citizen advisory committee members volunteer their time and energies and have no policy-making status. They lend their expertise to the mission of the committee and serve the district and the citizens through their advisory recommendations. Consider the skills and interests of the individuals that you ask to serve on an advisory committee. You need to be certain that the members of the group have the skills needed to accomplish the task. Balance the committee by selecting members who represent the broad spectrum of the community you serve.

Some groups are standing committees, others are ad hoc committees. Committees/advisory groups need to know what is expected of them and what they are responsible for. They need to have a mission statement, or charge, that clearly identifies what the expectations are. Negativism on the part of the administrator is counterproductive, as is relegating the council to deal with trivial matters that are of no consequence to the school/district. Give the committee something relevant and timely to deal with. Use specific language that is void of jargon in preparing the charge. Make certain that the committee members understand the charge; give it to them in writing.

The following are charges given by school districts to committees.

CHARGE
To the Dropout Prevention Task Force

The Dropout Prevention Task Force is composed of representatives from Danbury Community Groups, the Business Community as represented by the Danbury Community Education Advisory Council, and staff members in the Danbury School System during the 1987 – 1988 school year. They are charged with the following tasks:

    I. Advise and assist in the development of a plan to increase community awareness of existing efforts at Dropout Prevention in the school and community.

    II. Identify factors which should be included in developing a profile of who is dropping out of the Danbury Schools.

    III. Report on efforts that represented groups and others are currently using to prevent dropouts or assist those who have dropped out.

    IV. Identify unmet or under-served needs relative to Dropout Prevention.

    V. Present the findings of the Task Force to the Community Forum to be held in May 1988. Identify participants in that Forum.

    VI. Develop an action plan for reducing dropouts in the Danbury School System using the data collected by the Task Force.

Danbury Public Schools
Danbury, Connecticut

CHARGE
To the Educational Specifications Committee

The Educational Specifications Committee was formed to define building/space/facilities requirements as they relate to educational programs in the University City School District's elementary program. The specific charge to the committee was:

1. Develop a philosophy and purpose directed towards how the physical plant enhances the teaching/learning process.
2. Include a philosophy statement on the kinds of space needed to accommodate program requirements with consideration given to team teaching, large group, small group, continuous progress, self-contained, flexible groups, etc.
3. Include an overview of general elementary education to include areas such as math, science, language, reading, and social studies as taught by the classroom teacher. More specialized programs include art, music, physical education, etc.

For each program included in the elementary schools, identify the following:

1. Purpose/concept
2. Activities
3. Space/furniture/equipment recommendations

University City School District
University City, Missouri

CHARGE
Public Relations Advisory Board

This charge was given to members of the Public Relations Advisory Board of the South Central School District 406, King County, Seattle, Washington.

As a member of the Public Relations Advisory Board, you will be asked to:

- Give counsel on public relations strategies, general public relations, and other topics as requested by the School Board or administration.
- Give feedback on ongoing public relations programs in the district.
- Give advice on short and long range school/community relations plans and projects affecting the community.
- Share information about public perceptions of the district and bring related matters to the district's attention at bi-monthly PR Advisory Board meetings or as needed.

South Central School District 406
King County, Seattle, Washington

Identify a budget within which they can work and assign a staff member as liaison to the group. Encourage this staff member to work with the group to assure that the group does not stray far from the charge they were to examine. Make information available to them so that they can complete their mission. "Studies show that lack of information is a primary barrier to effectiveness of mandated councils. Low income and minority parents are especially disadvantaged by lack of access to information, and by the highly technical, jargon-ridden materials they are given" (Davies, 1980).

Give the group a lifespan and set reporting dates. Receive their report(s) and thank them. If they are an ad hoc committee as opposed to a standing committee, disband the committee once they have completed their mission. Very often you will find that members of a committee want to continue to be part of a watchdog group long after the mission is accomplished. Failure to thank and disband the group often leads members to think that they are, in fact, an ongoing group.

You will find that people will participate more readily when they know the specific charge to the committee and its lifespan. They can assess the commitment needed to participate. Where you have an ongoing advisory committee/board, appoint members for specific, staggered terms so that there can be continuity in their deliberations. When filling a vacancy on the committee, fill it for the remainder of the unexpired term. Do not upset the staggered terms by having a disproportionate number of people going off at the same time. It may be desirable to identify the number of times a person may serve on a committee.

Staff Advisory Committees

Staff advisory committees may be dealt with in a union contract that covers the staff of the district. Abide by the terms of the contract. If you find that the contract does not address the issue of advisory committees, and you would like to function with them, consult with the union representatives as a courtesy. Reassure members of the union that you do not intend to usurp their role in voicing concerns. Indicate that you are interested in opening lines of communication and resolving concerns. Do not deal with matters that are covered by, and can be grieved under, the terms of the contract.

Principals/Directors Advisory Councils

Building principals and program directors may opt or be required by union contract to work with advisory councils composed of representatives of the various grades/departments under their jurisdictions.

Ideally the Principal's/Director's Advisory Council (P/DAC) will meet at least once a month in a non-threatening environment to discuss matters of concern to either the staff or the administrator. Hopefully the areas of concern raised at these meetings which are under the control of the administrator will be taken care of within a reasonable time. Minutes of the P/DAC meetings should be kept and distributed to members of the faculty. A copy should be sent to the superintendent. You may wish to star (*) the items that are going to be raised at the next Superintendent's Advisory Council. There are generally two reasons that these items are placed on the agenda—(1) they do not fall under the purview of the administrator; or (2) the items have been on the P/DAC agenda for more than a reasonable time without being resolved, and are now being moved to the superintendent's level for resolution.

Superintendent's Advisory Council

Many superintendents have Superintendent's Advisory Councils (SAC) which meet with the superintendent once a month in order to maintain open lines of communication and to voice concerns that have not been resolved in the schools/departments. The membership of the SAC usually consists of one member elected by the staff of each building. In the case of a larger school, such as a high school, where there are many more staff members than in a smaller elementary or middle/junior high school, two or more representatives may be elected to the SAC. These individuals sit on their respective P/DACs and bring to the floor of the SAC the starred items from their monthly meetings.

Many times the superintendent will research some of the items in advance, and give a response at the meeting. The superintendent may bring a cabinet-level administrator with him/her to the meeting in order to respond. Many times the superintendent will use the meeting to obtain additional information, and bring a response to the next SAC meeting.

Problems that would traditionally remain unresolved or fester until they escalated to a point of contention, can be resolved in the P/DAC or SAC by virtue of the fact that they are aired in a non-threatening environment. Additionally, the move to site-based management goes hand in hand with the use of techniques such as the P/DAC and SAC.

Student Advisory Groups

Many buildings/districts have Student Advisory Groups (SAG) that represent the various grades. The SAG discusses matters of concern to the students. At the building level, the SAG is usually the student government. At the district level, the SAG is composed of elected representatives of the individual SAGs of each school. These meetings are held on a regularly scheduled basis, and otherwise as needed. They provide an excellent structure for two-way communication with students, whose voices are often ignored.

Consider Using Advisory Councils

Advisory councils have been very helpful in that their recommendations are generally balanced, because of the composition of the council, and the fact that they represent a group that has the expertise and the will needed to tackle a problem area.

CHAPTER 6

MEETINGS AND CONFERENCES

WE ARE A "MEETING SOCIETY." THE
MEETING YOU ATTENDED THIS MORNING
MAY HAVE BEEN IMPORTANT TO YOU,
BUT IT WAS ONLY ONE OF 11 MILLION
MEETINGS HELD IN THE UNITED
STATES TODAY.

Harvey J. Lifton
Human Resources Forum

M E E T I N G S are held in order to conduct the business of the school/district, to exchange information with the various publics, and to coordinate efforts. There are meetings called for any number of reasons, among which are:

- to conduct board of education business
- to speak with community groups
- to accomplish committee work
- to facilitate staff operations
- to orient newcomers to the school district
- to share information
- to set goals
- to solve problems
- to enable teams to work cooperatively
- to enable the PTA to function

Meetings may be conducted in public or private/executive session. Public meetings include: meetings of the board of education, public hearings, faculty meetings, Parent Teacher Association meetings, advisory group meetings, committee and various task force meetings, study group meetings, student organizations, and ad hoc work sessions. Private/executive session meetings include executive sessions of the board of education held in conformance with the Freedom of Information law and state sunshine laws. These sessions are usually restricted to matters dealing with personnel, and contractual or legal matters.

The decision as to whether or not meetings should be held, their frequency, participants, and agendas are controlled by the chairperson/administrator. The number of meetings can be reduced and their effectiveness improved as a result of careful planning.

Planning a Meeting: Why, Who, When, Where

Why

You have undoubtedly heard the old phrase that "meetings are where you keep the minutes and throw away the hours." Do not fall into that pattern. Recognize that all too many hours are spent on meetings during the course of a year—hours that could have been spent in a more meaningful way. Do not schedule a meeting for the sake of having a meeting. You will find staff, faculty, department, and committee meetings scheduled every week or so regardless of whether or not there is anything to discuss, or whether another vehicle might be better employed to accomplish the task at hand. Meetings should be scheduled for a specific reason. Clearly define the purpose of the meeting, the appropriate attendees, and the agenda before you call a meeting.

Ask yourself why you are having the meeting. Is there something that needs to be done? Do others need to be involved in order for a decision to be reached? Could you do so with one, or two others? by yourself? Could the matter be handled effectively without a meeting by using a memorandum or a telephone call? Once you decide that a meeting is necessary, set very clearly defined objectives, select the appropriate attendees, and let the participants know what it is that is to be accomplished and what is expected of them.

Consider how much time the meeting will take. People are very conscious of the time spent at meetings. Administrators are always looking for ways to manage their time better. Before you call a meeting and tie these individuals up, remember that a "key issue is not time management but making time to manage" (Chopra, 1989). Value time as others do; call a meeting only when it is the best vehicle to accomplish a purpose.

Who

A good rule to follow is to include only those people who need to be directly involved in accomplishing the objectives. The ideal number of participants for an effective meeting is five to seven; more than twelve people is generally too large. People need to be able to interact and be heard. The larger the number of participants, the more difficult and the longer it takes to reach the objectives (Bingaman, Graham and Wheeler, 1983).

Invite those individuals who can contribute to the essence of the meeting, are directly involved, or have a need to know. These individuals include those who are responsible for the topic, are politically involved, and/or can contribute to the deliberations of the group.

When

Having identified the people needed to reach a decision, find out the times that are most convenient for them to attend. Schedule a meeting that is mutually convenient for them. Notify them of the time and place of the meeting just as soon as you set it so that they can place it on their calendars. Send a written confirmation of the meeting to them asking for confirmation that they can attend. If you find that an individual(s) cannot attend, ask him/her to send a representative who can act on his/her behalf.

Where

Deciding where to hold the meeting generally has a direct relationship to the objective of the meeting. Do the participants need uninterrupted time away from others in the organization? Will you be meeting for a long period of time? Will you need break-out rooms? Will an off-site location provide the change of pace that the group needs to set the tone of the meeting? Do you need a retreat-type setting? Or, is it best to hold the meeting in your office or a school conference room?

Select a location that will accommodate the size of the group; have the equipment, such as easels, projectors, and VCRs available. Be able to serve coffee or lunch if needed, and be near restrooms.

Conducting a Meeting

A basic routine will lead to a more productive meeting.

(1) Start the meeting on time. When a meeting is called for a particular time, be on time yourself and start the meeting on time. Do not punish those individuals who come on time by catering to latecomers.

(2) Make certain that everyone knows one another. Introduce anyone who is new.

(3) Go over the reason why the meeting has been called and briefly state the objectives to be accomplished.

(4) Agree on the rules of order to be followed during the meeting.

(5) Appoint a recorder so that a brief record of action items or other needed data is assured.

(6) Go over the agenda.

(7) Review the time schedule.

(8) Respond to questions.

(9) Move the meeting along.

(10) Stay focused and on schedule.

(11) Listen actively and paraphrase complex points or ask clarifying questions for understanding.

(12) Encourage participation by all.

(13) Look at people's statements or data – minimize judgment or evaluation.

(14) Summarize decisions.

(15) Clarify actions required.

(16) Determine follow-up actions. Get a verbal commitment from the participants to follow through with their responsibilities.

(17) Close the meeting. End the meeting on an upbeat note and thank the group.

(18) Send out minutes of the meeting.

Meeting Agendas

Set a realistic agenda and send it out in advance of the meeting. Send the appropriate backup information along with the agenda, coded accordingly. This enables meeting participants to come prepared to discuss the agenda items. Handing out the agenda and backup materials at the meeting serves to slow down the meeting and generally results in a less productive atmosphere.

Arrange the agenda so that items requiring clear thinking are dealt with first, when people are fresh and eager to get on with the meeting. Group the agenda items so that all the ''action'' items are together and all the "information" items are together. Grouping the items facilitates the meeting and enables the meeting to proceed more efficiently. If no immediate action is required on an item and you have lead time in dealing with it, consider placing the item on the agenda as an "information" item the first time it is presented. Bring it back as an "action" item when you want it acted on. This enables the participants to raise questions that they have on the item prior to being asked to vote on it. It also enables non-participants to ask any questions they may have. Further, it negates the often heard accusation that an item was rushed through in relative secrecy and in less than an open, honest manner.

Figure 6.1 illustrates an agenda format used by many schools, districts, and professional associations. The agenda items are numbered so that you can tell the year that the item was introduced and the number assigned to it. For example, the designation "90-138" readily indicates that this item came before the board in the 1989−90 school year and was the 138th item dealt with by the board. This enables the tracking of the item over the course of time. This format is useful for groups such as boards of education, faculty, and committee meetings. It can be adapted to suit the needs of the organization.

Prepare a separate page for each agenda item, stating the background, a discussion of the item, and the action requested (Figure 6.2). Where there is supporting documentation for an agenda item, code it the same as the agenda item. Place the backup behind the agenda item or alongside it so that they can be viewed together.

If there is a problem that concerns one individual, have the courage to speak to that person directly. Do not simply place the item on the agenda. Staff members are offended when they have to spend time dealing with an item that is not applicable to them. This is especially so when they know that one individual is the guilty one. They quickly recognize that you are refraining from addressing the issue; this weakens your position as their leader.

Moving the Meeting Along

Monitor the pace of the meeting, and keep the discussion on track. Try to move the group together, both those forging out ahead and those falling behind. Encourage participation. Make certain that the members know that all ideas and suggestions are welcome. A guiding principle in working with a group is: "If you help write it, you underwrite it." If the

February 15, 1990   **8:00 p.m.**   **McKnight Administration Building**
                                      8346 Delcrest Drive

Order of Business	Agenda Item	Subject
Call to Order		
Announcements		
Citizens' Comments		

A period of thirty minutes will be allotted to residents of University City School District and staff at the beginning of the meeting to give the Board the opportunity to listen to citizens. The Board is very interested in citizen viewpoints and problems. We encourage citizens to work through problems at the building and/or administrative levels before coming to the Board. We ask that remarks be limited to three minutes and to one appearance, thus allowing a maximum number of participants in the allotted time. This is a period in which citizens are to speak to issues. Questions directed to the Board cannot always be answered immediately. All questions will be responded to by an appropriate person within the week wherever possible. Board meetings are neither trials nor testimonials. Persons wishing to discuss personnel matters with the Board should write the Board about the matter. Persons who wish to suggest items for the agenda should contact Board members or the Superintendent.

In the event there are more citizens wishing to make comments, an additional period of time will be set aside at the end of the business meeting. Citizens who have a comment about a particular agenda item will be allowed to address the Board at the time that agenda item is under consideration with the understanding comments would be made after the Board has concluded its own discussion, but before a vote is taken. The guidelines for comments on agenda items would be the same as for the beginning of the meeting. If it appears that the item will become a major issue, the Board will limit discussion at its discretion. Time can be provided in another forum.

Order of Business	Agenda Item	Subject
Approval of Previous Minutes		
Superintendent's Reports and Recommendations		
Action	90-138	Order for Drawing Checks/Fund Balance Report
Action	90-139	MO Comprehensive Guidance Program Model
Action	90-140	Gift/Class of 1954
Action	90-141	Pershing "Acceleration 1990" Funding Proposal
Action	90-142	National Fitness Alliance Grant
Action	90-143	Marching Band Uniforms
Action	90-144	Summer Youth Employment Program
Action	90-145	Roof Repair/Senior High
Information	90-146	Employee Evaluations
Action	90-147	Conference Attendance
Information	90-148	Conference Attendance

Executive Session
  Approval of Previous Minutes
  Personnel Actions
  Real Estate
  Legal Matters
  Pupil Personnel

Figure 6.1

AASA HIGHER EDUCATION COMMITTEE

American Association of School Administrators
Arlington, Virginia

SUBJECT: **RESOLUTIONS COMMITTEE REQUEST**

Date: October 27, 1989
Reason for committee consideration: Action

BACKGROUND: Each year the AASA Resolutions Committee convenes to study major education policy issues and develop a draft of policy statements (resolutions) for consideration by the Delegate Assembly at the AASA national convention. The committee met September 18-19, 1989. A draft of the 1990 resolutions **(see enclosure)** will appear in AASA's Leadership News. Comments, reactions, and additional resolutions will be considered at a second meeting of the Resolutions Committee prior to the 1990 convention in February.

STATUS: The chair of the AASA Resolutions Committee, James L. Auter, sent a letter, August 21, 1989, to Higher Education Committee chair, Irene Lober **(see enclosure)** to request from this committee any information or recommendations for the Resolutions Committee to consider when it convenes in February.

RECOMMENDATIONS: Review the proposed platform and resolutions and suggest changes or additions.

Item number: HEC-89-25
Enclosures: 2

Figure 6.2

participants have a say in the deliberations and the final product, they will support it because they were instrumental in putting it together. It is difficult not to support something that you helped create.

Do not dwell too long on any one point, and do not wander too far afield. Keep restating where the group is and where you want to get. Remember that you want to complete your objective and you can always get back to an area that comes up incidentally. There is nothing more demoralizing to a group than to sit through a meeting and find out that another meeting is needed because the group did not complete the agenda. Recognize that all participants may not agree on every detail; try to reach consensus. If additional work is needed, agree to send the proposal back in order to get the work done and to return to it when it is ready for reconsideration.

Your ability to keep the meeting on track will result from your ability to question, listen, and respond to questions. Early recognition of, and promptly dealing with, potential problem areas, conflicts, and behaviors that can negatively impact the meeting, will result in less stress and a more productive meeting.

You may want to use a form similar to that used by the committees of the American Association of School Administrators for keeping track of the progress of the meeting. This form outlines who is expected to do what by when (Figure 6.3).

Physical Arrangements

Pay attention to the physical arrangement of the room in which the meeting is to take place. The physical arrangement of the furniture sets the tone for the meeting. If you are interested in reaching agreement, consider seating participants at a round or oval-shaped table where they are able to see one another. There are no sides to the table, as there would be if the participants were seated in a confrontational/negotiating mode, opposite one another. If you want to resolve an issue, you want to set as conciliatory a tone for the meeting as possible.

Public Participation

If public participation is desired, adopt speaking guidelines prior to the start of the public's participation. Waiting until an individual has spoken too long before deciding on suitable time limits causes undue strain and resentment. Inform the public in advance about the meeting.

AMERICAN ASSOCIATION OF SCHOOL ADMINISTRATORS

Meeting Record and Follow-Up

During a meeting, use this form to craft specific, responsible, and complete decisions. Following a meeting, this form should be used to monitor follow through and accountability.

Meeting Of: _____
Date/Time: _____
Location: _____
Attendance: _____

Recommended Project/ Activity	Who Is Responsible?	Starting and Completion Dates	Is Project Consistent: S.O., Budget, LRP?	Purchase Cost And/ Or Income	# Of New Members It Will Attract/ Old Members Will Benefit	AASA Activity: Addition/ Replacement	Status

Reprinted with permission from the American Association of School Administrators, Arlington, Virginia.

Figure 6.3

For example, the University City School District's Board of Education encourages public participation early in the board meeting. A board-adopted statement identifies the limits of the public's participation (see "Citizens' Comments," Figure 6.1). Other boards of education have adopted similar statements that are made available to the public (Figures 6.4 and 6.5). Some boards require individuals wishing to address the board to complete a Speaker Request Form (Figure 6.6).

When boards find that the time allotted before the meeting is too short to accommodate the number of people who want to speak, they convene the regular meeting of the board and then recess the meeting in order to hear additional citizens' comments. At times, the board may continue listening to citizen comments at the conclusion of the meeting. There are some boards that allow citizens to speak as an agenda item is being considered by the board. Remember that in holding public hearings you may want to adopt the practice used by your board of education in hearing citizens' comments. There is much to be said when a district is consistent in how the various groups/schools secure citizen comments.

Public Hearings

Public hearings are held in order to hear from the public on a specific topic, such as the budget, school boundaries, extracurricular activities, and new programs. In a public hearing you are reaching out to the community in order to find out what their attitudes and opinions are relative to a specific topic.

Do not start a public hearing prior to adopting a set of guidelines for the conduct of the hearing. The hearing could get out of control without a set of procedures to guide its conduct. Have the guidelines available at the hearing; this minimizes conflict (Figure 6.7).

Publicize the hearing well in advance so that the community will know that it is being held and what the topic is. Send out news releases, send home flyers, and talk about the hearing every chance you can. Getting the word out is important (Figure 6.8). Set the time for the public hearing to start and *start on time.* Eliminate small talk, focus on the agenda and the topic of the hearing.

Exemplary Practice: One superintendent of schools recognized the fact that information was needed in order to determine the priorities of the community relative to the school district, prior to putting the superintendent's budget together.

We're Glad You Came!

Your presence at a school board meeting indicates your interest and concern in the education of Fort Knox children. The Board of Education and the staff of the Fort Knox Community Schools appreciate your interest in our schools and your attendance at board meetings. School board decisions affect our children's education and the well-being of the community. The Board can best represent its constituents when residents take the time to observe the Board in action, express their opinions, and raise questions.

We are pleased to have you here and hope you can attend meetings frequently.

School Board Meetings

Regular meetings of the Board of Education of the Fort Knox Community Schools are held once per month on the last Tuesday of the Month. The meeting location, time, and agenda are advertised in Inside the Turret, Channel 12 and the "Daily Bulletin".

Board meetings are held on the last Tuesday of each month (except July) at Pierce Elementary School at 4:00 p.m. The agenda is supplied to all visitors in addition to its pre-publication. The board Chair reserves the right to change the order of consideration of individual agenda items usually for the benefit of visitors interested in particular issues.

Occasionally special meetings are needed for board action outside regular meeting dates. The post Public Affairs Office is notified as soon as a special meeting has been established for publication.

At times the board may have to go into Executive Session, which means sensitive personnel matters, negotiations with employee bargaining units or items requiring closed sessions by federal law are to be discussed privately.

Most of the board action and informational items are staffed prior to the regular monthly meeting, requiring many hours of hard committee work. Research and analysis are critical to successful board meetings. Proposed board policy items are advertised in the Turret and Channel 12 to give adequate time for parent and staff input.

Participation By The Public

Individuals or groups are invited to address the board with their opinions, concerns, suggestions or complaints. The following procedure should be followed to allow the board to place your need on the agenda and to research the matter prior to the actual board meeting.

1. Submit a letter to the board Chair, through the superintendent, at least 5 days prior to board meetings, stating the nature of the matter to be discussed.

2. Matters of a personal nature will be discussed in executive session. FKCS employees being grieved will be given the opportunity to attend the executive session and allowed to participate in the discussion.

**Resolution of all matters involving an employee(s) of the FKCS must first be attempted through involvement of the grieved employee(s) immediate supervisor. If a satisfactory resolution is not reached with the grieved employee's supervisor, then an appeal should be sent to the superintendent of schools prior to board action.

The board chairperson may, at his/her discretion, recognize visitors from the floor to speak on agenda matters opened for discussion.

Board Meeting Schedule

Schedule for Fort Knox Board of Education Meetings SY 1987-1988

25	August	1987
29	September	1987
27	October	1987
24	November	1987
15	December	1987
26	January	1988
23	February	1988
29	March	1988
26	April	1988
31	May	1988
28	June	1988

The Board does not meet in July.

Responsibilities Of The Board

The Board of Education sets policy for the management of the district. The Superintendent and the district staff are responsible for the execution of these policies.

The general responsibilities of the Board are to:

- Select the superintendent of schools
- Establish policies for the operation of the district
- Appoint all school district personnel and approve salaries
- Adopt goals and objectives for the district
- Monitor and evaluate district progress toward these goals
- Decide use of district resources and approve the annual school budget
- Communicate the needs and progress of the district to the community, educational governing boards, and legislators.

Purpose:

To provide students of Fort Knox Community Schools an education so that they may become well adjusted, productive members of society.

Missions:

- To prepare Fort Knox students for responsible citizenship
- To prepare Fort Knox students for further schooling
- To prepare Fort Knox students for employment
- To instill a love of learning in Fort Knox students

Meeting Agenda

The usual order of business at regular business meetings is as follows:

- Call to order
- Board operation, administration, instruction
- Fiscal management
- Personnel (faculty and students)
- Facilities and transportation

Reproduced from *Welcome to a Meeting of Your School Board*, Fort Knox Community Schools, Fort Knox, Kentucky.

Figure 6.4

COMMON QUESTIONS	SAMPLE AGENDA

COMMON QUESTIONS

WHEN CONFRONTED WITH A PROBLEM IN MY CHILD'S SCHOOL, SHOULD I FIRST CONTACT A BOARD MEMBER?

The primary function of the School Board is to establish county-wide policy. The Seminole County School District adheres to a system called "school-based management" which places the responsibility of school administrative action with the principal and administrative staff of each school. If you have a concern about your child's school, communicate that concern first to your child's teacher, then pursue it further with the school's administration. County level administrators can provide assistance with interpretation of school policy and provide information about district programs and curriculum. If you believe your concern involves a problem with a county-wide policy, you may choose to address those concerns at a Board meeting.

HOW CAN I CONTACT A BOARD MEMBER TO EXPRESS A CONCERN ABOUT AN ISSUE OR POLICY?

You may reach any Board Member by leaving a message with the School Board Secretary at 322-1252, extension 201.

DO BOARD MEMBERS REPRESENT ONLY THE CONSTITUENTS FROM THEIR INDIVIDUAL DISTRICTS?

No. Although Board Members represent individual districts, they work toward common goals of the entire school system.

HOW CAN I DETERMINE WHETHER A BOARD MEETING WILL BE HELD IN THE AFTERNOON OR EVENING?

The School Board meets throughout the year on the second and fourth Wednesday of each month. Meetings which fall on the second Wednesday of the month convene in the afternoon at 2:00 p.m. Meetings which fall on the fourth Wednesday of the month convene in the evening at 7:00 p.m.

SAMPLE AGENDA

- AGENDA -
SCHOOL BOARD MEETING
COUNTY OFFICE BOARD ROOM

DATE - TIME

CALL TO ORDER
ROLL CALL
PRESENTATIONS AND REQUESTS
Includes any special presentations, awards or recognition of Seminole County students, personnel, business groups and community leaders. Members of the public who have previously requested to be represented on the agenda are heard at this time.
CATEGORICAL CONSENT AGENDA
This part of the meeting covers items that the Board is familiar with, or items that require little or no discussion. Staffing recommendations, bids and purchase orders, and inventory removal are some of the items presented as part of the Categorical Consent Agenda.
SUPERINTENDENT'S REPORT
Items which are a part of the Superintendent's Report must be presented to the Board Members for discussion and then approval or rejection. Seminole County is currently under a comprehensive construction program, so the report often focuses on capital outlay projects which include changes in building specifications, contract revisions and approval of like documents.
ATTORNEY'S REPORT
The School Board Attorney's report deals with legal issues in which the Board acts as contracting agent or litigant.
OLD AND NEW BUSINESS
Old business may include items that are carried over from previous Board meetings. New business includes items going before the Board for the first time. Members of the audience who wish to pose a question or make a statement may be heard at this time.
EXPULSIONS
Expulsion hearings are presented last, and are generally open to only those persons involved in the hearing.

Reproduced from *A Citizen's Guide to the School Board of Seminole County, Florida.*

Figure 6.5

Pinellas County School Board
SPEAKER REQUEST FORM

School Board Meetings

The public is invited to attend School Board meetings.
Meetings are held on the second and fourth Wednesdays
of each month in the Board Room of the Administration
Building, 1960 East Druid Road, Clearwater, Florida.
Special meetings are scheduled as needed.

If you wish to speak to the Board

1. Fill out the form below, list the item, and turn in to the Public
Information Officer five minutes before the item is
discussed.
2. If you wish to speak about a subject not on the agenda,
fill out the form below, list the subject, and turn in to the
Public Information Officer five minutes before the listing
of "Presentations from the Audience."

You will be called on by the Chairman at the appropriate time.

**Presentations are limited to five minutes. If there are
more than ten speakers on the subject, the limit is three
minutes per person. You may yield your time to another
speaker if you choose.**

Date _____

I wish to address the School Board about

Item No———— concerning ———————

_____

_____

Name _____

Address _____

_____

Figure 6.6

BOARD OF EDUCATION

Danbury, Connecticut

CONDUCT OF PUBLIC HEARING

The purpose of this hearing is to offer members of the community an opportunity to respond to the Superintendent's proposed budget recommendations and to share their thinking, interests and concerns about the school budget. Residents of Danbury and staff members are permitted to speak at this hearing. Comments may be directed to the chair, individual members of the Board and the administration. Clarifying questions will be asked. Responses to concerns will be dealt with during Board review sessions and every attempt will be made to respond to the individual raising the concern.

The meeting will begin promptly at 7:30 p.m. We hope that this hearing will provide a suitable forum for voicing ideas and information to help planning for the future. In order that individuals may have a fair opportunity to speak, we must, of necessity, follow these rules of order:

1. Each speaker must identify him/herself by name, address and group he/she represents, if other than him/herself.

2. Each speaker must be a resident of Danbury or a staff member and will be granted five minutes to present a position or raise a question. Speakers representing organizations will be granted 10 minutes.

3. No one will be allowed an extension of time or second time until all who wish to speak have had at least one opportunity.

4. A one-minute warning will be signaled.

5. When all who wish to speak have done so, and time permits, an additional five minutes will be granted to anyone who wishes to speak a second time.

6. Problems of a personal nature are not proper subjects to be discussed at this hearing. Anyone who has such a problem should contact the Superintendent directly, who will arrange a personal conference with the appropriate staff member who can assist in the matter.

7. Whenever the chairperson believes that statements made are derogatory or critical of Board members or school personnel or which cause argument, the discussion on the subject may be terminated.

8. Individuals having prepared statements are requested to leave a copy with Dr. Punzo.

We recognize that some individuals present may be here under a time constraint. If those individuals would come up front and be seated in the front rows, they will be recognized.

Figure 6.7

You are invited to attend a

Public Hearing

on the

Redistricting Plan

for the
School District of University City

Thursday,
February 23, 1989
7:00 p.m.

McKnight Building
Board Room
8346 Delcrest Drive
University City

Figure 6.8

The superintendent held "time to talk" sessions, at which time anyone in the community could come and talk about what the person would or would not like to see take place in the district. Opportunities such as these gave the superintendent an exposure to the community that was broad in scope, and showed the community members that the superintendent cared for their opinions, was ready to listen, and was available.

The meetings were scheduled on different days of the week, at different times of the day, and in different parts of the community. The rationale behind this was that if community members worked in the evening, they could come in the morning; if they could not come in the morning, they might be able to come in the afternoon; if they could not come on a Monday, perhaps they could come on Tuesday or Wednesday.

Two meetings were scheduled for staff: one at the end of the secondary school day, and one at the end of the elementary school day.

The information gleaned from the meetings gave the superintendent a great deal of information that would generally not have been available.

Exemplary Practice: A second series of meetings was scheduled using the same format, when circumstances dictated that the budget had to be cut. At these meetings, the superintendent and staff listened to recommendations for areas to be cut or trimmed. It was meaningful because the superintendent could hear firsthand how people felt about various issues and programs prior to identifying areas to be cut.

Closing the Meeting

Close the meeting once the allotted time has run out or you have accomplished the objectives of the meeting. If you find that enough has been accomplished by the group and that a few members can finish up the item, assign the task to the few members, and end the meeting. If you find that much more work needs to be done, or that you do not have the people you need at the meeting, then decide what needs to be done, give the assignments, and end the meeting.

At the conclusion of a meeting, succinctly summarize what has been accomplished, the outstanding items that need to be dealt with, assignments made, and due dates. Everyone should leave the meeting with a clear understanding of what transpired, the follow-up that is needed, and who will be involved.

Minutes of the Meeting

Minutes of the deliberations of the committee should be kept. General Henry M. Roberts gives good advice on how this can be done.

> In keeping the minutes, much depends upon the kind of meeting, and whether the minutes are to be published. In the meetings of ordinary societies and of boards of managers and trustees, there is no object in reporting the debates; the duty of the secretary, in such cases, is mainly to record what is ''done'' by the assembly, and not what is said by the members . . . where the regular meetings are held weekly, monthly, or quarterly, the minutes are read at the opening of each day's meeting, and after correction, should be approved. (Roberts, 1951)

Following the Meeting

The minutes of the meeting should be distributed to the attendees along with the materials as agreed upon at the meeting.

You may wish to adopt the use of an action letter form which is directed to a specific individual and serves as a reminder of the specific action that needs to be taken and the due date (Figure 6.9).

If you had invited speakers, send letters of appreciation to them along with their honorarium, if any. When you are covering travel expenses, include the necessary forms and explain the reimbursement procedure, if that had not been done prior to this time.

Arrange for the payment of all other expenses related to the meeting, including the rental fee, expenses for coffee or lunches, and the like.

In addition to sending the action letter, you should brief those individuals who would be affected in some way by the decisions reached at the meeting. Let them hear the news from you at the earliest possible time rather than through the grapevine.

The minutes of the meeting should include:

- beginning and ending times of the meeting
- attendees and the chairperson of the meeting
- location of the meeting
- agenda items discussed and the decisions reached relative to each item

```
                              ACTION LETTER


        DATE:


        TO:

        FROM:

        RE:


        ACTION NEEDED:













        DUE DATE:
```

Figure 6.9

- assigned tasks: what, to whom, and date due
- future meeting date(s), time, and place

Planning for a Major Meeting/Conference

Every so often a major meeting or conference is held. Planning for a large-scale meeting such as this is far more detailed than planning for a routine meeting in your office. Assuming that the objective, the intended audience, and the general format of the conference have been agreed upon, there is a need to adopt a conference theme. This theme should be carried out throughout the conference. Attention should be given to the details.

Dates

Select several dates on which the conference could be held, recognizing that certain times of the year would be more desirable for certain staff members. For example, you should not plan to have a conference for principals that would conflict with either a state or national principals' convention. Nor would you want to have one on a school or religious holiday. Hold the conference at a time of year when the pressures on staff are at a relatively low point. If at all possible, select a date that will not be in competition with any other major community event or holiday. Undue competition can result in a significant decrease in participation and media coverage. Consider holding the conference at a hotel or other choice location on the off-season, so that a high-quality atmosphere can be had for a relatively low price.

Key Presenters

Check the tentative dates with the key presenter(s) and determine several that are possibilities. Ask the presenter(s) to hold them until arrangements can be finalized with the facility in which you are going to hold the conference. When the dates are finalized, contact the key presenter(s) to lock in the specific dates. Issue formal letters of invitation as soon as possible. These letters should include the nature of the conference, your expectations of them, their honoraria (if any), and travel and housing arrangements. Ask them to confirm the dates and arrangements and sign and return a copy of the letter of agreement to you.

Facility

Contact several facilities that could accommodate the conference you are planning and make a site visit yourself. Work with a site coordinator who will be with you should you decide to hold the conference at that location. Discuss the conference, what you intend to accomplish, and who the audience will be. Talk about the ambience that you would like to have. Determine whether or not the location can accommodate the size of the group that you anticipate, in the manner you envision, on the dates that you would like to hold it, and determine whether it is accessible to the handicapped. Check the credentials of the facility with other conference clients.

Facility Check

When making your site visit, identify your needs with respect to the following and match your needs and their availability at the facility. Listed below are many items that you may need to consider.

Meeting rooms:

- Room sizes—Can they accommodate the large group in the configuration that you desire—banquet style with large round tables seating approximately ten people; theater style with rows of chairs, one after the other, with an aisle running down the middle of the room; circle(s) of chairs; rectangular tables with a head table arrangement?
- Break-out rooms available—Can they accommodate the format that you desire?
- Are they fairly close to restrooms and telephones?
- Is there an area that would be suitable for the press? Can telephones be made available for the press?
- Is there an area that would be suitable as a speakers' room?

Sleeping accommodations:

- singles available
- doubles available
- hospitality suites available

Catering capability:

- breakfast
- breaks—morning and afternoon
- lunch

• dinner
• menu selections (Recognize that their menus are guides and that you can usually plan your own menu with the banquet manager.)
• bar/bartending
• table decorations such as flowers, bunting, banners

Parking:

• Is it an in-house facility?
• Is it nearby?
• Is it valet?
• Is there additional cost, or is it available free to all house guests? Is it available for all lunch/dinner guests? Negotiate a package rate for parking.

Audio-visual support capability:

• public address system, microphone
• podium
• lecterns in the break-out rooms
• overhead projectors
• VCRs
• screens, stands
• backup equipment, bulbs
• limitations on the use of equipment as a result of a union contract(s)
• permission necessary to bring your own equipment

Support capability:

• signage available in the lobby
• personnel available on the day of your conference should anything go wrong, e.g., conference manager, custodial and/or maintenance staff, banquet manager
• recording services available
• duplicating capability
• telephone support
• room controls: heat, light, air conditioning, sound
• ability to receive shipments of materials/displays in advance of the conference
• coat checking capability

Reception area:

• Space—Is it large enough to accommodate your needs?
• Are table(s) available for registration and/or displays?

Display area:

- Size — Is it large enough?
- Is it accessible to the main conference area?
- Are there restrictions?
- Is there availability of tables?
- Is there availability of power?
- Are there limitations, i.e., safety/fire regulations?
- Security of area when exhibits are closed — Can they be secured or must you hire a security guard(s)?
- Is there ability to screen admission to display area?

During your site visit, find out whether or not there are competing functions scheduled concurrently that might cause you to select another site. Find out the extent of their insurance coverage in order to assist you in deciding whether or not you need to secure special insurance for your conference. Determine the color schemes that they can readily accommodate. If you have another in mind, discuss the matter and see if it can be resolved.

Discuss the cost of services and the gratuity structure. Remember that you can generally negotiate a package that is considerably lower than the individual items used separately. Do not feel squeamish about discussing each item if need be. Remember that you usually have a choice of location. Come up with a package that you can live with. Use your tax exempt status to further reduce the cost of the conference whenever possible.

Once you have determined the facility that has the accommodations that you require and whose charges are within the range that you can cover, secure a contract *detailing* all arrangements as agreed to during the course of your conversations. These arrangements should include specific room numbers or names, the physical layout of the rooms (tables, chairs, and the like), audio-visual equipment needed, and time that the particular room is to be used. Confirm the times of the breaks and breakfast, lunch, and/or dinner that you will be serving, where they will be served, what they will consist of, and the specific charges are stated. Identify the color scheme. Decide whether or not you will allow smoking and where; arrange to have/not to have ash trays available.

Make arrangements for payment of the bill. Make certain that expenses incurred by conference attendees are not billed to the conference. Indicate which charges you will cover. Give the conference manager a copy of your tax exempt certificate so that the district will not have to pay unnecessary taxes.

After a very careful check of the contract, sign and return it to the facility. Keep a copy for your records.

Conference Planning

Travel Arrangements

If you anticipate that the attendees at your meeting will be traveling by air, contact the group services desk of a major airline servicing your area and negotiate a discount for the attendees. This is not difficult to do, and the attendees will appreciate your efforts. Many times you will be able to coordinate ground transportation, rental cars, and side trips both before and after the meeting. If the airline cannot coordinate the ground transportation and side trips, contact a local ground transportation company.

Conference Costs

Determine in advance *all* of the costs involved with putting on this conference to include those identified to this point and the cost of items such as printing and mailing promotional materials, telephone calls, honoraria for reactors/moderators, folders, and name tags. Identify the number of people who will be attending gratis and anticipate the number of paying attendees. Set the cost of the conference to cover your costs.

Many times the district will subsidize the cost of the conference and thereby decrease the amount needed to be raised through registration fees. Costs may be cut by rearranging the format of the conference and eliminating the meals. Arrange the time frame so that the attendees have time to eat on their own. Determine whether or not there is a foundation that supports the goals of the conference; solicit it for support of the conference or any part thereof.

Advance Preparations

Planning is needed whether the conference is a professional conference or a major community-wide event/meeting. Prepare a timeline that you will use to keep you on track as you proceed with conference/meeting plans. Include all of the items in it so that you will not forget any as the pressures mount and the time draws near for the actual conference. Maintain a file of all materials related to the event.

Three to Four Months prior to the Event

Select and have in place the leadership team for the conference or event/meeting. The chairperson should be a well-known, well-respected leader who is able to bring to the event the clout and class that you want.

The chairperson and the leadership team should come to closure on the site of the event, and reach agreement on costs, number of participants, keynote speakers, and the like. Confirming letters to key presenters/speakers and reactors/moderators should be sent out; contracts with the facility should be signed.

The leadership team needs to identify a theme, logo, slogan(s), color scheme, and general procedure to be used in publicizing the event. If the participants are all local, a speakers' bureau should be identified.

The team needs to prepare an all-inclusive outline of what needs to be done tied to a timeline; identify a budget and the source of funding.

Planning needs to begin for the opening, kick-off event, and for the media coverage to include feature stories, store displays for local meetings, and regional/national coverage in magazines as appropriate.

Two Months prior to the Event

Prepare all promotional materials at least eight weeks in advance of the conference. Compile a mailing list of possible invitees. Secure any signs well in advance of the actual date of the conference/meeting.

Inform the media of the upcoming event by sending them materials and responding to their questions. Follow up by contacting local media and arrange for live interviews, both radio and television, and feature stories in the newspapers. Prepare radio and television public service spot announcements.

Five to Six Weeks prior to the Event

Send out promotional materials to the mailing list of possible invitees and send invitations out to preferred guests—key local, state, and national officials.

Hold a news conference to officially announce the event. Prepare and hand out press packets. Identify where additional information can be secured; give the telephone number and the location.

Distribute posters for window displays. Place notices on public bulletin boards.

Hold a meeting with the members of your speakers' bureau in order to give them the information they need prior to their going out to speak in behalf of the event.

Four Weeks prior to the Event

Touch base with the key presenters, speakers, reactors, and moderators. Secure transportation, if necessary. Make arrangements to meet them, pick them up, and/or for parking their cars.

Do another bulk mailing of promotional materials to a mailing list of possible attendees, to bolster registration.

If you have a speakers' bureau, solicit speaking engagements for them and arrange for them to speak as requested.

Obtain copies of the key addresses and send a copy to the reactors/moderators. Obtain a short biography of each presenter for use in introducing the individual. Give a copy to the leader of the session and keep one for your files.

Maintain contact with the press. Maintain the momentum by providing new materials to the press. Arrange for press interviews with the key presenter(s).

Make certain that the registrations are monitored and responses made as needed. Consider telephoning some of the people who have not responded. Many times, people will respond to a personal telephone call while they would not to a written invitation. Most people want that personal touch—to know that they themselves are wanted and are not merely names on the mailing list.

Have your support staff start preparing the folders of materials that you would like the participants to have at the time of registration.

Decide whether or not you want a photographer present to take pictures of the event and to work with the press. If you do, engage a photographer.

Send out reserved parking stickers to those individuals you are granting that privilege.

Two Weeks prior to the Event

Continue to monitor the number of attendees. Arrange for speakers to appear on radio and television talk shows and the local newscasts.

Prepare press releases, including photographs of the key presenters.

Visit the facility in which you are having the event.

Speak with the conference manager to review and confirm the arrangements that were agreed to — the physical, banquet, and audio-visual arrangements.

One Week prior to the Event

Review the registrations. Prepare a list of the attendees.

Decide on the final seating arrangements at key functions, such as the head table at a dinner function, the platform guests, and the like.

Convey the final physical arrangements to the conference manager at the facility in which the event is taking place.

Prepare identification badges for the conference attendees. If you are having break-out groups, you may decide to place the attendees in groups, in order to avoid cliques and to stimulate discussion. This can be easily done by placing a colored dot or a letter on their badges to correspond to their group during the break-out sessions.

Complete the compiling of the participants' folders.

Maintain contact with the press, releasing whatever new information you have. Maintain a clipping file for your records.

Meet with the members of your staff and confirm who is going to do what at the event. Line up several individuals who will be on call and serve as substitutes as needed. Arrange for someone to contact the key presenters soon after their arrival and escort them to their session.

Prepare a fact sheet on the event, listing key points that you would like known and disseminated.

Check with the photographer in order to review your understanding as to the pictures you want taken and the photographer's relationship with the press.

Day of the Event

Arrive at the facility early. Make certain that there is reserved parking set aside for those individuals who need it, and that the area is clearly marked.

Make certain that the registration area is set up with two distinct areas — one for preregistered participants and one for current registrants.

Check to be certain that the speakers' room has coffee and is comfortable.

Check the press room to be certain that copies of the speeches, with appropriate release dates and times, are available, as are coffee and telephones. Are the fact sheets available? Is there an interview area?

Day After the Event

Prepare a press packet that includes an abstract of the key events that took place, together with some good quotes. Include glossy prints for the press to use. Be available for personal interviews. Include a ''sorry you weren't there'' letter to those press people who did not attend.

Send ''thank you'' letters to the members of the press who attended, to key people at the facility who contributed to the success of the event, and to the participants, to include all of the individuals who had any part in making the event the success it was.

Mail the honoraria together with a thank you note to the presenters and others as appropriate.

Follow up on any promises made for additional materials. Pay all bills as received.

Call a meeting of the leadership team to debrief and make constructive suggestions for future meetings.

Prepare a report to the leadership team and close the file on the event until it is needed again.

CHAPTER 7

ELECTIONS

THE VAST MAJORITY OF SUCCESSFUL
ELECTIONS ARE BUILT ON THE
FOUNDATION OF A STRONG, ONGOING,
WELL-DEVELOPED AND ORGANIZED,
YEAR-ROUND PUBLIC RELATIONS
PROGRAM.
                National School Public Relations Association
                School Public Relations: The Complete Book

I N most communities, school buildings are used to hold national, state, and local elections because they are conveniently located, familiar to the general public, and no fee is charged for their use. Unfortunately, because the majority of the public does not have school-age children, they rarely come into school buildings at times other than to vote. The general public's impression of the schools is influenced by what they see and hear for themselves when they enter a school building to vote. Additionally, at this point in time, when choice is a viable option for parents of school-age children, the need to put your "best face forward" is more important than ever. Parents are influenced by what they see and hear.

First Impressions Count!

A clean, orderly school environment is a reasonable expectation. You can insure that this is so by following the guidelines below.

(1) Meet with the person in charge of running the election in your building in advance of the election. Find out exactly how the room is to be arranged and what is needed. Point out the proximity of the restrooms, the lounge area that the election workers can use, refrigerator space, a telephone, and the like. Keep the contact person informed in case anything is needed.

(2) Before you leave the building the night before the election, make certain that the custodian has arranged the voting area in accordance with the wishes of the election official (usually a precinct or

137

ward captain). If tables are to be set a certain way, see that this is done. Accommodate the needs of the election workers; make them feel comfortable. The individuals working at the polls are political appointees and have some clout in local party politics.

(3) Make sure that the night custodians pay particular care to the entrance and voting areas so that they are clean and look cared for; spray buffing the floors and wiping down the walls goes a long way to accomplishing the ''cared for'' look.

(4) Make certain that the bathrooms are clean and have a sufficient supply of toilet tissue, soap, and paper towels. Have any graffiti removed from the walls and stalls. If possible, have any graffiti removed from the outside of the school building as well.

(5) Arrange to have a day custodian in early enough on election day to clean up the grounds around the building, removing all papers, cans, and other trash that may have accumulated overnight. The first impression is created when the voter approaches the school building. Clean grounds impress voters.

(6) You may want to consider vacating parking spaces in close proximity to the voters' entrance, thereby making it more convenient for people to enter the building. People are much more inclined to have a positive mind-set when they are not inconvenienced. You will, of course, need to work with your staff to make certain that they understand why you are doing this. Identify accessible alternate parking areas for election day.

(7) Consider asking the staff and the custodians to keep the window shades at the same level in each room. This gives the voter a good impression of the building, as well as a feeling that a sense of order prevails.

(8) Recognizing that many elections take place in November, make certain that the windows are not wide open, as this leaves voters with the feeling that their tax dollars are being wasted to heat ''the great outdoors.'' It is better to temporarily move classrooms to other parts of the building rather than arouse the wrath of the community. Of course, it is far better to have the heating system balanced so that the temperature does not exceed tolerance levels.

(9) Arrange to have school activities that may not be understood by the occasional visitor moved out of the general vicinity of the voting

area. Trying to correct erroneous impressions is often difficult to do; eliminating the need to do so is far simpler.

(10) Stop by the voting area early in the morning, and then several times during the course of the day in order to welcome the voters and to make certain that everything is in order. The one thing that you do not want to have happen is to have complaints arising from conditions under your control.

The above guidelines should be followed for all elections held in your building. They are especially helpful when the district is going for a school board election, budget vote, tax levy or bond referendum. Community members need to feel positive about their schools on a year-round basis, not only at a time when the district wants something. Following the previous guidelines for all elections sets a continuing positive tone.

National, State, and Local Elections

Remember that it is inappropriate for schools to become involved in political battles. You have students from families on both sides of any given issue in your buildings. Do not favor one side over the other. As individuals, and after-hours, participate as fully as you please, but do not bring that involvement into the educational environment.

If in support of the educational programs in your building it is deemed appropriate to invite individuals running for various offices to your school, make certain that all sides of an issue are represented. Do not favor one individual over another. If there are speakers, suggest that they draw lots in order to set their positions on the agenda. Set a limit on the time that each person is to speak, and adhere to it; do not allow anyone to run over that limit.

If there is to be a question and answer period, make certain that the guidelines have been established and agreed to in advance by the speakers, and that the students understand these guidelines prior to beginning the question and answer part of the meeting.

Treat all candidates with equal respect; remember that from among the group running, there will be the successful ones who can, and will, have an influence either directly or indirectly over the functioning of the schools in the district. Even if the candidates do not vote directly on operational issues, they will undoubtedly vote on local, state, or national issues that will affect the operation of schools.

School Board Elections

Electing School Board Members

Be particularly careful not to take sides in a school board election. Be prepared to give equal access to information to all candidates who are running. Be very careful not to give preference to some of the candidates.

Recognize that incumbents generally have more information about the system than newcomers by virtue of having served on the board. If you are asked for information, it is better to respond in writing because you can then give the same information to all candidates who ask the same, or similar, questions. When a response is written, you generally have the ability to take the time necessary to prepare your response; you have far greater control over what is stated. In giving an oral response, you may not use the most precise or convincing language, because generally conditions are too demanding for deep thought. Take the time to prepare a written response whenever possible. It will pay off in the long run.

Most importantly, be neutral during meetings to elect members to the school board.

District Elections for Bond Referenda, Budgets, and Tax Levies

District elections have a very direct impact on the school district— either the proposed dollars are approved, or they are not. In these elections, decisions do not rest on the will of the board. The public makes very specific decisions, decisions that the district will have to live with until another election of like magnitude takes place. Going down to defeat can have devastating effects on the districts. If the time is not ripe, do not go for the vote; wait until the correct moment.

Many times the defeat of a proposal in a district election can be traced back to the fact that the public did not know very much about the philosophy of the district, and what it was trying to do. All too often the public becomes aware of the school district only when something very negative occurs in the district or when the taxes need to be raised. This results in a very negative attitude toward the district.

As a general rule, once one district's budget is defeated, surrounding districts tend to defeat their budgets. Many times school boards redesign some small portion of the budget and come back to the public some weeks later, only to meet defeat again. The attitude of the public is—if the schools show that they can do with less, let us defeat the budget again, and they will come back with still less, and our taxes will not go up as much as was originally stated. This is particularly true in the case of "empty nesters" (families with no children living at home) and senior citizens.

Recognizing that only 20 percent of the households have school-age children at this time, and that there is an ever-increasing number of senior citizens and empty nesters in our communities, it becomes clear that we have to reach these families without school-age children in order to gain their support. Our PR efforts have to be increased. Additionally, there are community members who have school-age children who have opted to send their children to private or parochial schools. The support of these groups is crucial to the district.

We can gain their support, but only when they know the why, what, how, where, and when of the district long before they are asked for their vote. We must communicate with them on a continuing basis.

Communicate, Communicate, Communicate

This cannot be overstated! We must communicate with the voters on a continuing basis, not just prior to an election. Members of the community need to be kept informed on a regular basis so that they can know what is going on and why. They need to know the good and the bad, as well as our aspirations, efforts, successes, and failures. Only by keeping them informed on a continuing basis will the community understand the school district.

Communication needs to be year-round and can take many forms: direct mailings going to the residences in the community, press reports, participation in radio talk shows by key members of the school district, and invitations to participate at public hearings/forums, to name a few. The next chapter, "Channels of Communication" contains countless ways to communicate with your many publics.

Running School District Elections

The elections referred to in this section are the elections that districts hold in order to pass a budget, increase a tax levy, and pass a bond referendum.

Well in advance of the time you plan to hold an election, initiate an effective communication plan. Make certain that the community has been hearing from you prior to the time you are ready to ask for their vote.

Citizens' Committee

Once you know that you need to have an election, and well in advance of the time of the election, organize a citizens' committee that will take charge of running the campaign to get the vote out. Select those individuals who have standing and clout in the community; those people who are looked at as community leaders and whose opinions are respected. Identify a prominent person to head this committee. That person can usually attract the support of outstanding individuals in the community. The more people you involve, the better.

This committee should operate with funds it raises under the direction of its leader, and not on school time. You can, and should, become involved with the efforts of the committee, being careful not to cross the line between community volunteer and school district employee.

The committee generates its own sources of income. This is generally done by means of donations to the committee for the specific purpose of running the district election. The funds are handled by the committee and are not commingled with district monies.

Involvement of District Employees

Encourage other district administrators and employees to support the efforts of the committee. District administrators and employees are excellent sources of support because they know the school attendance area better than anyone. They also know the parents and the community that the school serves. They can make the important personal contacts and the telephone calls to garner the support needed at election time. They can man the polls on election day in order to keep track of who has voted.

Plan, Plan, Plan

If there is one word to remember in order to run a successful campaign, it is "plan." You are never too organized.

Plan for every detail of the campaign, from the slogan that you adopt to identify the campaign, to the strategies to be used prior to the election, to election day efforts, and the post-election celebration. Every detail should be considered by the citizens' committee and planned. No detail is unimportant; every single vote counts, and many of the details zero in on voters in one way or another.

Once the broad parameters of the campaign have been identified, initiate a master timeline that allows you the time necessary to accomplish each particular item. Identify who on the committee will be responsible for seeing to it that the item is done on time.

Before placing an item on the timeline, consider how this item fits into your grand strategy. Make certain that the members of the citizens' committee know what each phase will result in and how the various parts support each other. The members need to see the relation of the parts to the whole.

Campaign Strategies

The major part of the planning process is to decide campaign strategies. Among the considerations should be the following.

Adopt a Slogan and Logo

Identify a catchy slogan that will reinforce the election item and that will be meaningful and easily remembered. Adopt a logo that will be used only for that purpose. You want people who see the logo—regardless of where they see it—to associate it with the upcoming election.

Voting Records

Decide if you want to find out the number of registered voters and the percent of the population they represent. If the numbers are low, you may decide to hold a massive voter registration drive prior to embarking on the election campaign.

Register Students

Many districts bring a registrar into the high school in order to register all eligible voters. Students will almost always vote in favor of the district, if they know what is at stake.

Absentee Ballots

Consider the number of former students who are currently attending colleges around the state. It may be advantageous to contact the students and have absentee ballots sent to them so that they can vote.

Exemplary Practice: One midwestern school district that needed a two-thirds vote in order to pass a tax levy (state law) used an 800 telephone number that was made available by a community member. Three members of the committee contacted scores of students attending the state university system's various campuses, sent the ballots to them and then went to the campuses and collected them. Where necessary, arrangements were made to register the students.

That one district had more absentee ballots than the twenty-two other school districts in the entire county combined. The district won the election, in no small part due to the efforts put forth to obtain the absentee vote.

Speakers' Bureau

Decide whether or not you will have people who would be willing and able to speak at various functions or group meetings. If you decide to have a speakers' bureau, make certain that the speakers are very familiar with the contents of the item(s) on the ballot, know the past history, and can speak with authority on the topic. If they are weak as to background facts, consider sending a district employee who is familiar with the item along with the speaker. The district employee will serve as a support to the speaker, assuring that the listeners receive the message as fully and completely as possible.

Solicitations

Decide how the community will be solicited – by telephone? in person? by mail? at the various churches and synagogues? at their social clubs?

If you are going to do any solicitation, make certain that the workers doing the soliciting are well trained. Prepare a guide for every worker, work out every detail that they will need. Give them the supporting materials to get the job done right. Do not let them go out without the training session.

PR Pieces

Identify who is responsible for the production of PR pieces. Where will they be done? What will they cost? Decide on a color scheme and the distribution scheme to be used. The PTAs (Parent Teacher Associations), using their resources, can send notices home to the parents saying things that school officials, using school resources, cannot do.

Involve and Inform the Staff First

Make certain that they are informed in advance of the community so that when community members approach them, they will know what the vote is for, why it is needed, and will be able to answer questions that individuals ask them. If they do not have the answers, they will know where to get them.

Explain the Reasons for the Election

Tell the community why you need the funds and what you will be able to provide for the children. State the facts, and do not threaten the community.

Run the Campaign Like a Political Election

Take lessons from the politicians who try to run campaigns that will get the bodies to the polls. Without the voters at the polls, you cannot possibly win.

Ignore the "No" Votes?

Many times election committees decide to ignore the ''no'' votes and go after the ''yes'' voters and the ''undecideds.'' That decision is made by the committee because it is generally felt that ''you will not change their minds; they will be there voting as they always do.''

Identify Your "Yes" Voters

This is done by a person-to-person or telephone canvass. You want to make sure that all of the ''yes'' voters do vote.

Monitor the Polls

Have community members who are familiar with the individual school community monitor the polls on election day. Those persons can keep tabs and will know who has and has not come in to vote. If a person does not show up, telephone the individual – two or three times, if necessary, just make certain that the person comes and votes.

Provide Help to Get Voters to the Polls

Identify those individuals who need rides to the polls and line up people who can drive them to and from the polls. If a person needs a baby-sitter in order to get to the polls, have someone available to allow the person to get to vote.

If you are facing winter months, consider lining up four-wheel drive vehicles that will be able to drive through the worst weather and bring people to the polls to vote.

PTA Involvement Is Essential

PTAs are an excellent source of support for district elections. Many PTAs will serve coffee near the entrance to the voting area. They usually ask for a small donation, but a prime reason for serving coffee is to be able to greet the incoming voter in a most positive manner and to keep tabs on who is coming in to vote.

Some PTAs traditionally serve a low-cost breakfast at the school on election day in order to entice the parents to bring their child to school, eat with the PTA, and vote. PTA involvement in monitoring the vote is critical.

Follow the Vote

Make certain that you keep tabs on the vote by getting hourly reports. That is the only way that you know how the vote is coming in and from which areas it is coming.

There was one school district in New York State that had a group of people who were very anti-school district. While the district's budget election was held all day long, no one took note that few, if any, of the individuals opposed to the school district had voted. Then, with just about one-half an hour left until the polls closed, hundreds of the opposition voters arrived at the polls and were strong enough in number to vote the election down. Had the district monitored the election, they would have been alert to the absence of these votes and worked at getting more of their ''yes'' votes to the polls. The district changed its strategy for the next election.

No Magic Formula

Just remember that there is no magic formula for conducting successful district elections. Use as many strategies as you can to assure success in your district. Whatever works for you is best for you.

And when all is said and done and you have won at the polls, do not take any of the credit. Thank everyone else for their support and give your committee the credit.

If you lose, be prepared to shoulder the blame. Get together and review what happened. Keep the good ideas for the next time and improve on those that did not work as well.

You will win—if you plan and communicate!

CHAPTER 8

WORKING WITH THE MEDIA

IN SIMPLE TERMS, NEWS IS SOMETHING
THAT INTERESTS MANY PEOPLE. . . .
Lin Grensing
''Start the Presses''

Working with the Press

W E recognize the power of the press to influence voters and communities. The particular emphasis that members of the media place on stories influences the opinion of their readers/listeners. What they choose to include, or exclude, can make a difference in how a situation is portrayed.

Ask newspeople what they feel their major purpose is and they will most often respond, ''To serve the community.'' Ask educators how they view their role and the response will be similar. Despite this commonality of purpose, I have always been amazed by the amount of animosity that exists between the two groups.

The litany of charges and countercharges has become almost a cliche. ''The media cover only negative news about schools,'' charge the educators. ''Schools are only interested in a whitewash of their problems,'' respond the media. There is a kernel of truth in both statements. Newspapers are in the business of news, and stories about drug raids in schools make news and sell more papers than stories about outstanding science fairs. (Zampolin, 1985)

We need to recognize that reporters are out to cover the major events of the day and are not ''out to get us.'' They want to gather the facts, interpret them, and turn them in to the appropriate editor. They are not interested in attracting advertising to the newspaper. Not all of them are writing from a preconceived notion of what the story is. As a group they are well-educated inquirers—honest and ethical. They will keep ''digging'' and asking questions as long as they feel that they do not have all of the facts or that some aspect of a situation is being withheld from them.

Be honest and straightforward with members of the press. Recognize that they want to be treated fairly, given the facts, and not misled. They like to be complimented when they have done a good job and recognize that there is a need to correct errors when one appears.

Establishing a good relationship with the press is very important. Find out the names of the reporters in your community who cover education. Set up a time for them to come and visit with you before anything happens in your school/district. Get to know them. Find out what their deadlines are, the best time for you to contact them, and what they may be interested in. Remember, as you deal with reporters and the press, that these people operate in different media and have different time and space constraints, depending on whether they cover the news for a newspaper, the radio, or television.

Exemplary Practice: One superintendent of schools established such a fine relationship with the anchor for the local evening television newscast that any time the reporter had some space to fill, he would call the superintendent. The superintendent made sure that she had some interesting items to share with him that were newsworthy and that the public would be interested in knowing. The topics she spoke about varied, but the fact is that the reporter could depend on getting a few minutes of videotape when he called. As negative stories about the district unfolded from time to time, the reporter treated them with a marked degree of caring and concern.

When we think of the press, we tend to think in terms of the daily newspapers, and the radio and television stations. We need to remember that many cities and towns have weekly and regional newspapers. There are also regularly scheduled newspapers geared to the interests of particular groups, such as unions and ethnic organizations, that focus on local news and community events. These local/regional/organization newspapers are generally read from cover to cover, because their area of emphasis is directly related to the interests of the readership.

Editors of daily, local, or regional newspapers are interested in receiving and publishing news, and we generally try to get their attention when we want news disseminated. Editors who publish house organs for institutions such as hospitals, local industries, chambers of commerce, public libraries, and the YMCAs and YWCAs are also interested in getting news of local interest. Their publications often reach thousands of people. Many editors will accept a well-written feature story or carry a news item covered in a press release. There are times when the news media will pick up a story from one of the house organs that is deemed as being a good news item for their readers.

Understanding the Operation of the Newspaper

Most newspapers, and particularly the daily and weekly papers, have editors who are responsible for particular areas of the paper (NARFE, 1987).

- The *city editor* is the individual who usually handles the day-to-day hard news. The city editor receives the news releases, decides what should make good copy, and sends the reporter out to cover the story.
- The *feature editor,* where there is one, makes decisions on releases other than hard news stories. The feature editor usually decides whether or not to cover different, first time programs, visitors to the district, unusual accomplishments by a staff member, and the like.
- The *editorial page editor* is responsible for the editorial page including the guest column, where there is one. Most newspapers will print letters to the editor provided they are signed and the writer is a local person. Some newspapers will not publish a letter to the editor if it is not signed and does not contain the address of the writer. Those newspapers call the writer to confirm that the person did in fact write the letter.
- The *reporter* is the person who is sent out to follow up on a news release. The paper may have a reporter assigned to cover the education scene. This person would cover the stories resulting from the news release and also cover the board meetings, open forums, and public hearings.
- The *news editor* is the person who oversees the reporters, and the rewrite staff, and supervises the coverage of the news on a daily basis.

Understanding the Operation of the Radio and Television Station

The staffing of a radio or television station is largely determined by its size. Several key positions are needed to accommodate the workload (NARFE, 1987).

- The *news director* is usually in charge of all news that comes to the station and, unless the station has a director that handles education, you should direct your calls to the news director.
- The *program director* is generally in charge of all the programming at the station including news, public affairs, entertainment, public service announcements, and editorials.
- The *public affairs director* is the person who is responsible for public affairs programs and documentary programs. This person usually works very closely with the news department in order to make certain that there is coordination in work assignments.

Radio and television stations have a far more difficult time covering the news. They are severely constrained by time, and have to cover a story in just about one minute or 150 words. They do not have time for long explanations; time is critical for them. They must hit the highlights and get to the point immediately. If they talk about the same story on various broadcasts, the presentations have to be different; they cannot repeat what they have said before. News has to be fresh each time it is presented.

Many stations sponsor editorials and give viewers an opportunity to reply. They often host public affairs shows, talk shows, and broadcast public service announcements.

The press picks up fast-breaking stories by following the emergency short-wave channels and the wire services, and from telephone tips. A determination is made by the editor as to whether or not a reporter and/or crew (reporter, photographer, broadcast van) is to be dispatched to the scene of a happening. For all other stories, they rely on press releases, stories that are submitted, and personal contacts. The press generally follows events of local, state, national, and international importance. The space they devote to a story is largely determined by the story's relevant importance in terms of other news of the day.

Press Releases

Far more press releases are submitted than can be printed in a newspaper or carried on the air. It is important that your release be as complete as possible so that an editor can make a determination with fairly little effort.

The first paragraph should contain the answers to the who, what, when, where, why, and how of the story. By reading the lead paragraph, the editor can determine what is going to happen with the news item. Great care needs to be taken to assure that, as succinctly as possible, the story is told in the first paragraph.

Use the inverted pyramid format where the lead paragraph is followed by paragraphs that provide additional facts. The most important information is mentioned in the first paragraph; the others would contain information in descending order of importance. When editors are limited for space, they cut from the bottom of the story, paragraph by paragraph. Availability of space and the newsworthiness of the story largely determine how much of your release will be printed in the paper.

In preparing the release:

(1) Use a distinctive masthead so that the press can readily identify the organization it represents (Figure 8.1).

(2) Use only one side of a sheet of paper; type and double-space all releases. Try to limit the release to no more than two pages.

(3) Use wide margins.

(4) Type headlines in capital letters.

(5) Date the release.

(6) Keep the sentences and paragraphs short and to the point.

(7) If your release is longer than one page, type ''MORE'' at the bottom of the page and ''ADD ONE'' at the top of the second page.

(8) At the end of the press release, type either ''30'' or ''###'' to signal that you have reached the end of the press release.

(9) Avoid using educational jargon.

(10) Use the complete name of each person; check spelling for accuracy.

(11) Give exact date(s) and time(s) of the event, to include A.M. and P.M. Use ''Wednesday, August 28, 1991'' as opposed to ''next Wednesday'' or ''on Wednesday.''

(12) Be certain to include in the upper right-hand corner of the release the name, address, and telephone number of the individual who can respond to any questions that may arise.

(13) Indicate when the information may be released at the top of the release: ''For Immediate Release'' or ''For Release August 31, 1991.'' You may decide that you do not want the information released prior to a board meeting; that you want to embargo the release. In that case use ''Embargoed until 9:30 P.M., March 2, 1991.''

Danbury Public Schools
NEWS RELEASE

Administration Building
Danbury, Connecticut 06811

Office of Information
(203) 797-4717

FOR IMMEDIATE RELEASE

September 8, 1989

DOWN ON THE FARM COUNTRY FAIR

On Saturday, October 7th, a "Country Fair" will be held at
Stadley Rough School to benefit the "Down on the Farm" project. The
Fair will be held from 10:00 a.m. to 3:00 p.m.

The community is invited to attend the Fair and spend a day at
the farm. There will be fun activities for the children as well as
craft items and food. Raffle tickets will be sold to support this
project to maintain the buildings and premises, as well as the care
and feeding of the animals. Come one, Come all for a fun day!!

# # #

For additional information, contact:

Judith E. Kreiger
Chairperson 1989
King Street Primary, 797-4744

Figure 8.1

154

Remember that the press is interested in "newsworthy" items, write your release that way.

Tip Sheet/Calendar of Events

Consider collecting the dates of events that will be occurring in your school/district during the next week or month and issuing a tip sheet or calendar of events. The sheet should identify dates, times, places, and events in chronological order. It then becomes a simple matter to know what is happening in the building(s)/district. Reporters rely on such information at times when there is a sparsity of news. Information for the tip sheet can be readily obtained by soliciting the members of the staff and providing them with a form on which to list the event (Figure 8.2).

Public Service Announcements

Radio and television stations will air Public Service Announcements (PSAs) (Figure 8.3). PSAs can be used to disseminate specific information in a short period of time and can run ten, twenty, thirty, or sixty seconds in length. These spot announcements convey messages to large audiences at times other than during a traditional newscast; they come right to the point. Despite the severe constraint on time, be certain to include the who, what, when, where, why, and how, the essence of your PSA release.

Television announcement copy must be accompanied by visual material. Normally, film, videotape, or one slide is enough for 10- or 20-second copy. For 30-second copy, if film or videotape is not available, two or more slides are necessary. Film or videotape must be used for 60-second television announcements.

If you don't have a stopwatch with which to time your copy, here are a few guidelines that may safely be used:
10-second spot has approximately 20 words
20-second spot has approximately 50 words
30-second spot has approximately 75 words
60-second spot has approximately 150 words
(Bortin, 1981)

East Ramapo Central School District
Barry Goldberg

CALENDAR OF EVENTS FOR MONTH OF _____

Date/Time	Brief description of activity	School/Location	Contact/Phone

Figure 8.2

Sioux Falls School District 49-5
Community Relations Office
1401 East 35th St.
Sioux Falls, SD 57105
(605) 331-7955

Radio Spot
Sample

PUBLIC SERVICE ANNOUNCEMENT   FOR USE MARCH 2, 1989
30 SECONDS
SCHOOL NEWS

PATRICK HENRY JUNIOR HIGH WILL SPONSOR A CENTENNIAL

FESTIVAL OPEN HOUSE THIS EVENING FROM 5-7. STUDENTS AND

THEIR FAMILIES HAVE BEEN INVITED TO PARTICIPATE BY SHARING

COLLECTIONS, DEMONSTRATIONS, DISPLAYS, MUSIC, OR FAMILY

HISTORIES. THE FESTIVAL IS OPEN TO THE PUBLIC. PATRICK HENRY

IS LOCATED AT 2200 SOUTH FIFTH AVENUE.

Figure 8.3

157

Many PSAs are generic and can be run over a period of time. Indicate the start and stop dates for running the announcement.

Photographs

While it is recognized that timeliness, impact, and relevance generally determine whether or not a story will be published, pictures add immeasurably to the value of the story. Photographs give added enrichment by providing a view of the story that can best be described when seen. While fast-breaking television coverage of events captures our imaginations at the moment, print media coverage provides the ability to read and decide the deeper meanings of what has been reported. Photographs enhance a story and enable readers to examine details over and over again at their leisure. ''Photojournalism sets the stage for newsworthy items. The pictures may add to the written article or offer a persuasive slant'' (Mercury, 1990).

> Pictures do a great job of capturing a reader's attention — a much better job than words alone can do. And if the picture and its caption can communicate the essence of your story, so much the better. You see, not only do more readers see pictures and read captions than read stories, readers also remember pictures better and longer. And stories with pictures are read more often than stories without pictures, which is one reason editors prefer them. Another reason is that pictures help break up the all-gray look of a page that's mostly typeset words, and editors are very sensitive to the look of a page.
>
> Pictures also add a sense of reality to a piece of information. In announcing a new product and discussing its attributes, a picture can help give form to the concepts that your words are trying to convey. (Winston, 1982)

Photographs may be used at the time of announcing an event, in anticipation of the event, when reporting at the time of the event, and at a later time when the event is followed up. You can get added publicity by using interesting photographs of the event. Pictures can be run by themselves with a caption describing the essential facts of the event that was held.

Photo Memos

If you would like to bring your event to the attention of the editor, do so by directing a photo memo to the editor of the section in which your story would be included. The photo memo is similar in content to the traditional press release, while it highlights the fact that the event would be a photo opportunity (Bortin, 1981).

Photographers

Most newspapers send their own photographers to take pictures. They prefer to have their people go out to the scene and take the angle that the newspaper is interested in featuring. The editor needs to know what the story is, as well as where and when the photographer needs to be there.

If you know that the newspaper is sending a photographer, be sure that you are on time. Photographers are usually on very tight schedules and cannot wait around for you to gather the group together, or to set up. Be prepared. If students are involved, secure permission slips from their parents beforehand. Be prepared to give the photographer the names, addresses, and other pertinent information about the individuals being photographed.

When the newspaper cannot send a photographer, the editor may rely on your photograph. You may decide to hire your own professional photographer, or get someone to take photos for you. Make certain that the individual doing the photography is skilled. You may have/want photographs that are suitable for use prior to the event or during follow-up on the event.

Meaningful Photos

In order to convey a message through a photograph, the photographer must view the scene through the eyes of the camera. Shapes, lines, patterns, textures, and light, or lack thereof, affect a picture.

A viewer is attracted to a photograph by the initial impact it has on him/her. This is usually determined by the shape or basic outline of the object. Isolating, by visually cropping the photo, can eliminate unnecessary details. Changing the angle of the camera can achieve a different effect (Mercury, 1990). Busy pictures have no central focus and tend not to be used. If action is taking place, remember that the eyes travel from the lower left hand corner of a photograph to the upper right hand corner; movement in photographs goes to the right. Make certain that the action that you want to capture moves in that direction.

There is power within a photograph. Pose the subjects of a photo interestingly. The lower the angle, the more powerful the picture. Standing is more powerful than sitting. However, do not have the subjects standing as if they were receiving a citation. By turning slightly to the side, you obtain a more relaxed look. If the photograph is to be taken at a desk, leaning slightly forward results in a more relaxed look as well. Try to have the person you are photographing engage in some action — newspapers like action shots. Do not have the individual look at the photographer. Encourage them to turn slightly from the camera.

If photographed from a low angle, a prominent nose or chin may be pictured. If photographed from a high angle, the head is out of proportion to the rest of the body. If a full length picture is taken from an eye-level viewpoint, the subject will appear shorter. If the photographer uses a squatting position, a more realistic picture will result.

The angle that is used in shooting the picture determines the center of interest. Lines show direction and distance. Be aware of patterns in the form of repeated shapes, lines, or colors in pictures. Such repetitions need not be identical to present a pattern. Texture can project a three-dimensional sense. It appeals to the tactile viewing and offers a suggestion of the object's weight, as well as its softness. While best illustrated in close-up shots, it can also be very effective in pictures shot at a distance. Yvonne Mercury gives some good advice on taking photographs:

> Pictures can be shot from above, below, or at eye level. A shot from above eye level produces a dominant tone. In using this approach, you may rid the shot of a cluttered background. By shooting upward, on the other hand, you shoot the subject against the sky or plain wall and rid any foreground detail. Both of these angles then eliminate excessive detail and simplify the subject. An eye-level shot evokes a sense of realism. (Mercury, 1990)

It is best to have no more than three or four people in any photograph. Try to avoid having women wear busy prints. Gentlemen, in a professional setting, should wear their jackets; a red tie is a power tie and makes a statement. Red, as a color, stands out, while something like beige fits right in. Dark stripes blend in; women in suits make powerful statements. If the American flag is pictured, it should be on the right-hand side, over the individual's right shoulder. You may recall that politicians usually stand with the American flag. The message they are trying to convey is that ''this person is an American, this is the person we want.''

Submitting Photographs

Follow the guidelines above and submit your best results to the newspaper. Most newspapers prefer to receive 8 × 10 glossy prints, although they will accept 5 × 7 glossies. The photograph must be of very good quality, focused, and have good contrast. Submit clear, crisp originals. Black and white photographs are preferred over colored photos. Make certain that there are no smudges, cracks, fold marks, or writing on the photograph.

Submit a cutline that tells clearly and specifically the who, what, where, when, and why of the picture. Do not write on the back of the photo, do not clip anything to it. Type the cutline on a piece of paper, and fold it so that the typing appears at the bottom of the photograph and fold the rest of the sheet of paper behind the picture. Tape the rest of the sheet to the back of the photograph. Always include your name, address, and telephone number on the cutline so that the editor will be able to contact you should there be any questions (Bortin, 1981). If the photo contains people, clearly identify who they are and give their names from left to right.

Do not send identical photographs to several newspapers. Take different shots of the same event and send them out. Editors will not take too kindly to using the same picture that another newspaper is using. They will report on the same event, but with different photographs.

Photographs can pack a powerful punch. Use them again and again to illustrate a point. Replace those that are outdated and continue to feature and celebrate the good! Remember—a picture is worth a thousand words.

Press Relations

Good press relations are critical to assuring fair treatment and the coverage you want. Walling (1982) identified six tips in dealing with the "Fourth Estate":

(1) Develop positive relationships with editors and reporters. Get to know them personally. Meet and discuss upcoming projects. Learn what the newspaper needs in order to serve the schools well.

(2) Adhere to deadlines and style requirements. Press releases that need little or no revision in the newspaper's editorial room will merit the best treatment and will earn results.

(3) Make certain that school news really is news—up-to-date and important material of interest to the community.

(4) Play fair with press releases. Where more than one newspaper is involved, make sure all newspapers get the same material at the

same time. If one paper wants to ''scoop'' another, it is up to that paper to gather additional facts, background information, interviews, and the like. But the PR leader cannot play favorites in the initial release without losing valuable credibility and, in the long run, damaging relationships with all the news media.

(5) When releases are sent (as they sometimes must be) to different departments of a single newspaper, inform both reporters/editors so that conflicts and duplication of effort within the newspaper staff can be avoided.

(6) Be ready for questions. Make sure reporters know who to call and, when they do call, make certain that factual information is at hand to answer their questions. Reporters live with deadlines and cannot afford delays caused by unpreparedness on the part of the school PR people.

Recognize that the press has constraints under which they work, guidelines, and timelines to honor. Respect them, meet them halfway, level with them, and you can rest assured that you will enjoy fair coverage of your school/district news events.

Press Conferences

It is useful to call a press conference when an important announcement should be handled on an immediate basis, or is of sufficient importance that it will raise questions on the part of the press. If you have the time, and can plan for it, schedule the press conference at a time that is convenient for the press. Hopefully you will have an idea as to what their time constraints and their deadlines are. If it is of an immediate nature, give the press a reasonable time to get there. Recognize that the television stations may want to send camera crews.

The physical setup for the conference should be such that the surroundings would not interfere with the essence of the conference and is close enough to the reason for the press conference, if that is possible. Make certain that adequate seating is available. You may want to have telephones available for their use should the story need to be covered immediately.

Be prepared for questions based on the information shared at the press conference. Make every effort to have supporting staff available to assist you so that questions can be answered at the time of the conference. You do not want to leave the press with unanswered questions which invite them to "fill in the blanks."

Press Packets

A very useful tool to use at the time of a press conference is a press packet, which contains background information, detailed information about the event, and charts and photographs as appropriate. By providing a press packet you are giving members of the media the background to put their stories together as they see fit. They can then make their reports as long or as short as they wish. It generally insures that the reporter's story more accurately reflects the information that was shared at the press conference.

Many superintendents provide press packets for the press at the time that the school budget is released. In that packet superintendents place summary sheets of the highlights of the budget, a breakdown of revenue sources, and expenditures by category. Charts reflecting changes from year-to-year and comparisons with other districts/states are other items that may be included. Information contained in the press packet should serve to add accuracy to the statements of the press, and reduces the incidence of inaccurately shared information.

Other times that press packets come in useful are when redistricting of school boundaries is being proposed, school closings anticipated/recommended, and the grades being housed in various schools are under consideration.

Interviews

Be comfortable when you are being interviewed. Remember that the reporter wants a balanced story just as you want the interview to be a positive one. Prepare for the interview by gathering the facts that may be needed. Have them ready and share them with the reporter. Make certain that the most important facts are presented up front, do not bury them. Whenever possible, give the reporter a hard copy of facts, figures, and statements from which the reporter can prepare the story, quoting as the reporter sees fit.

Always be honest and discuss the story to the extent that you can share information. If you do not have answers to some of the questions, say so, and get back to the reporter with the answers as soon as you have them. Do not forget to get back to the reporter.

Whenever possible speak "on the record" and avoid educational jargon. Doing so enables the reporter to prepare a story in language that both the reporter and the reader readily understand. If you are dealing with a sticky issue, prepare a short comment and either read it, or hand it to the reporter. Try to avoid a "no comment" response to a question. The shortest prepared comment is far better than a "no comment" response.

Recognize that the print media is often limited as to space, and the radio and television media are limited as to time. Shorter sentences can be quoted more readily, particularly in the broadcast media. Always think before you speak. You may hear yourself, or read what you said, again and again.

Crisis Situation

At the time of a crisis you need to provide accurate and timely information to the press and the community. Having a crisis management plan in place helps you know the specific steps that you should take at the time of a crisis—i.e., what the district expects of you under trying circumstances. It is far easier to think through a plan prior to a crisis than it is at the time of a crisis. Chapter 9 discusses the contents of a crisis management plan.

During any crisis, you will have to deal with the press. A spokesperson should be identified. That person should immediately notify all local media from a roster that has been compiled well in advance of any occurrence, requesting strict adherence to the district's crisis information management plan. Either the superintendent of schools, the personnel relations person, or the board chairperson should be designated as the district's spokesperson. If none of them is available, then the chief administrator at the building may be designated. All questions pertaining to the crisis situation should be referred to the spokesperson who will make every reasonable effort to provide timely replies.

A room, either at the site of the crisis, or at another location, should be designated to serve as a news room for media personnel. Make certain that the press has access to a telephone(s). If telephone access is limited in the news room, you may wish to indicate that reporters may use the telephone on a rotating basis for local calls, not to exceed five minutes per news organization per rotation. Brief the press on the situation and provide periodic updates.

Reserve one telephone line at the site for incoming calls from district personnel. Designate another telephone line at the site as the crisis information line. Make certain that an operator is available to respond to incoming calls, routing them as appropriate. When the determination is made that a crisis no longer exists, the spokesperson should notify the press.

Dealing with Critics

We are subjected to criticism in many forms, both written and oral. As a general rule, the individual who gets media attention will continue to pursue an issue. When the attention stops, the individual generally calms down.

There are times when we are asked questions for which we do not have the answers on hand. Do not hesitate to say that you will get the answer and get back to the individual. Just make sure that you find out where and how you can contact the person. At other times you cannot respond because you may be dealing with a personnel matter, or a legal or contract issue. Do not feel defensive. Know that you are not at liberty to speak to certain issues. You cannot always respond.

At all times, be calm and be honest.

Professionals Doing Their Jobs

In dealing with the press, remember that they are professionals doing their jobs. Recognize that they have constraints and deadlines. Recognize that they will generally be fair in their coverage of a story. Be available, open, cooperative, and level with them.

If they feel that there is a cover-up, they will dig and get to the bottom of a story, possibly speaking to all the wrong people. You are a far better, and more reliable source than an individual who may have an ax to grind. Maintain good working relationships; they pay off time and again.

CHAPTER 9

BEING PROACTIVE
RATHER THAN REACTIVE —
PLANNING FOR PUBLIC RELATIONS

ONE POSSIBLE REASON WHY THINGS
AREN'T GOING ACCORDING TO PLAN . . .
IS THAT THERE NEVER WAS A PLAN.

Anonymous
Planning Your School PR Investment

A L L too often we feel that everything is moving along and that things are going well at the school/district. We feel that "nothing is broke, so we won't fix it." And then something happens in the district — we find that the school budget is defeated, that a bond referendum is not passed. And then we are shocked! Shocked that the public does not support us, shocked that we cannot go forward with our plans, and distressed that we have to go back to the drawing board and start to build public confidence and rethink and redo portions of our proposal before we present it to the public again.

Very often the prime reason why people do not support a bond referendum or turn down a school budget is because they do not have enough information about what is being proposed or they do not have confidence in the school district. They have little or no information about the district, its programs, its successes. A question that voters always answer for themselves is "Why should I vote the school district more money? Why should I believe what they are telling me now?"

Recognizing that it is far easier not to do anything, we also need to recognize that public relations does not take care of itself if left unattended. It is often too late to start winning friends and influencing people when the chips are down and the decision must be made.

What is needed is a planned and systematic approach to school public relations. You need to be proactive and plan a public relations program that will move your district in a forward direction. Once you recognize the need for a planned public relations program, you need to determine what it is that you want to accomplish and who the target audience is. It is then that you can proceed to identify how you will accomplish your objectives and evaluate whether or not you have accomplished them.

167

Determine Priorities

Does the system or school have goals and objectives that they would like to accomplish? If they do, keep them in mind as you plan your program. Publicize them, reinforce them, and try to gain support for them. If there are no goals or objectives, decide whether or not you will determine them from your vantage point. You gain credibility when you set goals and objectives that correspond to the concerns of the community you serve. You need to know what is going on and what people are thinking; you need to be tuned in and not turned off.

You can determine public sentiment as a result of talking to people, working with advisory groups, listening to key communicators, or getting responses to questions by doing a survey or needs assessment. Whatever form the survey takes, do not survey the community unless you intend to do something. To do a survey and then do nothing can be deadly. Perceptions of your leadership ability will lower, as your drive for change loses credibility.

First ask yourself what it is that you want to know and why you want to know it. What will you do with the information once you have it? Do you need this information to help you run an effective school, and to assist in the planning process? You may decide that you would like to identify the community's perceptions of the academic programs; the future direction that the program, school, or district should be taking; the programs that are considered important to the community; or the public's concerns relative to certain aspects of the program. Find out where you can get this information. Is this information available in the system? Is there another way to get the information other than conducting a survey? Only when all of these questions are answered should you move on to the survey itself.

Conducting a Survey

If you decide to conduct a survey, whom will you survey in order to get feedback? Parents? Staff members? Students? How will you select the individuals that you survey? Often the credibility of a survey rests largely with the group that is asked to respond. Make certain that you have a broad base that reflects the various sides of the issue(s) you are addressing.

What type of survey will you use—a written questionnaire, personal interviews, or personal telephone calls? Each form of survey has its strong and weak points.

Consider the length of time that it will take to do the needs assessment. Wording of questions has to be carefully considered. Then materials must be printed, the instrument must actually be administered, then finally the responses have to be tabulated and evaluated. Additional time needs to be added if you are going to mail a questionnaire. Set a realistic timeline for the accomplishment of the survey and establish benchmarks for the accomplishment of the various phases. Identify the key people who will be working on the survey and the budget to support the operation. Monitor the process to be sure that it proceeds according to plan.

Telephone Survey

If a telephone interview is selected as the method to use in collecting the data, make certain that the interviewers are trained in advance of the actual telephoning. Anticipate questions that may be asked and train the interviewers in the appropriate responses. Instill in the interviewers the need to be neutral in their approach to the responses to the questions. Their tone of voice can influence the outcome of the survey. A telephone survey can generally be accomplished with speed and dispatch.

Personal Interviews

The same general guidelines hold for individuals conducting personal interviews. Here the tone of voice and the non-verbal communication skills of the interviewer can very materially influence the outcome.

Decide whether the interviewers will record the data as they receive it, or wait until after the interview is over to do so. If they will record as they go along, which is best in most cases, construct the form so that the interviewer can easily mark the form and proceed to the next question in a logical, orderly fashion.

Guidelines for Planning and Conducting the Interview

The following are guidelines which you can use in following through when using interviews:

(1) Decide who will be interviewed.
(2) Decide upon the type of interview you will conduct—structured, semi-structured, or unstructured.

(3) Decide how the interview information will be recorded – tapes, notes, post-interview report.

(4) When planning the interview:
- Prepare direct unambiguous questions.
- Avoid threatening questions.
- Avoid leading questions.
- Ask only those questions the person has the capacity and background to answer.
- Pretest your interview questions.

(5) When conducting the interview:
- Establish rapport with the person.
- Briefly explain why you are conducting the interview.
- Do not forget to record the information provided.

Questionnaires

If you decide to use a written questionnaire, you need to decide if you will send it home with the students, send it to all the homes in the community using bulk mail, or publish it in the newspaper. Where and how will the questionnaires be returned? Will you be expecting that they will be returned to the school by students or community members, sent back postage paid by addressee, or will there be a need for the respondent to place a stamp on the envelope?

What will the form of the questionnaire be like? Will it be so imposing that readers/responders will balk at responding? Will the responders have an opportunity to comment on the process, the questions asked, or to state their opinions on topics not covered in the questionnaire? In selecting the questions to be asked, make certain that you do not use educational jargon. Keep the questions straightforward and simple. Once the questions have been written, try them out on a target group who will give you feedback so that you can modify the questions as needed. Select only the best questions to go into the questionnaire. Format the response sheets so that they can be tabulated by computer. Consider using optical scan sheets.

Identify how the analysis will be done and how the information gleaned from the survey will be disseminated. Set a target date for the process to conclude and monitor the benchmarks for the accomplishment of the various phases.

The following guidelines can aid you in constructing a questionnaire.

Cover Page

Create a cover page that has a title on it and states the reason for the questionnaire. Explain how the information derived from the questionnaire will be used, and indicate when and where the results will be available.

Indicate whether the response is anonymous, and explain how the questionnaire should be returned. Say thank you, and sign your name.

Questionnaire Items

Develop specifications as to the kind of information you want. Decide upon the item types you wish to use.

When constructing the questionnaire items:

- Make them short and direct.
- Minimize the need for lengthy evaluation or interpretation on the part of the respondent.
- Avoid threatening questions.
- Avoid leading questions.
- Avoid questions in which there is an obvious socially desirable response.
- Pretest the questionnaire items.

Collating the Questionnaire

Group the items by type and topic and develop directions for each item and type.

Type the questionnaire neatly in an organized format and pretest the questionnaire.

Administering the Questionnaire

Set the date, place, and time.

Make arrangements for reproducing, mailing, and collecting the completed questionnaires. Make certain that the data is analyzed, conclusions drawn, and recommendations made.

The University City School District, University City, Missouri conducted a needs assessment involving the entire school district prior to identifying the school district's goals and objectives (see the Appendix at the end of the book). Every household in the city was surveyed by the questionnaire, as were staff and students. Valuable information was gleaned from the results. The data was disaggregated along many lines and conclusions were drawn, from which goals and objectives were adopted by the board of education. The process worked well.

Planning for Public Relations

Members of the general public know only what they read in the newspapers, hear on the local radio station, and see on the local television program. All too often they are not aware of what you are doing because there is little or no recognition of how important it is for them to know what is going on. There generally has been no concerted effort to celebrate the good. Planned communication has not been viewed as a high priority by many administrators. Administrators can offer many reasons for not paying attention to this very critical area, such as the fact that there is not enough time, people do not care, people do not want to know, and what difference will it make.

This situation must change. Attitudes towards sharing information must change. As school staffs move into using shared decision making as a viable organizational strategy, staff and parents must have information to make intelligent decisions. Administrators must open communication lines so that there is give-and-take, which results in building understanding and support.

As parents are provided an opportunity to choose which school their student is to attend, they will be looking at the schools much more critically. They will want to know about the school's programs, staff, attitude towards their students, test scores, and the like. Administrators will have to share that information with the public, and will need to promote a positive image to convince the parents to stay in their current school rather than selecting another one. Maintaining student enrollment is critical in many schools, and it could well become a matter of survival for the poorer-performing ones.

The only way that the community will become aware of the positive programs and results in the schools is through the PR put out by the school. The public finds out about the negative happenings by reading the daily newspaper or watching the local news. The media is quick to pick up the negative, since negative press sells newspapers. Administrators can no longer sit back and think that the public automatically knows what is going on in the schools. Nora Palmer Gould (1989) points out how this process has impacted early childhood programs:

> Early Childhood Programs have suffered profoundly during the past few years from negative publicity. Newspaper headlines have screamed about sex abuse being rampant in day care centers. The Federal Administration in Washington has implied that good mothers stay home and don't "warehouse" their children. Pediatricians issue reports on *Good Morning, America* and other TV shows about the "raging" epidemics of childhood diseases inherent in group settings for young children. Positive external communication is terribly important for Early Childhood Programs. It is important for parents to feel good about leaving their children in day care. It is the director's job to promote an image within the community which will make all Early Childhood Programs an attractive idea to parents and the general public.

Positive press will assist the school in its staff and student recruitment efforts. Recognize that choice is available in many states and that everyone wants to be part of a winning team. Given the choice between a school that is viewed as a winner and a school viewed as mediocre, staff and students will naturally opt for the winner. Start now to plan your PR program. Be proactive, and celebrate the good that is happening at your school!

Planning for positive PR involves more than simply getting information to the public earlier and more frequently. Decide whether you want to share information or influence opinions. Target your efforts to accomplish your goals and recognize the audiences you need to address.

Establish an Operational Plan

Establish an operational plan that will accomplish your objectives. Set forth what you want to accomplish, how you plan to accomplish it, and what it will take in terms of people, money, and time.

Adopt a Theme and/or Logo

Consider a theme and a logo that will be eye catching and memorable, and that people will be able to link to your school or district. Examples from industry are: "We Bring Good Things to Life" (GE), "Quality is Job 1" (Ford), "We Love to Fly and It Shows" (Delta), and "Good to the Last Drop" (Maxwell House coffee).

Several years ago the Oklahoma City Schools, Oklahoma adopted the theme "Our Hearts Are in the Public Schools, and So Are Our Children." The bumper stickers and posters all carried the theme and a large red heart. It was catchy and meaningful. It was reinforced again and again as it appeared in different places and on different PR pieces.

Fort Knox Community Schools, Fort Knox, Kentucky adopted the theme "Quality Education in *Mint* Condition" (Figure 9.1). Kelso Public Schools, Kelso, Washington adopted "Celebrate Learning!" as their theme, and incorporated an apple as part of their logo (Figure 9.2). Consider your district and come up with one that meets your objectives and ties in with a local characteristic, such as "mint" for Fort Knox, and apples for the state of Washington. In a short, well-worded phrase you can capture the essence of your district in a way that will be picked up and remembered.

Identify the Target Audiences

Decide the audiences to whom you are going to address your efforts, both internal and external. These are the individuals or groups that need to know where the school is and where it is heading. Then, if you feel that you want to communicate information, use mass media techniques such as bulletins, flyers, news releases, newsletters, and brochures. Many people can be reached fairly easily once the material is put together. If you want to change attitudes, you would use face-to-face communication techniques such as meetings, discussion groups, workshops, telephone conversations, conferences, dialogues, receptions, and seminars. Face-to-face, interpersonal techniques enable us to get closer to the people and influence them on a more personal basis, responding to their concerns and answering their questions.

Identify Viable Channels of Communication

There are channels of communication or strategies that can be used to reach your intended objective. Once you have decided on the audience you want to reach, identify the channels of communication that will best accommodate your need (see Chapter 10). Will you use bumper stickers, newspaper articles, letters to the editor, newsletters, brochures, or posters?

Fort Knox Community Schools

Quality Education in Mint Condition

Figure 9.1

Figure 9.2

Identify a Budget

Decide how many dollars will be needed to accomplish your plan, recognizing that you may need to be flexible as to the final product. A well thought out plan, properly documented, will generally be supported. Be realistic as to the availability of people to get the job done and the finances of the district. Do not overlook contributions that can be obtained from community businesses. Remember that these businesses have a vested interest in the community and want the school district to do well, because as a school district goes, so goes the community.

Action Plans

Planning documents to deliver a PR program may take several formats. A marketing plan, for instance, identifies:

- objectives to be accomplished
- activities to be supported
- evaluation component to judge the strategies' success
- person(s) responsible for carrying out this phase of the plan
- timeline needed
- detailed cost analysis

Communication Grids

Once you have a marketing plan, translate it into a communication grid, which shows visually and clearly who will get what piece of PR that is produced. This grid is a road map that outlines the plan. The details are generally contained in supporting materials. Communication grids can be drawn to address whatever the intent is, and can address a particular program, school, or district.

The following three communication grids are representative of various formats. Each addresses a specific need: to share information on magnet schools, to promote a dual language program, and to organize parent information day (at a not-for-profit residential facility). In addition to each grid is an explanation of the designated channels.

MAGNET SCHOOLS OFFICE
Newburgh Enlarged City School District
Newburgh, New York
Marsha Sobel

Objective: Aid the Magnet Schools Office in its quest for better public relations with the community, its schools, parents, staff, the media, other communities, and the New York State Education Department.

Explanation of Communication Channels:

- *Brochures* — Several different brochures are published throughout the calendar year. Some are to explain different programs, such as the Magnet Summer Laboratory School. Others are to describe magnet schools that are currently in existence in the school district. These are distributed to parents for informational purposes and used to publicize the schools in outside communities. Copies are distributed to other publics for information purposes.
- *Magnet attractions* — A monthly newsletter composed of articles submitted by the staffs of the magnet schools, by its students, and by parents is published. These are sent to all magnet schools and administrators, and are used for public relations purposes for visitors to the district.
- *Press releases* — News releases on newsworthy items are sent to the media for informational purposes with the intent of reaching a wide audience quickly.
- *Policy Advisory Council meeting notices and minutes* — Monthly meeting notices are sent to the Policy Advisory Council, which is composed of parents, teachers, administrators, and Magnet Support Staff. Monthly minutes of the meeting are issued.
- *The media* — The media is used to publicize events that are open to the community. Newspapers and cable television advertisements are used to inform and attract the public to these events.
- *Reports* — Midyear and end-of-the-year reports are produced. These are available for the community to read and are sent to the New York State Education Department for review.
- *Staff development workshops* — Information is sent to the schools regarding staff development topics. Workshops are organized for

Magnet Schools Office Communication Grid

CHANNELS	Students	Teachers	Administrators	School Board	Media	Parents	Community	Other
Informational Brochures - Programs	X	X	X		X	X		
Informational Brochures - Schools	X	X			X	X	X	
Community Newsletter	X	X	X		X		X	
News Releases					X			
PAC Meeting Notices and Minutes	X	X	X		X			
TV Advertisements					X			
Newspaper Advertisements					X			
Reports - Mid-Year / End-of-Year		X	X			X	X	
Staff Development Notices	X	X						
Interviews	X	X	X			X	X	
Tours of Magnet Schools	X	X			X		X	
Informational Meetings	X	X	X		X	X		
Program Fact Sheets and Applications	X	X	X	X	X	X		
Open Houses	X	X	X	X	X	X		
Surveys	X	X			X	X		
Phone calls	X	X	X		X	X	X	

Figure 9.3 Magnet Schools Office communication grid.

teachers and administrators. The information is available to the teachers and community.

- *Tours* — Visitors to the district are taken on tours of the various magnet schools, providing these guests with information concerning the programs at each site.
- *Informational meetings* — Informational meetings regarding programs and issues are held. These are open to anyone interested in attending — parents, teachers, students, and community members. These meetings are publicized through the print media and television ads.
- *Program fact sheets and applications* — Fact sheets regarding various programs that originate from the staff are produced. These fact sheets give concise facts regarding a particular program; an application form is printed on the reverse side.
- *Open houses* — Open houses are held at various sites to promote the magnet schools. The community is invited to visit the site and get a feeling for the program at that school.
- *Surveys* — Surveys are conducted periodically to receive information regarding programs, issues, needs, and evaluation.
- *Telephone calls* — The Magnet Schools Support Staff speak with members of the community and other school districts on a continuing basis.

DUAL LANGUAGE PROGRAM
Beacon City School District
Beacon, New York
Debra Hogencamp

Objective: Increase the Dual Language Program's visibility in the district as well as in the community by:

- publicizing program goals
- highlighting program accomplishments
- sharing program resources
- encouraging parent/community/business participation

Explanation of Communication Channels:

- *Newsletter* — will be specifically directed to the parents of students participating in the program. It will be bilingual and include such items as student accomplishments, field trips, guest

DUAL LANGUAGE PROGRAM
COMMUNICATION GRID

KEY:
DL: Dual Language
DW: District Wide
SA: South Avenue School
BETAC: Bilingual Education
Technical Assistance Center

CHANNELS	Superintendent	Board of Education	Principal (SA)	Administrators (DW)	Teachers (DL)	Assistants (DL)	Teachers (SA)	Assistants (SA)	Teachers (DW)	Assistants (DW)	Students (DL)	Students (SA)	Secretaries	Custodians	Food Service	SED, Division of Bilingual Education	BETAC	Parents (DL)	Parents (SA)	Parents (DW)	Non-parent taxpayer	News Media	Local Businesses	Community Organizations	Other Educational Facilities
Newsletter -District	✓	✓	✓	✓	✓	✓	✓	✓	✓	✓	✓	✓	✓	✓	✓	✓	✓	✓	✓	✓	✓		✓	✓	
-DL Program	✓	✓	✓		✓		✓	✓	✓	✓	✓		✓	✓	✓	✓	✓	✓	✓	✓					
Informational Presentations		✓	✓	✓	✓	✓	✓	✓	✓	✓	✓	✓	✓	✓	✓	✓	✓	✓	✓	✓	✓	✓	✓	✓	✓
Newspaper Articles	✓	✓	✓	✓	✓		✓	✓	✓	✓	✓	✓	✓	✓	✓	✓	✓	✓	✓	✓	✓	✓	✓	✓	✓
Press Releases	✓		✓		✓	✓	✓	✓	✓	✓						✓	✓	✓	✓	✓	✓	✓	✓	✓	✓
Surveys		✓	✓		✓											✓		✓							
Parent/Teacher Reception	✓		✓	✓	✓	✓								✓	✓	✓	✓	✓	✓	✓					
Video	✓	✓	✓	✓	✓		✓	✓	✓	✓	✓		✓	✓	✓	✓	✓	✓	✓	✓	✓	✓	✓	✓	✓
Poster Contest	✓	✓	✓		✓	✓	✓	✓	✓	✓			✓	✓	✓	✓	✓	✓	✓	✓		✓	✓	✓	✓
Board of Education Meeting		✓	✓	✓	✓	✓					✓					✓		✓	✓	✓					
DL Advisory Committee Meeting		✓	✓		✓	✓					✓					✓		✓							
Parent Phone Call "Check-in"			✓		✓	✓												✓							
DL Informational Brochure	✓	✓	✓	✓	✓	✓	✓	✓	✓	✓	✓		✓	✓	✓	✓	✓	✓	✓	✓	✓		✓	✓	✓
Parent Recognition Luncheon	✓	✓	✓		✓	✓										✓	✓	✓				✓			
DL Student Recognition "Tea"	✓	✓	✓		✓	✓										✓	✓	✓				✓			
Staff Development Advisory Council			✓		✓	✓	✓	✓	✓	✓						✓		✓				✓			✓

Figure 9.4

181

speaker presentations for cultural events, parent workshops and activities, and teacher recognition.

• *Informational presentations* — These will outline the program to various publics. Other channels such as a program video or brochure may be employed. These presentations will be done frequently for different audiences such as those at faculty meetings (district-wide), district administrative council meetings, the Head Start Center, City Council/Mayor's Office, real estate agencies, churches/religious institutions, the public library, Hispanic Society, Martin Luther King Center, IBM, Texaco, and other local businesses, State Association for Bilingual Education, and the State Education Department two-way bilingual meetings.

• *Newspaper articles* — Newspapers will be contacted for special events, such as student performances, guest presentations for cooperative culture classes, and special parent activities. This will occur approximately five times per school year.

• *Press releases* — They will be issued for each scheduled activity, inviting parent and community support. Included are Parent Advisory Committee meetings, parent/community workshops, and program performances. Announcements of new staff and requests for volunteers will also be included.

• *Surveys* — They will be disseminated to both internal and external publics such as parents, community, and district-wide staff to determine perceptions about the program. This will assist program staff in identifying what information needs to be clarified and what issues are of the greatest concern. A team consisting of dual language teachers, assistants, administrators, and parents will prepare the surveys. Parents whose children participate in the program shall be surveyed three times a year (September, January, June). The community and district staff will be surveyed twice during the year (October, May). The first survey will serve as a needs assessment for the public relations program and the second as an evaluative tool.

• *Parent/teacher receptions* — These will provide an informal setting for parents and teachers to get together to discuss classroom activities, curricula, and concerns. They will occur twice a year (November, February).

• *Video* — This will be developed illustrating instructional, parental, and staff development activities provided by the program.

- *Poster contest* — A poster contest with a theme will be sponsored. Entries will be displayed at a local business and a panel of judges from the community will be assembled. Prizes will be sought from local businesses. This will be a yearly event.
- *Board of education meetings* — A presentation on the program's progress is given to the Board of Education. In addition to this requirement, the assistant director along with a member of the staff or parent advisory committee attends regular board meetings (bimonthly) to maintain visibility by mentioning upcoming events and/or accomplishments.
- *Parent advisory board* — This board acts as a liaison with other program parents in order to encourage their participation. The board will become versed in how to run meetings and strengthen the parent organization. Meetings of the board are held once a month.
- *Parent phone call check-in* — Teachers make telephone calls to the parents of their students with at least one positive comment about the student's progress in order to cultivate positive home-school relations. Invitations to volunteer or attend parent meetings are extended. Calls are logged. If a household is without a phone, a brief note is mailed.
- *Information brochure* — A brochure aimed at parents, community and non-dual language staff is disseminated. This publication is used to enhance other channels such as presentations and meetings. It is placed in the central registration office, real estate agencies, district schools, and local businesses.
- *Parent recognition luncheon* — An annual recognition luncheon is held at a local restaurant. Awards for outstanding support of the program are given. A guest speaker presents a topic selected by the parent advisory group.
- *Dual language student recognition tea* — This event is held for parents, teachers, and students in honor of student accomplishments within the program at the end of the school year. Awards are given by building administrators. A reception and cultural presentation follows.
- *Staff Development Advisory Council* — This council, comprised of teachers, assistants (school-wide), and building administrators, develops a list of educationally relevant themes. A schedule of workshops and presenters is formulated and disseminated to building staff. If space permits, the workshops are opened to all district staff. Some eight sessions are held throughout the school year.

DEVEREUX PARENT INFORMATION DAY
Devereux Center
Rhinebeck, New York
Candace H. Shyer

Objective: To organize a Parent Information Day with workshops to be held on guardianship in New York State, transitional funding, and SSI benefits.

Explanation of Communication Channels:

- *Invitation letter* — This will inform and/or invite guest speakers, officers of the Parent's Association, parents, staff, and agencies to the Parent Information Day. The day consists of workshops and a buffet lunch. The letter is written by the cochairmen and approved by the campus director. One mailing is needed.
- *Information release* — An insert information page is attached to the invitation letter which briefly describes the workshop speakers and their topics.
- *Schedule of events* — This is an easy to read schedule chart showing time, location on campus, and speakers for the workshops and lunch.
- *Response card* — An RSVP card and envelope are included for parents, agencies, and speakers.
- *Phone calls* — These are a continuous method used to communicate with guest speakers, cochairmen, campus director, and President of the Parent's Association. They will also be used initially to contact guest speakers.
- *Memos* — Memos are a continuous method to request and inform various department heads of events, numbers attending, equipment needed, and personnel needed to set up, run, and clean up after the workshops and buffet lunch.
- *Organizational meetings* — These are planning and information meetings held by the cochairmen, campus director, department heads, and officers of the Parent's Association at least once a week prior to the event.
- *Staff meetings* — At weekly department meetings one of the cochairmen gives the current status regarding Parent Information Day.
- *News releases* — News releases written by the cochairmen and approved by the campus director, are mailed to the in-house newspaper, Devereux Foundation newsletter in Pennsylvania,

Communications Grid
Devereux Parent Information Day
May–89

Publics:

Channels	Co-Chairperson	Parent's Association	Campus Director	Department Director	Parents	Guest Speaker	Students	Agencies	Devereux Staff	In-House Media	Out-of-House Media
Organizational Meetings	*	*	*	*							
Phone Calls	*	*	*	*		*					
Invitational Letters	*	*	*	*	*	*		*	*		
Information release	*	*	*	*	*	*		*	*		
Schedule	*	*	*	*	*	*		*	*		
Response Card	*	*	*	*	*	*			*		
Memos	*		*	*					*		
Staff Meetings	*		*	*					*		
News Releases	*	*	*	*		*		*	*	*	*
Direct Verbal Communications	*	*	*	*		*	*		*		
Thank You Letters		*	*	*		*			*		

Figure 9.5

and to the President of the Parent's Association. Releases are mailed one month prior to and at the conclusion of the event.

- *Direct verbal* — This is a continuous method used to communicate with students, staff, officers of the Parent's Association, campus director, department directors, and guest speakers about the event.
- *Thank you* — "Thank you" letters are written by the cochairmen following the event to people assisting with the project.

Lead Time Required

Consider the amount of time needed to bring your ideas to fruition. Include time to involve the appropriate people, secure the funding, prepare the materials, do the mailings, and the like. Walling (1982) estimated lead time needed to accomplish various PR strategies as follows:

Letters	1 − 2 weeks
Flyers and newsletters	1 − 4 weeks
Pamphlets and booklets	2 − 6 weeks
Newspaper inserts	2 − 6 weeks
Conferences and informational gatherings	2 − 6 weeks
Meetings involving meals (breakfasts, luncheons, etc.)	4 − 8 weeks
Large programs, banquets, etc.	6 weeks − 6 months
Press releases (standard)	1 − 2 weeks
Press releases (special events)	1 − 4 weeks
Public service spots	2 − 4 weeks
Advertising	2 − 6 weeks
Posters and bulletin boards	1 − 2 months
Free-standing display units	2 − 6 months
Slide shows and videotapes	4 − 12 months

Checklist for Principal's PR Plan

The National School Public Relations Association (1986) recognizes that "the responsibility for planning and executing a long-range public relations program at the building level rests with the principal." The NSPRA identified check points to "help judge an existing program or initiate a new one," shown in Figure 9.6, which is reproduced with permission.

Crisis Management

> A crisis is an unstable time or state of affairs in which a decisive change is impending – either one with the distinct possibility of a highly undesirable outcome or one with the distinct possibility of a highly *desirable* and extremely *positive* outcome. (Fink, 1986)

Crises occur time and again when we least expect them and without apparent warning. A crisis is an incident that escalates quickly in intensity, interrupts the normal flow of events in the school, and interferes with learning. It usually draws media attention to the school, and can readily damage a school's image in the community.

Crises happen quickly – a fire, an explosion, a burst pipe, a suicide, a bus accident. They happen when we least expect them. Try as we may to avoid them, crises occur.

There are steps you can take to help you plan for a crisis before one occurs. With a detailed crisis management plan in hand, and known to your associates and staff, situations should be handled much more easily and with less stress.

Identify a Crisis Management Team

This will be a small team consisting of your key administrators, key teachers, secretary, head custodian, physical plant manager, and public relations person.

Inventory the School's Vulnerability

Working with the team, inventory the possible vulnerable areas and plan how these crises would be managed – who would do what, where, when, and how.

Based on the tentative strategies identified to handle these vulnerable areas at the time of a crisis, identify the common elements in your responses and incorporate them into an overall response plan that would undoubtedly apply to most crises.

CHECKLIST FOR PRINCIPAL'S PR PLAN

The final responsibility for planning and executing a long-range public relations program at the building level rests with the principal. These check points will help judge an existing program or initiate a new one.

1. In planning a public relations program are you careful to:
   ___ a. allot an equally adequate amount of time to planning and systemizing a long-range program as you do for the instructional program?
   ___ b. involve your staff in planning, preferably through a committee of teachers and non-teaching personnel?
   ___ c. tailor a program to meet your community's unique needs and characteristics instead of adopting some other school's program?
   ___ d. keep the plan simple, and on paper, so that it is easily understood and operable?
   ___ e. move slowly, not stirring up community and staff suspicion?

2. Do you indicate to your staff the importance you place on good school-community relations by:
   ___ a. your own attitude, actions, and time devoted to this area?
   ___ b. providing the time, materials, and facilities your staff needs to carry out its responsibilities?
   ___ c. assuming responsibilities for school-community relations that can best be handled through the school office?
   ___ d. developing school policies, rules, and procedures that promote good school-community relations?

3. In working with the staff do you assume responsibility for:
   ___ a. conducting continuous in-service programs for all employees which will increase the understanding of the need for public relations and develop the skills needed to fulfill these needs?
   ___ b. promoting staff morale?
   ___ c. encouraging constructive staff associations with pupils, parents, and community?

4. In working with the community do you:
   ___ a. conduct a continuous survey of its needs and attitudes?
   ___ b. keep the people regularly informed on all phases of the school program?
   ___ c. provide channels for school-parent relations?
   ___ d. enlist the assistance and cooperation of lay leaders and organizations?
   ___ e. maintain regular contacts and flow of information with the local newspapers, radio, and television stations?

Source: National School Public Relations Association, Arlington, Virginia.

Figure 9.6

Establish a Crisis Headquarters

This will be the place from which the crisis team can operate at the time of a real crisis. Have readily available the equipment needed to communicate during a crisis including telephones, typewriters, battery operated walkie-talkies, shortwave radios, and a copy machine and paper.

Draft a Crisis Management Plan

Distribute this crisis management plan to the staff. This plan should indicate whom to contact, what to do, what the staff can expect, where things are, and the immediate steps to take in the event of a crisis. The plan should also indicate who will be in charge and make decisions. The names and telephone numbers of the crisis team should be included in the plan. Review the plan with the staff early in the school year, each year, before anything happens. Post the plan in conspicuous places so that it is readily available in case of need.

Designate a Spokesperson

Only one person should speak for the school/district. That person should have access to all of the information about the crisis, and should release the most current information available that is authorized for release. At times there may be information that needs to be withheld for legal or other purposes. A rule of thumb is that the person would always state the date of the occurrence, location, persons involved (if it is possible to release this information), what happened, and the probable cause if it is known at the time.

Often the superintendent of schools is the designated spokesperson. The spokesperson may also be the district's public relations person or the building principal. Whoever does the speaking needs to be viewed as credible, well informed, and able to speak well. That person must not panic under stress.

The designated spokesperson should have available the names, addresses, and telephone numbers of the news reporters. News releases should be used, as should fact sheets about the district.

The spokesperson will notify the board of education in accordance with an agreed plan. Some boards feel that all that is needed is for the board chairperson to be notified. The chairperson then notifies the rest of the board. Other boards want each board member called. In that case it is best to prepare a written statement that is read to each board member as he/she is called. In that way you are sure that each member has the same information.

The spokesperson should contact the district's key communicators and relay appropriate messages and status reports to them. They will be able to spread the information through the community and often dispel rumors that may be circulating.

In releasing information to the media and the key communicators, give the facts as you know them—what has taken place, what has/is being done to contain/repair/limit the impact of the crisis, and who is involved. Respond to questions honestly, but do not feel pressured into saying anything you should not say. Feel comfortable with the statement you have prepared. The chances are that you prepared it fully aware of its implications and had an opportunity to assess what you wrote.

St. John (1986) recommends that as soon as the crisis occurs, and before any details are known, the spokesperson should make an immediate statement to:

- Indicate that school officials are aware of and on top of the situation.
- Assure that details are being investigated.
- Assure all interested persons that all appropriate information will be shared as soon as possible.
- Explain why, if you cannot discuss something; "no comment" is a red flag to news media.

Notify key community support groups such as the fire department, police department, local hospital(s), key local government officials, and utility companies.

Whatever you do, do not panic, lie, cover up, minimize to the extent that you are viewed as lacking credibility, assess blame, or deviate from your agreed-upon crisis plan.

Once the crisis has subsided, meet with your key administrators and crisis team members in order to assess the crisis plan, the actions taken, and the changes that may need to be made to the crisis plan so that future incidents can be handled more smoothly.

Thank those who were helpful, nurture those who need support, acknowledge any losses, and work to bring the school back together as a functioning whole. This may take time. Be prepared, and be patient.

A crisis generally does not happen overnight, the healing may take a little longer.

Just as planning is needed to run a school/district efficiently, so too is planning needed to manage crises. The more adept we are at handling crises, the better our image will be in the community.

IMPLEMENTING THE PLAN—
CHANNELS OF COMMUNICATION

T H E R E are many channels that you can use in communicating with the publics you serve. They are not mutually exclusive and should be incorporated into your communication plan to help you achieve your goals.

The channels identified in this chapter have been used very successfully by schools/districts across the nation. They have been reproduced with the permission of the school district.

District-Wide Channels

Newsletters

Newsletters can be used very effectively for sharing information with parents and the community. They can convey information about the district, its staff and students, and its programs and policies. They can be issued from the various offices within the school/district and are not mutually exclusive. Newsletters are often issued by the central office (Figure 10.1), the building principal (Figure 10.2), and guidance departments (Figure 10.3). PTAs, student groups, and booster clubs often issue newsletters.

In deciding whether or not to issue a newsletter, consider the audience you want to reach and what you intend to accomplish. Do you want to let the readers know what is going on? to report on progress? to solicit input prior to making a decision, such as in the case of preparing for a bond referendum? or perhaps to influence them to support a specific issue? Do you wish to address the students? the in-house faculty and staff? the parents? the community at large?

193

A NEWSLETTER FOR PARENTS OF KIRKWOOD SCHOOL DISTRICT R-7 STUDENTS

Kirkwood Celebrates 125 Years

The Kirkwood R-7 School District and the city of Kirkwood are gearing up to celebrate their 125th anniversaries.

The city of Kirkwood received its charter of incorporation from the State of Missouri on February 20, 1865. This charter made Kirkwood the first planned residential community west of the Mississippi. The Kirkwood School District was established three days earlier on February 17.

To celebrate its birth, the Greentree City is hosting festivals and special events filled with fun for the entire family.

September 30, 1989 - All Kirkwood volunteers are invited to be part of a huge promotional photograph—Kirkwood High School—10 a.m. (school district volunteers are encouraged to participate)

November 18, 1989 - Kickoff dinner—$62.50 per person/$125 per couple; 6 p.m. at Greenbriar Hills Country Club.

February 20, 1990 - Public invited—dinner sponsored by senior citizens—$20 per person; 6 p.m. at the Viking

June 15-16, 1990 - Historical pageant—Theme: "We Touch the Future"—the week after school is out—students and parents are encouraged to participate, Kirkwood High School-8:00-9:30 p.m.

All year long -"Project 125"- Kirkwood clubs and organizations identifying and completing one or more of 125 projects of improvement, beautification or promotion of Kirkwood.

The R-7 School District has organized a committee that is in the process of gathering ideas for classroom activities, fund raisers and assemblies to celebrate the district's 125 years of existence.

School Opens September 5

The 1989-90 school year will open Tuesday, September 5. School hours are as follows:
High school: 7:30 a.m.-2:30 p.m.
Middle school: 8:35 a.m.-3:05 p.m.
Elementary school: 8:55 a.m.- 3:35 p.m.

Morning kindergarten session:
8:55 a.m.- 11:55 a.m.
Afternoon kindergarten session:
12:35 p.m.-3:35 p.m.
Full-day kindergarten session:
8:55 a.m.-3:35 p.m.
School lunch prices will be:
Elementary: $1.00   Secondary: $1.10
Adults: $1.25

Volunteers Make A Difference

How would you like to have fun, meet new and exciting people and make a genuine difference in your child's education? You can by becoming a Kirkwood School District volunteer.

You can help make school a better place to be by joining a group of volunteers who contribute over 20,000 hours of their time each year in many capacities.

They assist classroom teachers, work one-on-one with students, perform clerical duties, plant flowers on school grounds and assist the school nurses and librarians. The list goes on and on.

If you would like to volunteer, please contact your school's office or call Sandy Miller at 965-9500. You'll be glad you did.

Reproduced from *School, A Newsletter for Parents of Kirkwood School District R-7 Students,* Kirkwood, Missouri.

Figure 10.1

WARREN ELEMENTARY SCHOOL
Newsletter #9
October 16 - 20, 1989

DATES TO REMEMBER:

October 20	Parent/Teacher Conferences 10:00 a.m. - 5:00 p.m.
October 23-27	Red Ribbon Week - SAY NO TO DRUGS
October 23	Cub Scout Pack Meeting, 7:00 p.m.
October 25	Picture Retakes

HALLOWEEN TRICK OR TREAT

Little ghosts and goblins are invited to Trick or Treat in Greenwood Mall this Halloween! Many of the stores will be giving individually wrapped candy or certificates good for food products or games (while supplies last). Everyone 12 and under may Trick or Treat in the mall on Tuesday, October 31, 5:00 - 7:00 p.m.

Reinforcing Learning
YOU CAN HELP GIVE CHILDREN THE WRITE STUFF

Children who can express their thoughts in writing have a head start in school. Writing is a skill that improves with practice. Here are some ways to encourage your child to write at home.

1. Show your children how writing can help them stay in touch with people they care about. Encourage your children to write letters to friends or family.

Write notes to your children, and leave them on the refrigerator or in a lunch box. These notes can be practical - "Don't forget Scouts today" - or just for fun - "I hope you're having a great day."

Encourage your kids to write notes to you. There's nothing like finding a note that reads, " Mom, I love you" to brighten your day.

2. Give your child the tools for the job. Some nice paper or a special pen or pencil will make writing more fun.

3. Let your children see you writing. If you write letters, or if you do some writing for your job, let your children read what you've written.

4. Praise your child's writing. The best reward for a writer is an appreciative reader. Let your child know that reading what he writes makes you happy...and proud.

When You Need Help

REPORT CARD TIME IS TIME TO TALK

Report card time is one time many parents want to know where to turn for help with their student's school work. Here are some tips that can help:

• **Talk with your child about each grade - calmly.** Does she know why she got that grade? Can she explain it to you? What does she think needs to be done?

• **Talk with the teacher to get her views on needed improvements** ans suggestions for ways to improve. The teacher will be glad to work with you and your child.

• **Find out what help your school offers.** Tutoring may be available or after-school classes on study skills.

• **Consider getting outside help.** Perhaps an older student will work with your child. A neighbor might be glad to help.

• **Remember that grade cards report on only a few things.** They can't tell about a child's dreams or ambitions or what the child will become in the future. Grades are not a measure of a child's worth, just a picture of current school performance. Talking together, planning needed changes, and keeping grades in perspective can help.

PARENT QUIZ
Setting the Stage for Success

The children who do the best in school usually have parents who encourage them to do their best-and who expect nothing less.

Here's a quiz to help you see how well you are communicating about your expectations about school to your child. **Answer Yes or No:**

_____ 1. I make it a point to learn about my child's schoolwork.

_____ 2. I let my child know I am interested in what goes on in school. I ask questions and listen to the answers.

_____ 3. My child knows I expect him to do his best work in school.

_____ 4. I help my child make plans for high school and after. I sometimes talk about how what he is learning now will help him later on.

_____ 5. I think my child is great, and I let him know it!

How Did You Score?

Four or five "Yes" answers is very good. Three is just fair. Less than three means you can do more to let your child know what you expect.

Reproduced from *Warren Elementary School Newsletter #9*, Bowling Green, Kentucky.

Figure 10.2

JUNIOR JAZZ

Published By: MINISINK VALLEY HIGH SCHOOL COUNSELING DEPARTMENT

March, 1989

COUNSELORS
Maria Diana
Maureen McGeady
Donald Przytula

3/20/89 - Junior Homeroom Teachers - Please announce and post.

S.A.T. SIGN-UP

The S.A.T. exam will be given May 6 here at Minisink High. The counselors strongly urge college-bound Juniors to take this exam. Applications are available in the Counseling Office and must be filled in and mailed with payment by **MARCH 31.** Cost: $14.00.

After March 31, the cost goes up. Don't delay - pick up application and information booklet **now.**

IMPORTANT UP-COMING EVENTS

March 21 to May 8 - **BOCES Visitations:**
If you are interested in a BOCES course for next year you must sign up to visit the center.

April 7 & 8 - **The 1989 Engineering Open House at Rutgers University**
See the facilities at Rutgers and find out what engineering is all about.

April 18 - **SERO** - **National Scholarship Service and Fund for Negro Students,**
Inc. is sponsoring its annual student - college interview sessions in N.Y.C..

April 24 - **Junior Parent Night**
The college admissions process will be explained to you and your parents. Letters will be sent home announcing time and place.

Reproduced from *Junior Jazz*, Minisink Valley, New York.

Figure 10.3

Newsletters allow you to be proactive and share the message you want your public to receive. Do not wait until you need to respond to negative press or need to correct erroneous information conveyed by the media. With newsletters you can share information and selectively address topics of your choice. The format puts you completely in control of the information that is released.

The timing, number of issues, and format of the newsletter(s) will be influenced by your objectives, the expertise available to publish the newsletter, and available funding. For example, if you intend to issue a monthly update in order to inform the reader of what is and will be happening at your school, and to share students' work on a regular basis, you may decide to use both sides of one sheet of 8 1/2 × 11 inch or 8 1/2 × 14 inch paper, or you may decide that you will use an 11 × 17 inch sheet folded in half, which would afford you the equivalent of four 8 1/2 × 11 inch sheets of paper. One size or format does not usually fit all circumstances. Again, consider the intent of the newsletter, the message that you wish to convey, and your budget allowance.

Logo, Masthead, and Format

Once a decision is made as to the focus of the newsletter, as well as when and how often it will be issued, you should adopt a logo, masthead, and format that reinforces the image you want to portray. The logo may be the school's mascot or the district's logo, it could incorporate an award won by the school, or illustrate a sense of purpose (Figure 10.4). You may want to design a logo specifically for the newsletter. Select the finish, weight, and color of paper that complements the color ink you will be using in the newsletter. Multiple color inks, used carefully, can make a newsletter very attractive and convey a sense of the school; they can set a tone that influences the opinions of the reader.

Once you are pleased with the appearance of the newsletter, reserve use of the masthead and color of paper for the newsletter so that the readers will, at a glance, recognize it as coming from your office and not cast it aside as some junk mail that is being sent home.

Designing Newsletters

The design of the newsletter should attract readers. There is no one design or format that fits all circumstances. Initially the readers need to

Figure 10.4

be drawn to the newsletter. This can be done by making it attractive, letting them know at a glance, that it contains information that may be of interest to them. Try to give the feeling that it is a person-to-person letter. Responding to the needs of your public will often insure a continuing readership. You want to secure reader loyalty; you want people to be eager to read your newsletter.

Use headlines that capture the attention of readers so that they will be moved to read the article(s). Headlines help readers to focus attention. Use graphs, charts, and tables in conjunction with articles to make the newsletter easier to understand, and more attractive. A strong focal point in the newsletter will attract readers and lead them through it.

Remember that a picture is worth a thousand words. Consider using photographs and/or clip art. Clip art is readily available in many of the computer graphics programs and in copy shops and stationery supply houses. Use camera-ready copy and art; materials should be first-generation and clean.

Consider the audience that you are addressing. Small type generally turns off the audience and may, therefore, affect readership. Type styles may vary within a newsletter, but as a rule use no more than three different styles. Use columns in order to break up the printed matter and make it more readable. Paragraph breaks help as well.

Use of Computers

The ability to design clear, attractive newsletters at greatly reduced cost has been tremendously enhanced by the use of computers. It is no longer necessary to set type in order to change type styles and to arrange and rearrange the parts of the newsletter. There are outstanding desktop publishing programs available that can be used even for very small jobs. There are printers on the market that rival set type and defy your ability to recognize the difference.

You may decide to do the entire newsletter on the computer, or to paste up the newsletter once you have the copy ready. Use a special light blue pencil that is not readily picked up by the cameras, and use paper on which you can place very light markings to assure proper placement. There are pencils specifically made for this purpose. Use glue that enables you to lift the item and place it in another location. Rubber cement is excellent for that purpose, but be careful to remove any excess glue so that you do not have smudges, or dirty spots and marks, on your final pasteup. Spray glues are available, as is ''post it'' glue.

When you are satisfied that the materials are the way you want them to be, place a clean sheet of paper on top of the pasteup to insure that it will remain clean and have it printed.

Special Purpose Notices

All too often, matters arise that need to be brought to the attention of parents and community members. Consider issuing a newsletter for that very purpose, but use a masthead, color of paper, and format that will be easily recognized as coming from your office and being fairly important.

Programs that do not routinely issue newsletters find that they need to communicate with parents from time to time. These information pieces should have distinct mastheads that identify the program, and should follow the guidelines identified in the newsletter section.

An example of an information piece released by a district for a special purpose is *Construction Corner,* issued by the University City School District in order to keep the community informed as to how construction was progressing; they passed a major bond referendum to upgrade their schools (Figure 10.5).

School/District Calendars

Many districts prepare school-year calendars during the course of the summer months and include in them the important dates that parents and community members need to know: opening and closing dates, school holidays and vacation dates, major exam days, PTA/PTO meetings, school board meetings, concerts, choral shows, and performance group dates (Figure 10.6). When the interscholastic schedules are available, they, too, are included in the yearly calendars (Figure 10.7).

Sports Calendars

Athletic Directors usually prepare a seasonal sports calendar, on which they list the dates that the team is playing, the location of the games, and the teams they are playing. At times the calendars will feature action shots of the teams and players.

These poster-sized calendars feature the school colors and are posted throughout the community in locations where they will get the widest possible readership (Figure 10.8). In order to offset the cost of printing,

Construction Corner

An Update on Repairs and Improvements throughout the University City School District

March 21, 1988   Volume 1   Number 2

EXPLANATION OF PLANNING, DESIGN PROCESSES

Many of you have called, written or approached members of the Board of Education and/or the Administration with your concerns about "why aren't we seeing more progress? After all, we passed the bond issue in November of 1986."

Despite the complexities which go into any $18.8 million project, the answer is simple. It takes planning and on-target designs to insure a project of this nature is compatible with District needs and funds.

Architects from the Wm. B. Ittner firm have been involved with planning even prior to the bond issue ballot proposal in November, 1986. At that time, the District came to the conclusion that its three year capital improvements cycle was accomplishing too little with too few funds.

With a vote of confidence from the University City community in November, 1986, the Board and Administration proceeded in confidence with a bold capital improvements program. The charge was to repair and renovate buildings so they would be a source of pride to all.

This is no small task. It takes planning. What does planning entail? It includes many walking tours of each building, assessing the strengths and weaknesses of the particular item needing repair or renovation. With over 860,000 square feet, it takes some time to inspect each and every door, for example, to see if it is worth repairing or if it needs replacing.

Planning also includes discussions with contractors and consultants to determine ball park cost figures so that when it comes time to bid, the District will be able to make cost effective decisions on what should or should not be in the specifications.

It also means talking to those persons directly affected by the changes - principals, teachers, parents and students. For example, when it comes time to renovate science labs at the High School and Brittany Woods this summer, the contractors will need to know the details of a modern, 21st

Century science lab.

Good planning takes the District right up to the design, bidding and construction process.

What constitutes the design process? Once the District makes a decision on what is to be repaired and/or renovated, it is time to design the project using results from design meetings, talking with the various groups and then making the schematic drawings.

The architects are now at this point with many projects in the Capital Improvements plan. Mr. Dwyer has appointed a committee at each school to work with the architects to give input on what is needed, discuss and decide on options and how the proposed work will mesh with the school program.

Throughout the entire Capital Improvements program, the architects and District have tried to compile work into large packages in order to secure the best prices along with quality work.

In addition, the District and architects have hosted one design meeting with others scheduled to hear input and comments from parents and the community on design factors for the work.

Once the design process is complete, it is time for the package to go out for bid.

PROJECTS TO COME

- Interior work
  (ceilings, paint, light fixtures, etc.)
- Site Work
- Life Safety
- Heating and Ventilation
- Windows

Figure 10.5

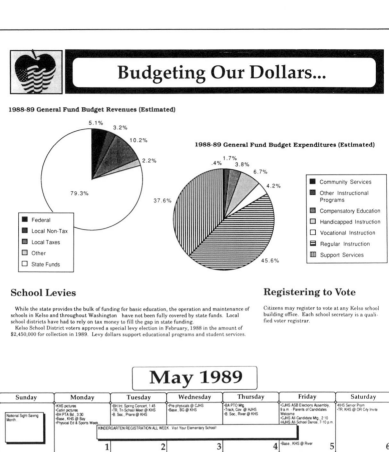

Budgeting Our Dollars...

1988-89 General Fund Budget Revenues (Estimated)

5.1%
3.2%
10.2%
2.2%
79.3%

- Federal
- Local Non-Tax
- Local Taxes
- Other
- State Funds

1988-89 General Fund Budget Expenditures (Estimated)

1.7%
.4% 3.8%
6.7%
4.2%
37.6%
45.6%

- Community Services
- Other Instructional Programs
- Compensatory Education
- Handicapped Instruction
- Vocational Instruction
- Regular Instruction
- Support Services

School Levies

While the state provides the bulk of funding for basic education, the operation and maintenance of schools in Kelso and throughout Washington have not been fully covered by state funds. Local school districts have had to rely on tax money to fill the gap in state funding.

Kelso School District voters approved a special levy election in February, 1988 in the amount of $2,450,000 for collection in 1989. Levy dollars support educational programs and student services.

Registering to Vote

Citizens may register to vote at any Kelso school building office. Each school secretary is a qualified voter registrar.

May 1989

Sunday	Monday	Tuesday	Wednesday	Thursday	Friday	Saturday
National Sight Saving Month.	•KHS pictures •Catlin pictures •BH PTA Bd., 3:30 •Base., KHS @ Bay •Physical Ed & Sports Week. **1**	•BH Int. Spring Concert, 1:45 •TR, Tri-School Meet @ KHS •B. Soc., Prairie @ KHS KINDERGARTEN REGISTRATION ALL WEEK. Visit Your Elementary School! **2**	•Pre-physicals @ CJHS •Base., BG @ KHS **3**	•BA PTO Mtg. •Track, Cov. @ HJHS •B. Soc., River @ KHS **4**	•CJHS ASB Elections Assembly, 9 a.m. - Parents of Candidates Welcome •CJHS All-Candidate Mtg., 2:10 •HJHS All-School Dance, 7-10 p.m. •Base., KHS @ River **5**	•KHS Senior Prom •TR, KHS @ OR City Invite **6**
•Mother's Day **7**	Teacher Appreciation Week. National Music Week. •National Family Week. Be Kind to Animals Week. **8**	•Barnes Book Fair •Teacher's Day USA **9**	•BBB Exec. Mtg., 3:30 p.m. •TR, Fort @ KHS •B. Soc., Ev. @ KHS **10**	•Pre-physicals @ HJHS •School Board Mtg. **11**	•Track, CJHS/HJHS/Cas. @ Schroeder •RV PTO, 9 a.m. **12**	•BH PTA Carnival **13**
☙ **14**	•Educational Bosses' Week. **15**	•BA Spring Program •TR, Qual. Meet @ KHS **16**	•Pre-physicals @ KHS, BOYS **17**	•Pre-physicals @ KHS, GIRLS •Carrolls Spring Program, 7 p.m. •Jr. High Track, Sub. District @ Shroeder Field **18**	•9th Grade Party 8-11 p.m. @ KHS •Wallace Spring Program, 9:15 a.m. •TR District, KHS @ Ev. **19**	•TR, District, KHS @ Ev. **20**
21	•Jr. High Spring Concert @ KHS, 7:30 p.m. **22**	•CJHS ASB Induction & Awards Assembly, 1:30 •School Board Mtg. •Catlin 4th Grade to Fort Vanc. **23**	•BBB Gen. Mtg., 7 p.m. (Election of Officers) •Jr. High District Track @ McKenzie Stadium •BA Volunteer Tea **24**	•Barnes 6th Grade Party •RV Science Fair •HJHS ASB Installation Assembly **25**	**26**	**27**
Memorial Day NO SCHOOL **28**	•CJHS Track Awards Dessert, 6 p.m. **29**	•CJHS Club Officers Elected •CJHS Publications Sale, 9th •Last Elem. DEEP Class **30**	**31**			

Celebrate Learning with Kelso Public Schools!

Reproduced from the *Kelso Public Schools 1988–89 Calendar/Handbook*, Kelso, Washington.

Figure 10.6

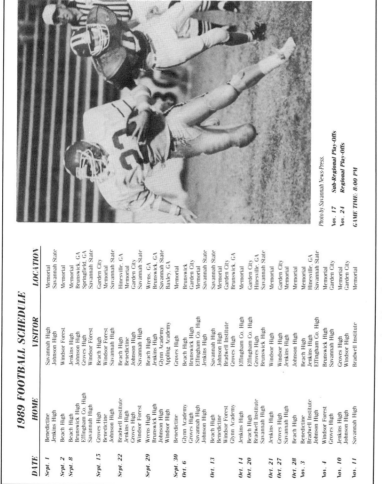

1989 FOOTBALL SCHEDULE

DATE	HOME	VISITOR	LOCATION
Sept. 1	Benedictine	Savannah High	Memorial
	Jenkins High	Johnson High	Savannah State
Sept. 2	Beach High	Windsor Forest	Memorial
Sept. 8	Beach High	Jenkins High	Memorial
	Brunswick High	Johnson High	Brunswick, GA
	Effingham Co. High	Groves High	Springfield, GA
	Savannah High	Windsor Forest	Savannah State
Sept. 15	Groves High	Beach High	Garden City
	Benedictine	Windsor Forest	Memorial
	Johnson High	Savannah High	Savannah State
Sept. 22	Bradwell Institute	Beach High	Hinesville, GA
	Jenkins High	Benedictine	Memorial
	Groves High	Johnson High	Garden City
	Windsor Forest	Savannah High	Savannah State
Sept. 29	Wrens High	Beach High	Wrens, GA
	Brunswick High	Jenkins High	Brunswick, GA
	Johnson High	Glynn Academy	Savannah State
	Windsor High	Appling Academy	Baxley, GA
Sept. 30	Benedictine	Groves High	Memorial
Oct. 6	Glynn Academy	Beach High	Brunswick
	Groves High	Brunswick High	Garden City
	Savannah High	Effingham Co. High	Memorial
	Johnson High	Jenkins High	Savannah State
Oct. 13	Beach High	Savannah High	Savannah State
	Benedictine	Johnson High	Memorial
	Windsor Forest	Bradwell Institute	Garden City
	Glynn Academy	Groves High	Brunswick, GA
Oct. 14	Jenkins High	Effingham Co. High	Memorial
Oct. 20	Beach High	Effingham Co. High	Garden City
	Bradwell Institute	Groves High	Hinesville, GA
	Savannah High	Brunswick High	Savannah State
Oct. 21	Jenkins High	Windsor High	Memorial
Oct. 27	Groves High	Windsor High	Garden City
	Savannah High	Jenkins High	Memorial
Oct. 28	Beach High	Johnson High	Memorial
Nov. 3	Benedictine	Beach High	Memorial
	Bradwell Institute	Jenkins High	Hinesville, GA
	Johnson High	Effingham Co. High	Savannah State
Nov. 4	Windsor Forest	Brunswick High	Memorial
	Groves High	Savannah High	Garden City
Nov. 10	Jenkins High	Groves High	Memorial
	Johnson High	Windsor High	Garden City
Nov. 11	Savannah High	Bradwell Institute	Memorial

Photo by Savannah News-Press

| Nov. 17 | Sub-Regional Play-Offs |
| Nov. 24 | Regional Play-Offs |

GAME TIME: 8:00 PM

Reproduced from the *Savannah-Chatam Public Schools 1989–1990 Calendar*, Savannah, Georgia.

Figure 10.7

CROSS COUNTRY GIRLS & BOYS

Mon	Sept	19	4 00	Montcello & Minsink	H
Tues	Sept	27	4 00	Invitional At Bear Mt	A
Tues	Oct	4	4 00	Goshen	A
Tues	Oct	11	4 00	Warwick & Burke	A
Tues	Oct	18	4 00	Valley Cent & Cornwall	A
Tues	Oct	25	4 00	O'Neil & Washington	H
Fri	Oct	28	3 00	OCIAA Championships	A
Fri	Nov	4	4 00	Section IX Meet	A

* Weekend invintationals not included

FOOTBALL

Sat	Sept	17	1 00	Port Jervis	H
Sat	Sept	24	1 00	Goshen	A
Sat	Oct	1	1 00	Valley Central	H
Sat	Oct	8	1 00	Minsink	A
Sat	Oct	15	1 00	Monroe Woodbury	A
Sat	Oct	22	1 00	Middletown	H
Sat	Oct	29	1 00	Washingtonville	H
Fri	Nov	4	7 00	Kingston	A
Sat	Nov	12	1 00	Pine Bush	A
Sat	Nov	19	1 00	Championship Game	TBA

GIRLS TENNIS

Wed	Sept	14	4 00	Washingtonville	H
Fri	Sept	16	4 00	Valley Central	A
Mon	Sept	19	4 00	Monticello	H
Thurs	Sept	22	4 00	Minsink	A
Fri	Sept	23	4 00	Monroe Woodbury	A
Mon	Sept	26	4 00	Kingston	H
Wed	Sept	28	4 00	Middletown	H
Fri	Sept	30	4 00	Washingonville	A
Mon	Oct	3	4 00	Valley Central	H
Wed	Oct	5	4 00	Monticello	A
Fri	Oct	7	4 00	Minsink	H
Wed	Oct	12	4 00	Monroe Woodbury	H
Fri	Oct	14	4 00	Kingston	A
Mon	Oct	17	4 00	Middletown	A

GIRLS SOCCER

Fri	Sept	9	4 00	Walkill	H
Tues	Sept	13	4 00	Valley Central	H
Thurs	Sept	15	4 00	Pine Bush	A
Mon	Sept	19	4 00	Highland	H
Sat	Sept	24	10 00	Goshen	A
Tues	Sept	27	4 00	Washingtonville	A
Thurs	Sept	29	4 00	Monroe Woodbury	H
Tues	Oct	4	4 00	Kingston	H
Thurs	Oct	6	4 00	Middletown	A
Tues	Oct	11	4 00	Valley Central	A
Thurs	Oct	13	4 00	Pine Bush	H
Tues	Oct	18	4 00	Minsink	H
Thurs	Oct	20	4 00	Washingtonville	H
Tues	Oct	25	4 00	Monroe Woodbury	H
Thurs	Oct	27	4 00	Kingston	A
Mon	Oct	31	4 00	Middletown	A

BOYS SOCCER

Fri	Sept	9	6 00	Tournment	H
Sat	Sept	10	11 00	Tournment	H
Wed	Sept	14	7 00	Middletown	A
Fri	Sept	16	4 00	Valley Central	H
Mon	Sept	19	4 00	Pine Bush	A
Thurs	Sept	22	4 00	Suffern	A
Mon	Sept	26	8 00	Ketcham	H
Wed	Sept	28	4 00	Washingtonville	A
Fri	Sept	30	4 00	Monroe Woodbury	H
Wed	Oct	5	4 00	Kingston	A
Fri	Oct	7	4 00	Middletown	A
Wed	Oct	12	4 00	Valley Central	H
Fri	Oct	14	4 00	Pine Bush	H
Wed	Oct	19	4 00	O'Neil	A
Fri	Oct	21	4 00	Wassingtonville	A
Mon	Oct	24	4 00	Spring Valley	A
Wed	Oct	26	4 00	Monroe Woodbury	H
Fri	Oct	28	4 00	Kingston	H

GIRLS SWIMMING

Thurs	Sept	22	4 00	Warwick	H
Tues	Sept	27	4 00	Middletown	A
Thurs	Sept	29	4 00	Monroe Woodbury	H
Tues	Oct	4	4 00	Kingston	A
Thurs	Oct	6	4 00	Washingtonville	H
Tues	Oct	11	4 00	Pine Bush	H
Thurs	Oct	13	4 00	Middletown	H
Fri	Oct	14	8 00	Elmira Invit	A
Tues	Oct	18	5 30	Monroe Woodbury	A
Thurs	Oct	20	4 00	Kingston	H
Tues	Oct	25	4 00	Cornwall	H
Thurs	Oct	27	5 30	Pine Bush	A
Sat	Oct	29	9 00	Fairport	A
Tues	Nov	1	4 00	Marlboro	H
Thurs	Nov	3	4 00	O'Neil	A
Wed	Nov	9	4 00	Dive Champ	H
Thurs	Nov	10	4 00	Swim Trials	H
Sat	Nov	12	9 00	Swim Champ	H

NFA FALL SPORTS '88

Source: *NFA Fall Sports '88*, Newburgh, New York.

Figure 10.8

and to help the team, many athletic directors solicit community businesses to place ads on this calendar sheet. Recognizing that this is an
excellent cause, businesses readily support the endeavor. These ads are
usually clustered around the border of the page or arranged at the bottom
of the poster.

Annual Reports

Annual reports are prepared and released to the public by most school
districts. The most important release is usually the superintendent's
report to the board on the condition of the district, which addresses the
goals that were set for the district, and the extent to which they were
achieved. The format, quality of paper used, inclusion of pictures, and
number of copies printed and distributed depends on the financial
capabilities of the district. Annual reports are an excellent means of
sharing the gains made during the course of the year just completed
(Figure 10.9).

It is important to release the annual report as close to the end of the
reporting period as possible. Releasing an annual report six months
following the close of the school year is difficult to explain and not as
meaningful as it would have been had it been released earlier.

Welcome to New Residents

The public utilities maintain lists of new residents. Consider writing
to the new residents, welcoming them to the community, telling them
something about the school/school district, and inviting them to visit
your school(s) (Figure 10.10). Newcomers respond favorably to being
cared for as individuals and welcomed into the community. They tend to
respond negatively if the first time they hear from the district is when
the taxes are going up, or when they are requested to vote on a bond
referendum. Such first impressions are hard to break. Share information
with them (Figure 10.11), and continue to encourage parents to participate in their children's education (Figure 10.12).

Newspaper Ads

If you find that you are not getting your message out the way you
wanted it, or if you want to reach a larger readership, consider placing
an ad in the local newspaper. As with the newsletter, you have complete

The Rye Public Schools

Annual Progress Report
1988-1989

Figure 10.9

DANBURY PUBLIC SCHOOLS
School Administration Building, Mill Ridge
Danbury, Connecticut 06810
(203)797-4700

Irene M. Lober, Ed.D.
Superintendent
797-4701

John A. Wolfkeil
Assistant Superintendent
Instruction-Curriculum
797-4710

Walter E. Skowronski
Director School Business Affairs
797-4704

Dear New Resident:

I would like to extend to you my personal welcome to the
City of Danbury. Danbury is a fine community of family living.
Our highly rated schools contribute to the good life we enjoy in
this very pleasant city. We are proud of our outstanding staff and
the achievements of our students. Approximately 63% of the students who
graduate from Danbury High School continue their education at colleges,
universities, technical institutions and schools throughout the country.
Thirty-five percent of our students enter the ranks of the employed upon
high school graduation. Many employment opportunities are a direct result
of courses and preparation given at the high school.

I would like to take this opportunity to invite you to visit the
school in your attendance area in order to become acquainted with the
principal and staff so that you may see, first hand, the outstanding
opportunities available for your child. It is generally best to call you
principal(s) in advance so that they can set aside time to visit with you
and answer your questions about their schools(s).

We look forward to having your children enroll. We cordially
invite you to join the ranks of our parents who enthusiastically support
our schools. When you become acquainted with our schools, I am confident
you will share their enthusiasm.

Sincerely,

IML/jgh

Irene M. Lober, Ed.D.
Superintendent of Schools

Figure 10.10

207

WELCOME

CHINESE

本書的編排是專為了幫助你了解火魯奴ι
區公立學校所為你兒女開辦的各種教育課程. 書
中的每一節均備有資料以輔導你參與你兒女的教
育. 使你成為你兒女的教育中一重要份子.

ILOCANO

Daytoy nga libro ket naaramid tapno makita yo dagiti prog-
rama iti Distrito ti Honolulu nga inkayo maisagut iti anak yo.
Tunggal maysa nga seksiyon ikkan na kayo iti impormasyon nga
mangtulong kadacayo tapno makipaset ti pannakaadal ti anak yo.

KOREAN

이 책은 자녀들에게 제공하는 호노룰루 구역 학교 들의
교육 프로그램에 대하서 부모님께서 아실수 있게끔 돕는 의미에서
편제 됐습니다. 각 부분은 당신이 자녀의 교육에 참가 할수 있는 정보들을
제공하고 있습니다.

LAO

ປຶ້ມນີ້ຖືກຈັດຂຶ້ນ ເພື່ອຊ່ວຍໃຫ້ທ່ານຮູ້ຈັກຖິ່ງວກັບໂຄງການຕ່າງໆ ໜ່ວຍໂຕ ເພື່ອຊ່ວຍລູກທ່ານ
ໃນການສຶກສາ ຢູ່ໃນອງຄ໌ມຕ່າງໆ ໃນເຂດເມືອງອອນໂນລູລູ. ແຕ່ລະວັກຈະຊ່ວຍຂະຍັນບາຍ ກ່ຽວ
ກັບວທທທ່ານຈະຊ່ວຍລູກຄ໌ການສຶກສາຂອງລູກ.

SAMOAN

Ua fa'avasegaina lenei tusi ina ia fesoasoani iā te oe, e
te silafia ai polokalama fa'a-le-a'oa'oga ua tu'uina iai lau
tama i le Itumālō o A'oga i Honolulu. I totonu o vaega
ta'itasi, o le'a mafai ona 'e maua ai ni fa'atonuga ma nisi
fa'amatalaga tāua, o le'a mafai ai ona 'avea oe ma vaega o
fesoasoani malosi i le a'oga a lau tama.

TAGALOG

Ang aklat na ito ay binuo upang matulungan kayong
matuklasan ang mga programang iniaalay ng mga Paaralan ng
Purok Honolulu sa inyong anak. Ang bawa't bahagi ay
magbibigay sa inyo ng impormasyon/pabatid kung paano kayo
makatutulong sa kanilang pag-aaral.

VIETNAMESE

Cuốn sách này làm ra để qui vị thấy rõ nhưng gì mà chương trình
giáo dục của Quận Honolulu giúp các em học sinh. Mỗi phần trong cuốn
sách này sẽ giúp qui vị nhưng hiểu biết để qui vị trở nên một thành
phần trong việc giáo dục con, em.

Reproduced from the *Honolulu District Handbook*, Honolulu, Hawaii.

Figure 10.11

A MESSAGE FROM THE HONOLULU DISTRICT SUPERINTENDENT

Dear Parents;

The Honolulu District's motto is "Onward to Success; Every School a Winner!" A corollary to this is "Onward to Success; Every Child a Winner!" We want all children to learn all that they are capable of learning.

The district's top priority, therefore, is to set goals that inspire excellence in each classroom. The major objectives for the next few years are to continue our quest for effective teaching and effective schooling which promise enhancement of learning.

To help our students succeed, we need parents and the wider community as partners in our educational endeavors. In fact, much of the strength of our schools stems from the support we receive from all sectors of our community. The business community provides us with their specialized knowledge, skills, worksite experiences, as well as materials. Parents and others volunteer many hours each year, tutoring children and supporting school activities such as the bazaar and carnival.

We encourage you to get to know the school your child attends, its programs and activities. We encourage your support and guidance in the day-to-day learning experiences of your child. We ask parents to also join us in placing excellence in learning as a top priority.

This Handbook is intended to provide information about the Honolulu District schools, as well as guidelines and suggestions on what parents can do to help motivate and guide their youngsters. In addition, we invite you to visit our schools and see what they are accomplishing. We welcome your questions as well as your support.

Together, in partnership, we can help every child become a winner.

Sincerely,

Margaret Y. Oda

Margaret Y. Oda
District Superintendent

2

Reproduced from the *Honolulu District Handbook*, Honolulu, Hawaii.

Figure 10.12

control as to its contents, format, and timing (Figure 10.13). One superintendent of schools places an advertisement in the newspaper prior to the opening of school each year (Figure 10.14).

Transportation Schedule/Newspaper Inserts

Instead of placing the traditional bus pickup schedule for the school year in the local newspaper each August, consider preparing an insert for the newspaper – a quarter-fold. The insert is included in all issues of the newspaper, both newsstand and home deliveries, and will reach far more households than if it were distributed only to the parents of students. Take advantage of this, and use the insert as an opportunity to supplement the bus schedule with information about the system, its program offerings, school calendar, snow closing information, names of the members of the board of education, and the like. Include all of the items that schools are legally required to inform their parents of, such as the Buckley Amendment, Freedom of Information Act, and the school's affirmative action position. The cost of a quarter-fold is generally not much more expensive and can do a tremendous public relations job for the school district.

Exemplary Practice: One school district published a quarter-fold insert that was very well received by the community. The Parks and Recreation Department of the city government approached the school district and asked them to consider including their schedule in the district's quarter-fold. They paid a proportionate share of the cost of publication. This insert soon became a very valuable resource for the community (Figure 10.15).

The district realized that this was indeed a valuable selling tool for the city and had several thousand extra copies of the insert run at the time of publication. Several hundred were distributed to the schools. The district then sold the insert to the local realtors at a nominal cost, twenty-five cents each. The bus contractor was asked, and did, contribute to the cost of the insert because the company's name was featured in a prominent place in the bus schedule section of the publication. The revenue generated by the sale of these inserts, shared costs, and contribution was enough to offset the slight increase in costs from year to year.

Today's Graduates
are
Tomorrow's Future!

to the

Middletown High School
Graduating Class of 1989

The Board of Education, the Superintendent of Schools, and the faculty and staff of the Enlarged City School District of Middletown acknowledge the graduates' hard work and wish them success.

Figure 10.13

A MESSAGE FROM THE SUPERINTENDENT OF SCHOOLS

Dr. Carole G. Hankin

Enlarged City of Middletown

TOMORROW, SEPTEMBER 9, IS THE OPENING DAY OF SCHOOL.

As classes resume, you can be certain that teachers and administrators alike have resolved that the coming year will be the best one ever. We want to do everything we can to help your children succeed.

AS PARENTS, WE NEED YOUR HELP . . .

ENCOURAGE REGULAR ATTENDANCE. It is difficult for young people to learn when they are not in class.

ESTABLISH PRIORITIES. This may be the perfect time to sit down with your child to let him or her know that you feel that school is important.

MONITOR HOMEWORK. Let your child know that you will assist in any way that you can. Show an interest in work being done. Set aside a quiet place for study and designate a time when homework can be done without interruption.

COMMUNICATE WITH THE TEACHER. Plan to attend open house, as well as regularly scheduled parent conferences. Your cooperation is invaluable.

As the year begins, we all look to the future to be bright. Successful education is a step in the right direction.

Carole G. Hankin

Carole G. Hankin

THE MIDDLETOWN BOARD OF EDUCATION

Martin Dlugatz, President   Dr. Paul Johnson, Vice-President
Edith Weiss   Thomas Grecco   Evelyn Isseks
Dr. Oscar Sotsky   Edward Godwin   George Sands

Figure 10.14

212

Reproduced from *Back-to-School Guide and Parks & Recreation Program,*
1989–90, Danbury Public Schools, Danbury, Connecticut.

Figure 10.15

Translation of Materials

Materials sent home in English to a multi-lingual community may not meet the needs of the constituents, particularly if the receivers cannot read English. Consider publishing a statement in the predominant languages in your community indicating where constituents may go to have the document translated. The ethnic community groups are usually pleased to be of service, and the constituents are pleased that their needs are recognized (Figure 10.16).

Impact Statements

Involving staff and affected community members and groups at the time of the development of policy statements, rules, and regulations is helpful in addressing the needs of the groups and assures that the new policy or regulation, if enacted, should not cause major problems. Solicit input by means of an impact statement attached to a written copy of the proposed policy, rules, or regulations. The individuals solicited should be made aware that you are sincere, and that the item in question is not cast in concrete. Make changes deemed advisable as a result of the responses to the statement.

The respondent may remain anonymous. If the respondent does sign the impact statement, get back to the individual and indicate the disposition of the recommendation made on the impact statement. If the item is going to the board of education, attach the impact statements to the recommendation, so that the board knows the reaction to the proposed policy, rule, or regulation, in advance of taking any action.

Bumper Stickers

Consider adopting a slogan that quickly identifies a theme or a program. Some that have been used are:

- ''My child is an honor student at Main High School.''
- ''My heart is in the public schools, and so are my children.''
- ''Our schools are in *mint* condition.''
- Save Our Schools
- Vote YES for Kids

Very often groups such as the PTA and booster clubs will sell or distribute these bumper stickers.

INDEX

TRANSLATION SERVICES

In order to facilitate the availability of the information in this publication to community members whose native language is not English, the district has made arrangements with several individuals and civic organizations to provide translation assistance. We greatly appreciate this service to the community.

KHMER

បើសិនឪ្នកស់លោករិចៈ
បវកៈម្ចូបៈវ្ញានៃលៈឆ្វ,
សូបៈបេតៈ ទានៈ្តៈ

ARC, 213 Main St., Danbury, Ct. 06810 — Phone 792-9450

LAO

ຖ້າຫາກທ່ານຜູ້ໃດຕ້ອງການຄວາມ
ຊ່ວຍເຫຼືອຫຼືວ່າທ່ານຢາກບເຂົ້າໃຈໃນພາສາ
ອັງກິດ ກະລຸນາໄປຫາ

ARC, 213 Main St., Danbury, Ct. 06810 — Phone 792-9450

PORTUGUESE

Qualquer pessoa ou familia que precise de ajuda para falar em Ingles para resolver qualquer problema nas Escolas por favor contacte Manuel Cipriano na Igreja Portuguesa a partir das 4 horas de tarde — 797-1821 ou na Administracao Beaver Brook Center telef- 797-4710 — das 8 horas a 4 horas da tarde.

SPANISH

Si Necesita ayuda con la traducion de esta publicacction, por favor communiquese con el Sociedad Cultural Hispana 798-2855.

VIETNAMESE

NẾU MUỐN DỊCH SANG TIẾNG VIỆT NAM, XIN VUI LÒNG LIÊN LẠC VỚI HỘI A.R.C. ĐỊA CHỈ 243 MAIN ST., DANBURY, CT. 06810 SỐ ĐIỆN THOẠI: 792-9450.

40

Figure 10.16

Public Participation at Board Meetings

It is helpful to have guidelines that have been adopted and disseminated prior to having a meeting at which citizens are able to comment. That segment of the meeting can be managed if guidelines are in place. All who wish to speak respond to the same set of rules (Figure 10.17).

Follow-Up to Board Meetings

Issue a summary of the action taken by the board to the staff and community following the board meeting. Distribute the summary as soon after the board meeting as possible (Figure 10.18).

Public Hearing Guidelines

Just as it is helpful to adopt guidelines for citizen comment at meetings, so is it helpful to adopt guidelines for conducting public hearings.

Board Meetings

The tone for the district is very often set by the board as a result of the manner in which it conducts its meetings. Inasmuch as they are public meetings, members of the public should feel welcome. They should be able to see and hear the board members, and should have some idea as to who the individual board members are and what topics are on the agenda. It would be helpful if people attending the board meeting had an idea as to how the board conducts its business.

Arrange the board's table so that in addition to the board members being able to see each other, the community members can also see who is talking. Have microphones at the board members' places and name plates so that the public can identify them (Figure 10.19). Have extra copies of the agenda for the evening available for anyone who attends the meeting. It is helpful to community members if there is a guide to the board meeting and its members available.

Orientation – New Professional Staff, Substitute Teachers, Support Staff, and Board Members

Individuals who have not been employed by the district are not generally aware of how it operates, what its organizational structure is,

FRONTIER CENTRAL BOARD OF EDUCATION

POLICY # 1345

Public Participation at Board Meetings

Board of Education meetings are conducted for the purpose of carrying on the business of the schools. Board meetings are generally conducted in public, so that the public can observe its school government in action. The Board meets in private to discuss only a narrow range of legally defined issues.

The members of the Frontier Central Board of Education see themselves as a representative body, and also wish to provide an avenue for all citizens to express their interest and concerns for the schools. Therefore, time is set aside at the beginning, and at the end of each agenda to provide the "privilege of the floor" to citizens and staff members of the district.

Because the Board has a responsibility to conduct the business of a multi-million dollar education enterprise in an orderly and efficient manner, it requires that public participation be limited to a reasonable length. (If a matter is especially controversial, the Board may schedule a special meeting or hearing.) In all meetings the President of the Board shall manage the time allowed for public discussion, the appropriateness of the subject, and the amount of time allowed individual speakers.

The Board will not act immediately upon requests put before it from the floor, if those requests have not come through the administrative chain of command. Such matters shall be referred to the Superintendent for study and appropriate follow-up.

The full agenda of the Board meetings, and a publication explaining this policy and the operations of the Board shall be made available to the public and press immediately upon its mailing to the Board. (In addition, a limited number of copies of the agenda will be made available to the public at the meeting.)

Reproduced from *Welcome to a Frontier Central School District Board of Education Meeting*, New York.

Figure 10.17

Board Notes

A Summary of the University City Board of Education Meeting
Prepared by the Communications Office

For the Staff

JUNE 8, 1989

Reproduced from *Board Notes, A Summary of the University City Board of Education Meeting*, University City, Missouri.

MEETING OF JUNE 1, 1989

ANNOUNCEMENTS
Gary L. Dwyer, Superintendent, made the following announcements:
The Class of 1989 participated in graduation exercises on Tuesday, June 6 in the High School Stadium. Valedictorians were Brendan Cummins and Makota Ogura. Julie Baglan was the salutatorian.

Arlene Antognoli and David Ackerman are among 31 principals selected to participate in a three-week summer institute at Webster University. The institute is designed to help principals incorporate the humanities and classics into their curriculum. Professors from local universities, materials and resources will be made available for the 1989-90 school year.

Greg Voigt, Latin teacher at Brittany Woods and McNair, has received a $1,000 McKinley Scholarship from the American Classical League to attend graduate school this summer at Millersville University in Pennsylvania. Mr. Voigt will be a graduate assistant in the foreign language department.

CHECK ORDER APPROVED
The board approved the order for drawing checks.

GIFT ACCEPTED
The board accepted, with appreciation, a gift from Rep. Sheila Lumpe of a wooden chest filled with materials for science instruction.

TO SUBMIT CHAPTER 1 FUNDS APPLICATION
The board approved the submission of an application for Chapter 1 funds in the amount of $470,500.

DISTRICT PURCHASES COMPUTER EQUIPMENT FOR UCHS CLASSES
The board approved the purchase of computer equipment at a cost of $23,987.49. The Department of Elementary and Secondary Education will reimburse the District for half of the cost.

APPLICATIONS FILED FOR SCHOOL, TRANSPORTATION, EXCEPTIONAL PUPIL FUNDS
The board authorized the filing of the applications for State School Money, State Transportation Aid and Exceptional Pupil Funds.

TO REPAIR GYM DOOR
The board approved the repair of the electrical operable wall in the large gym of Brittany Woods at a cost of $13,000.

LAWLESS PLAZA WORK CONTINUES
The board approved a bid from Oreo and Botta Company in the amount of $64,800 to continue work on Lawless Plaza. The board also accepted, with appreciation, a gift of $34,800 from the Lawless Plaza Fund.

CONFERENCE ATTENDANCE SET
The board approved a conference attendance.

PERSONNEL ANNOUNCEMENTS

Appointments:
Chester Bluett, UCHS assistant principal (1989-90)

Sheila Moore, UCHS Attendance office secretary

Cafeteria personnel for 1989-90

UCHS coaches for 1989-90

1989 Summer Institute staff

Reassignment:
Suzanne Grow, UCHS secretary

Resignations:
Carl Zerweck, Jr., project manager

Jeanette Wode, Pershing teacher

MEETING OF MAY 18, 1989

ANNOUNCEMENTS
Gary L. Dwyer, Superintendent, made the following announcements:
Teddy Hermelin, head secretary at Flynn Park School, was named a winner in a contest sponsored by KMOX Radio to recognize outstanding secretaries. She received two tickets to the Muny Opera production of "A Chorus Line."

CHECK ORDER APPROVED
The board approved the order for drawing checks.

GOALS, OBJECTIVES DISCUSSED
The board discussed the District's Goals and Objectives for the 1989-90 school year.

BOARD MEETING DATES SET
The board approved meeting dates for the 1989-90 school year - July 6, August 17, September 7 and 21, October 5 and 19, November 2 and 16, December 7 and 21, January 18, February 1 and 15, March 1 and 15, April 5 and 19, May 3 and 17, June 14 and 28 (if needed).

GIFT ACCEPTED
The board accepted, with appreciation, a gift of a computer, disk drives and accessories from Burton Leinwand.

M.S.B.A. DUES RENEWED
The board approved renewal of M.S.B.A. dues of $2,566.80 for 1989-90.

TO PARTICIPATE IN READING IS FUNDAMENTAL PROGRAM
The board approved the submission of an application for federal funds of $1,803 for the Reading is Fundamental project.

P.L. 94-142 PLAN SET
The board approved submitting the District's Compliance Plan for PL 94-142 which outlines services available to handicapped students.

TO PURCHASE GYM SEATS
The board accepted a bid of $11,935 from Roger J. Hutchinson and Assoc. for new seating in the High School gym.

DISTRICT BUYS SHADES
The board accepted a bid of $4,276 from St. Louis Shade and Hardware for shade replacement at Daniel Boone School.

DAIRY BID ACCEPTED
The board approved the purchase of milk and dairy products for the 1989-90 school year from Pevely Dairy Co. in the amount of $73,832.50.

JACKSON PARK BID ACCEPTED
The board accepted a base bid of $1,297,000 from Albers Construction Co. for repairs and renovations at Jackson Park School.

Figure 10.18

The School Board of Pinellas County

Robert L. Moore
Chairman

Dr. Moore was elected to the Board in 1986. Prior to this, he was a teacher and principal in Pinellas County Schools. He has served as president of the Florida Association of Secondary School Principals, was a member of the Florida Professional Practices Commission, and served on the Board of Directors of the Florida Association of School Administrators.

Barbara J. Crockett
Vice Chairman

Mrs. Crockett, a native of St. Petersburg and a graduate of local schools, was elected to the School Board in 1986. Active in school and community affairs, she is a member of the St. Petersburg Junior League and the St. Petersburg Board of Realtors. She currently serves on the Board of Directors of Latchkey and the District Advisory Committee of H.R.S.

Albert G. Blomquist

Dr. Blomquist has been a member of the School Board since 1980, and served as Board chairman 1984-86. He was selected for the All-Florida School Board, and is a member of the Florida Education Practices Committee. He is associate pastor of the First United Methodist Church of Clearwater.

Lucile O. Casey

Mrs. Casey was elected to the Board in 1988. She was a foreign language teacher in Pinellas County schools and St. Petersburg Junior College. She is involved in civic, school, and church voluntarism in Clearwater, and founded The Compassionate Friends of Pinellas. She is an active associate with Number 1 Realty.

John R. Espey

Mr. Espey served on the Board from 1976 to 1984, when he was the Board chairman. He was re-elected in 1986. A former teacher, he is now active in the real estate firm of Bower and Espey, Inc. He was a member of the state Council on Teacher Education and the Education Practices Committee.

Corinne Freeman

Mrs. Freeman was appointed to the Board by the Governor in 1988 to fill a vacancy due to the death of a member. She successfully ran for election to fill the remaining two years of the term. The former mayor of St. Petersburg, she is now a stockbroker with Thompson McKinnon Securities.

Ron Walker

Mr. Walker was elected to the Board in 1984, and was re-elected in 1988. He was Board chairman in 1986-87. He serves as a director of the Florida School Boards Assn., is active in civic affairs, and is minister of education at the North Dunedin Baptist Church. He is vice-president of a computer consulting firm.

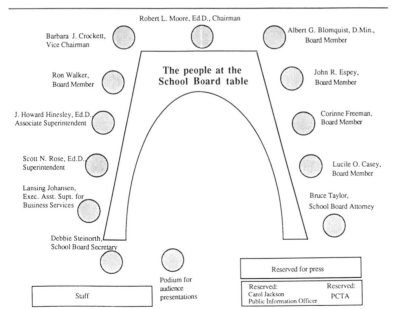

Robert L. Moore, Ed.D., Chairman

Barbara J. Crockett, Vice Chairman

Albert G. Blomquist, D.Min., Board Member

Ron Walker, Board Member

The people at the School Board table

John R. Espey, Board Member

J. Howard Hinesley, Ed.D., Associate Superintendent

Corinne Freeman, Board Member

Scott N. Rose, Ed.D., Superintendent

Lucile O. Casey, Board Member

Lansing Johansen, Exec. Asst. Supt. for Business Services

Bruce Taylor, School Board Attorney

Debbie Steinorth, School Board Secretary

Podium for audience presentations

Reserved for press

Reserved: Carol Jackson Public Information Officer

Reserved: PCTA

Staff

Figure 10.19

219

what the community is like, and what is expected of them. Very often they are not familiar with the district or the building they are going to be working in. Plan an orientation for newcomers in order to make them feel at home, and to allay any concerns they may have. Explain the essential routine procedures to them, and give them the support they need to feel secure.

Do not assume that new board members know the district. Plan an orientation for them as well. Theirs, of necessity, should be different in that you will be stressing board practices and procedures as well as how the district operates. The new board members should know who the key administrators are and their areas of responsibility.

Halftime

Once the new employee is working, do not forget that the person is still new to the district. Consider inviting new employees to an informal coffee at the end of the semester in order to have an opportunity to see how things are going, and to let them know that you have not forgotten them. Invite them to share Halftime with you.

Billboards

Solicit the local owners of the billboards and ask them to put up a billboard supporting the schools at no cost to the district. A billboard makes a tremendous impact on the community, and when placed in a strategic location it reaches many of the constituents (Figure 10.20).

Town Meetings, We're Listening, and Time to Talk

Recognize that it is important to solicit input from the community. The community members must have an opportunity to make their concerns known, and therefore they should be able to attend at times that meet their personal work schedules.

- *Town meetings* are valuable in that they are informal and give people an opportunity to speak to a particular subject, if one has been designated. There is generally a feeling of community at town meetings, and people tend to look to them with anticipation as being meaningful. When one is held, do not be overbearing – listen, and be responsive to what is said. Many good ideas surface at such meetings.

Figure 10.20

- *We're listening:* One superintendent of schools held meetings in the community on different days, at different times, and at different locations prior to preparing the preliminary budget. The superintendent had an opportunity to receive input from the community. Meetings were also scheduled at times that were convenient for the staff.
- *Time to talk:* These meetings, scheduled in the same manner as the "we're listening" meetings, were held after the board approved the budget and prior to recommending cuts to the board. Again, people were pleased that they had an opportunity to comment before actions were taken.

Dedications

Boards are usually afforded very positive press when dedications are held. Take advantage and dedicate a building; an area, such as a playground; or a center/wing of a building. Inviting the public and public officials affords the district yet another opportunity to get together in a very positive way. The cost of a dedication need not be prohibitive (Figure 10.21).

Student Artwork

Place student artwork on display in such areas as the principal's office, the superintendent's office, the mayor's office, in banks and utilities, libraries, hospitals, and the like. Having standard size frames makes it easy to change the exhibits. Students do some fabulous work. Put it on display along with the student's name, school, and art teacher's name.

Recognition Ceremonies

Consider holding recognition ceremonies at various times of the year where awards are given for such things as outstanding length of service to the school district and exemplary volunteer work in the district. Select different awards for various lengths of time, then invite the individuals, their families and friends, and the school district personnel that have been involved in their service to the district. A program listing their contributions and the presentation of a certificate will contribute to the meaning of the ceremony (Figures 10.22 and 10.23).

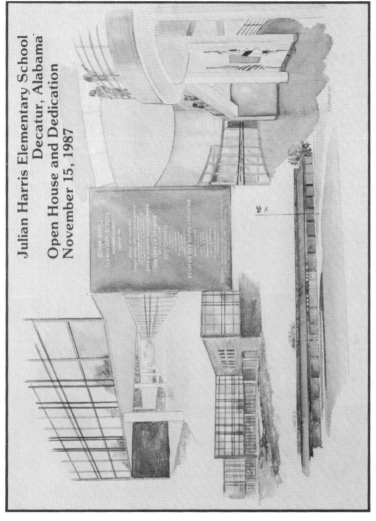

Julian Harris Elementary School
Decatur, Alabama
Open House and Dedication
November 15, 1987

Figure 10.21

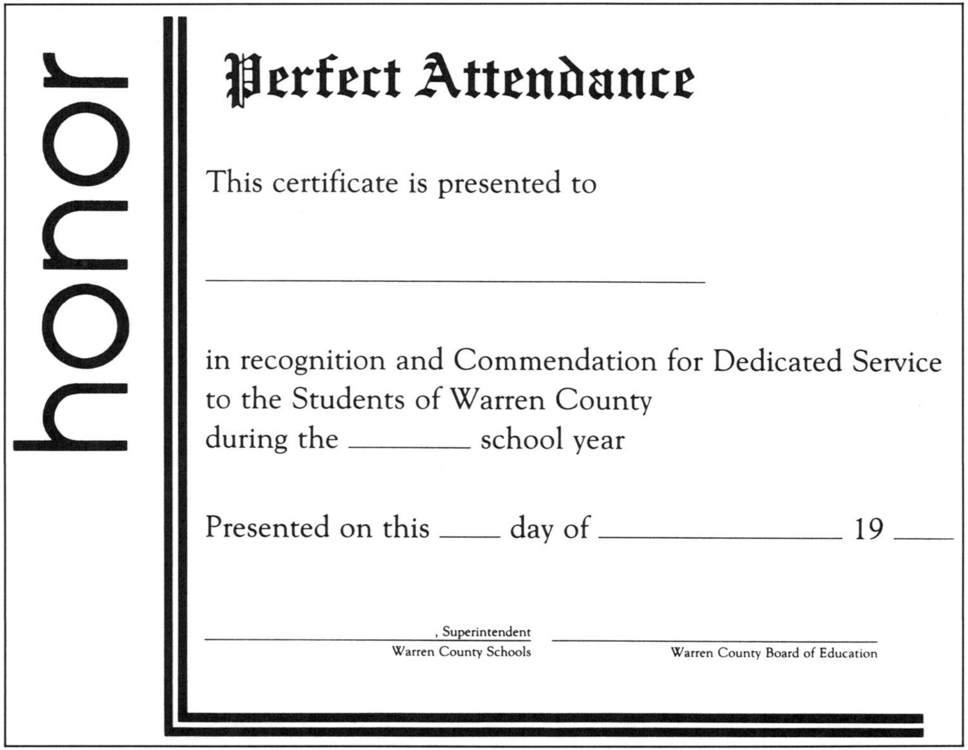

honor

Perfect Attendance

This certificate is presented to

_____

in recognition and Commendation for Dedicated Service
to the Students of Warren County
during the _____ school year

Presented on this _____ day of _____ 19 ___

_____, Superintendent
Warren County Schools

_____
Warren County Board of Education

Figure 10.22

224

Certificate of Appreciation

presented to

for your support of public education

Robert L. Moore
School Board Chairman

Scott N. Rose
Superintendent

Figure 10.23

District Budget

Make certain that a copy of the budget is available for review at each school district office building, each school building, and in the public library. Give a copy to every PTA president. Make it available to the public. You have nothing to hide, and the budget is a public document.

Policy Book

Make it possible for the staff to review the board's policy book any time it wants to. Place one copy in the principal's office and the other in the professional library, usually housed in a section of the media center at each school. District staff can then consult the policy book any time they have a question without arousing suspicion on the part of the principal.

Building-Based Channels

Telephone Calls

Ask your teachers to contact their students' parents within the first three weeks of school. The teacher is able to introduce him/herself to the parents and talk about the student while everything is going well. As a result of an early contact, such as this, a parent feels more at ease to call the teacher and ask a question when in doubt. Concerns do not build and become problems.

Report Cards

Report cards serve to let the parents know how their child is doing in school. Use of both interim and quarterly reports enables the parents to be informed on a continuing basis, usually no longer than some five weeks between reports.

The reporting process should be explained to the parents as close to the opening of school as possible; they need to know what to expect. If at all possible, identify the dates on which the reports will be sent home and the manner in which they will be sent. Decide whether you want to mail them or send them home with the students. In most cases, the younger students hand carry their report cards, while the report cards for junior and senior high school students are mailed home. It is felt that the younger students are far more reliable in getting information home to their parents.

Make certain that the parents know the marking system that you are using. A short explanatory paragraph generally serves to identify what it takes to earn a particular grade, as well as the meaning of the grade. It is helpful to be consistent within the school as to the type of report card used. It is disconcerting to have to adjust to various reporting practices. At an open house, take a few minutes to explain the reporting practice in use in the school and how it relates to the district's policy on reporting to parents. Have a copy of the reporting schedule and the meaning of grades to distribute to the parents.

Allow space on the report form for a message from the teacher and a space for the parent to comment. Teachers should be encouraged to use this space, since even a short note on the student's progress means a lot to parents.

Conferences

Invite the parents in to conference with their child's teacher(s) in order for them to know firsthand how their child is doing. Ask your teachers to schedule a conference early in the year so that the parents and teacher can get to know each other. Conferences held early in the year lead to good working relationships between parents and the teacher.

Glad Notes

Provide a supply of glad notes to your staff so that they may have them handy to send a note to a staff member or a student when a short, nice note is appropriate.

Back-to-School Night

Plan a program that is meaningful to the parents. Work with your staff and PTA in order to make certain that the parents are informed of their child's program, have an opportunity to meet the teachers, feel that they are welcome, and have a fairly good idea as to the attitude of the school towards children and what the school is all about.

Parent Teacher Association/Organization

Work with the Parent Teacher Association in your building. If none exists, take a leadership role and work with your key parents to form one. The PTA can be very helpful in supporting the efforts of the school. The executive board can also serve in an advisory capacity.

Room Mothers/Fathers

Ask the PTA to identify room mothers/fathers who can be called by the classroom teacher to assist in any number of instances. Parents volunteer to help and give valuable support to the teachers.

Chaperones

Recognize that chaperones on field trips and school events are usually very supportive of the school. Make certain that the students going on a field trip, or participating in a special event, know the rules of conduct that are expected. Set the number of chaperones needed based on the type of field trip or event, the age of the children, and whether there are any special circumstances involved in the trip. Brief the parents as to their responsibilities, and make certain that the emergency care cards are sent along with either the teacher or one of the parents.

Assemblies and School Programs

Invite parents, senior citizens, and members of the community to attend programs put on by the students, such as musicals, plays, dramas, concerts, spelling bees, and science fairs as appropriate (Figure 10.24). Assemblies are held for many different reasons. Invite parents to attend award ceremonies and special events, and to hear invited speakers. Take advantage of space at dress rehearsals for plays and invite senior citizens at no cost to them.

Athletic Competition

Invite parents to attend the interscholastic competition at your school. If you charge a modest admission fee, it can be used to support the program. Invite parents, senior citizens, and the community at large to attend field events in addition to the at-home games.

Scholar
Awards Dinner

Pine Bush High School
June 6, 1990 6:30 P.M.

Reproduced from *Scholar Awards Dinner*, Pine Bush High School, Pine Bush, New York.

Figure 10.24

Gold Cards

Issue ''gold cards'' to senior citizens which entitle them to attend at-home games, athletic events, and certain other events without charge. The senior citizens will be most supportive of the school and feel that they are remembered at a time other than when their vote for a school budget is required.

Thank You Coffees

Consider inviting the crossing guards and bus drivers in for coffee once the winter is over. They generally live in the community and may well be political appointees (crossing guards). Invite the mayor and local legislators as well. All invitees will be very pleased that you cared enough to host this modest thank you.

Letters and Personal Notes

Promptly send personal notes recognizing accomplishments and congratulating staff and students as warranted, as well as letters of condolence and thank you notes. The length is not important, and the thought is appreciated.

Coffees

Hold informal coffees at scheduled times so that parents can drop in for an informal chat with you. Maintain an open door, have no set agenda.

Special Meetings

Hold special meetings in the evening that are of interest to parents. Topics can include parenting, guidance services, college applications, financial aid, and various curriculum areas. Parents will come out if they feel that they will learn something of value.

Calendar of Events

Publish a calendar of events so that the parents can know what is taking place in your school. You may wish to send it home with the monthly menu, using the back of it, or you may include it in a newsletter that you send home on a regular basis.

Bulletin Boards

Bulletin boards in the building and in the classrooms should reflect the educational program. Make certain that they are changed in a timely manner and that they will send the message that you wish to parents and visitors to the building.

Home Visits

You and/or your staff members need to consider the advisability of making home visits to talk with parents about their child and/or to meet with small groups of parents in an informal setting for the purpose of informal conversations.

Volunteers

Work with staff and identify where they would like to enlist the assistance of volunteers. Community members can serve as tutors and translators, and can assist in the library, office area, and the classrooms.

Speakers Resource Guide

Survey your parents and community in order to find people who have special talents and are willing to share them with your students. Catalog the particular talents and distribute the names and addresses of the volunteers.

Advisory Councils

Work with, and make use of, advisory committees. Make them feel that you value their input and that they do make a difference.

Parent Advisory Council

Select your parent advisory council from either the PTA or your school at large. Make certain that the various elements represented in the student body are reflected by the parents who serve on the council.

Principal's Advisory Council

Ask the staff to select/elect their representatives to this council. The members should be spokespersons for the staff and be able to bring problems and suggestions to the group. This group could also respond to ideas that you are considering.

Student Advisory Council/Student Government

Work with a group of students to receive their input and to identify and respond to their concerns. Decide the grade level (in an elementary school) that you would like to have representation from. Meet on a continuing basis and respond to the concerns of these students.

Public Address System

Use the PA system in a judicious manner. Do not keep interrupting the classes to make announcements during the course of the day. If there are morning announcements, consider asking the older students in the building to make them each day. Their peers will often listen to them more carefully than to an administrator.

Lunch with the Principal

Invite ten or twelve students to have lunch with you once a week throughout the school year. Have an open agenda and listen to them. Respond to their concerns, and get to know them on a more personal basis.

Deal with Reality

Since schools are such highly visible public institutions, they are easy targets for politicians and pundits seeking a cause for the decline of American society. It is time that we as educators fight back against this storm of criticism with an aggressive public relations program. The many successes of our educational system have to be recognized and praised. We can not go on allowing ourselves to be viewed as losers by a society that does not know what is going on in our schools. Until we start telling our story, and telling it the way it should be told, we will continue to be the scapegoats for all the ills that surround us.

Be aggressive! Pick and choose those public relations vehicles that you feel most comfortable with and use them. Tell your story so that everyone in your district can appreciate the tremendous job that your schools are doing. Open the doors to your schools, and reach out for the respect that you have earned. Remember that if people do not know what is going on, it is difficult for them to support you.

Tell your story. Tell it loud and clear. Tell it over and over again. The benefits sown by a good public relations program will soon be reaped by your district—in terms of funding, jobs, and the good will of your community.

CHAPTER 11

SHOWCASING: FAIRFAX COUNTY PUBLIC SCHOOLS

F A I R F A X County Public Schools (FCPS)* is the tenth largest school district in the country, covering 399 square miles, with a student population of over 130,000 housed in 186 schools and centers. That number includes several schools at Fort Belvoir and in the city of Fairfax, Virginia. It is an affluent suburban school district located in the greater Washington, D.C., area. The county population of 764,800 has a median family income (projected for 1989) of $69,600, median age of 33.5 (1988) years with 6.3 percent (1988) of the community 65 years of age and over; the median school years completed (1988), 16.2; and a 13.9 percent non-white population. The school district has a 24.7 percent minority population.

The composition of the community is largely influenced by the political scene in Washington, D.C.; many federally elected and appointed officials and foreign dignitaries live in Fairfax County, as well as many employees of federal agencies. Students in the system represent all of the fifty states and 150 foreign countries. Many industries that do business with the federal government have offices located in Fairfax County.

The school district is overseen by a ten-member school board appointed by the County Board of Supervisors for staggered, two-year terms with one member representing each of the county's eight magisterial (election) districts and two at-large members. In addition, there is a non-voting student representative to the board who sits with the board at all meetings and participates in discussions. The chief

*Robert R. Spillane, Ph.D., Division Superintendent.

executive officer of the school district is an appointed division superintendent.

The school board has no taxing power; it submits its budget to the County Board of Supervisors for funding. Bond referenda are initiated by the County Board of Supervisors based on considerations determined in the Capitol Improvement Program (CIP), a five-year plan for school facilities. The FY 1990 approved budget is $1,083,260,146, with average cost per pupil of the general education program anticipated at $5,419 and the average cost per pupil of the special education program anticipated at $6,192.

In the school year 1989−90 the district employed 8,602 classroom teachers, and ran 1,001 school busses transporting 95,000 students a day, with 73.1 percent of the students bussed each day. Its academic program is broad and all-encompassing, recognizing that its students come from many different cultural backgrounds. Its English as a second language program assists foreign students, new to Fairfax County Public Schools (FCPS), who collectively speak a total of seventy-five foreign languages. Program offerings include: programs of study for grades K−6 (elementary), grades 7−8 (intermediate), grades 9−12 (high school), vocational model occupational programs, vocational foundation projects, special education programs, gifted and talented programs, Chapter 1 programs, family and early childhood education programs, English as a second language programs, alternative education, alternatives for high school completion, and adult and community education.

FCPS also has the Thomas Jefferson High School for Science and Technology, a unique school offering a comprehensive college preparatory program emphasizing science, mathematics, and technology. As the Governor's School for Science and Technology in northern Virginia, the school serves qualified applicants from Fairfax County and other participating school districts in northern Virginia.

The student mobility rate available from the school district measures the change in student membership between the first and the last day of the school year and is expressed as the percent of students who enter or leave a school. The elementary schools experienced 22 percent mobility in 1987−88; the intermediate schools, 15 percent; and the high schools, 16 percent. Student mobility in some schools was as high as 47 percent at the elementary level, 26 percent at the intermediate level, and 27 percent at the high school level. The high school dropout rate (grades 9−12) was 2.62 percent in 1987−88. Ninety percent of the graduating class of 1988 went on to post-secondary education, 160 seniors were selected as semifinalists in the 1989–90 National Merit Scholarship Program, 22 FCPS seniors were selected as semifinalists in the 25th annual National Achievement Program for Outstanding Negro Students, and an estimated $31 million in scholarships and grants were awarded to 1988 high school graduates (Office of Community Relations files, 1989).

The district has a strong commitment to keeping the public informed about its goals and objectives, students, employees, programs, needs, and successes. The school board established its ". . . commitment to the development and maintenance of positive relationships between the school division and the County community at large, and between local schools and their respective communities" in its Board Policy 1501. The policy statement, adopted by the board on July 1, 1986, states the following.

In fulfilling this commitment, the School Board shall:

A. Conduct its business in public sessions, except for matters discussed in executive session in accord with the Virginia Freedom of Information Act.

B. Inform the community about policies, plans, and programs of the school system, and achievements of its students and employees.

C. Invite and encourage the advice and counsel of County citizens.

D. Recognize the responsibility and right of the news media to seek, analyze, and report to the public, information about the school system; and assist the media in so doing.

This board policy is made operational by Regulation 1501, Staff Development, Planning, and Evaluation, July 1, 1986, which identifies its purpose as: "To establish guidelines for the release of information to citizens." The regulation deals with such topics as:

• distribution of board meeting agendas
• distribution of board meeting agenda materials
• public access to minutes
• public access to other official records
• fees for document copies

The board and Superintendent Spillane recognize the need to "inform the community about policies, plans, and programs of the school system, and achievements of its students and employees" (Board Policy 1501). In order to facilitate the two-way communication process, the school district established the Office of Community Relations, located in the main administration building. It is headed by Assistant Superintendent Dolores Bohen and has nine full-time employees.

"The Office of Community Relations performs one of the school system's most important functions by taking its message to the people and then serving as a conduit to relay the public's concerns back to the school system as to what citizens want to see happen in *their* schools," says Dolores Bohen, assistant superintendent for communications. "Our citizens are very involved in their schools," she continues, "and we realize that a dynamic, responsive, two-way communications process is crucial to promoting and maintaining a successful school-community partnership. This is a real challenge in Fairfax County because only one-third of our voters have school-age children. That leaves a large audience that we must reach through non-school channels" (Bohen, 1989).

In addition to countless personal appearances by the superintendent, board members, and members of the staff, the school district makes extensive use of a "family of publications" and cable television Channel 21, which is devoted exclusively to school-related public affairs programming.

The publications, issued through the Office of Community Relations, are varied and intended to carry out the board's policy and inform the public. Some of these are as follows.

- *Logo* — The school district has a distinctive logo (Figure 11.1), which appears on all of the publications of the district. Distinctive two-color mastheads have been adopted for the various publications, making it easier for the press or reader to identify the nature and source of each communication.
- *FYI — For Your Information* — News releases are issued regularly to encourage media coverage of FCPS activities. They cover a

Reproduced from *The Fairfax County School Board Meeting Summary,* Fairfax, Virginia.
Figure 11.1

wide variety of topics, such as the selection of the school board's chairman and vice-chairman, the accomplishments of students and staff members, and the release of county-wide standardized test scores. The releases are distributed to a media mailing list that includes selected community organizations and individuals (Figure 11.2).

- *Press conferences* – As deemed advisable, press conferences are held by the division superintendent. As appropriate, the press conference may be carried on public television Channel 21. Depending on the issue, the chairman of the school board or a program director may join the superintendent in a press conference. Press packets are prepared and distributed by the Office of Community Relations.
- *Media Tips* – This publication is issued on a weekly basis to all media to prompt coverage of feature ideas that are submitted to the Office of Community Relations by individual news liaisons in each school. It provides brief accounts of potential feature stories to help the media find the good local school stories that might be missed in such a large school system (Figure 11.3).
- *Supergram* – A newsletter called *Supergram* is distributed weekly to all employees. This contains job announcements and other information such as staff appointments, transfers, retirements, regulations that were issued, changes in procedures, coming events (speakers), etc. (Figure 11.4).
- *Agenda* – One week prior to each of the school board's business meetings, the *Meeting Agenda* is distributed to staff, county agencies, schools, the media, and members of a mailing list that includes community organizations and leaders. The agenda identifies that the board meeting has a time for citizen participation early in the meeting. Citizens wishing to address the board are asked to arrange to be placed on the speakers' list prior to the meeting (Figure 11.5).
- *Meeting summary* – The day after each business meeting of the board, a summary of the highlights of the meeting is published and sent to the same individuals who receive the *Agenda* (Figure 11.6).
- *"Speaking of teaching . . . ."* – This is a monthly publication from the division superintendent that is distributed to teachers and school staffs in order to inform them about board decisions, research, and other issues affecting education (Figure 11.7).

 **For Your Information**

ROBERT R. SPILLANE, Superintendent
DOLORES BOHEN, Assistant Superintendent
Office of Community Relations

FAIRFAX COUNTY PUBLIC SCHOOLS
10700 Page Avenue Fairfax, Virginia
Phone 246-2991

FOR IMMEDIATE RELEASE
REVISED

May 3, 1991

FAIRFAX COUNTY PUBLIC SCHOOLS
MAY CALENDAR

Following is the calendar for the Fairfax County Public Schools for the month of May. For information about any event listed, call (703) 246-2991.

May

6	. Annandale pyramid meeting, 7:30 p.m., Annandale High School
7	. School Board work session (Personnel Committee), 7:30 p.m., Burkholder Center
8	. Stuart pyramid meeting, 7:30 p.m., Stuart High School
9	. School Board business meeting, 8 p.m., Jackson Intermediate School
13	. Falls Church/Oakton pyramid meeting, 7:30 p.m., Falls Church High School
14	. School Board public hearing (budget), 7 p.m., Jackson Intermediate School
	. Minority Students' Achievement Advisory Committee meeting, 8 p.m., Burkholder Center
15	. School Board work session (Instruction Committee), 7:30 p.m., Burkholder Center
16	. School Board public hearing (budget), 7 p.m., Jackson Intermediate School
17-19	. School Board annual conference, Dulles Ramada Renaissance
21	. School Board work session (budget), 7:30 p.m., Jackson Intermediate School
22	. Human Relations Advisory Committee meeting, 8 p.m., Personnel Services Center
23	. School Board business meeting, 8 p.m., Jackson Intermediate School
27	. Memorial Day holiday, all personnel
29	. FCPS Annual Retirement Banquet, 6 p.m., Robinson Secondary School

# # #

Figure 11.2

FAIRFAX COUNTY PUBLIC SCHOOLS   10700 Page Avenue · Fairfax, Virginia 22030

ROBERT R. SPILLANE, Superintendent   PHONE: 246-2991
DOLORES BOHEN, Assistant Superintendent
Office of Community Relations

May 19, 1989

- **Clifton Elementary** will bustle with activity on Friday, May 26, as students don colonial dress and participate in crafts such as tin punching, making pomander balls, sewing–cross stitch items, stenciling, practicing calligraphy, whittling, and fashioning handkerchief dolls. Following a colonial feast, the children will enjoy Early American dancing, followed by an old-fashioned ice cream social. Contact principal Patricia Heiselberg or news liaison Karyl Garn, 830-2088.

- Kindergartners at **Clifton Elementary,** who will be members of the class of 2001, have researched and written a science fiction play, "2001: The Adventure Begins," which they will present on Thursday, May 25, at 7:30 p.m. The drama opens in Clifton where the children are visited by a spaceship from the planet Pluto. They answer the aliens' questions about the area concerning its history, culture, and geography. Then they join the aliens and travel through the universe in the spaceship. During the voyage, everyone learns fascinating facts about the earth and the universe. The production will feature costumes, scenery, and special effects. Contact principal Patricia Heiselberg or news liaison Karyl Garn, 830-2088.

- Cuddly critters will visit **Garfield Elementary** on Friday, May 26, from 9 a.m. to 3:30 p.m. The stuffed animals will come to school with their masters and mistresses. During the day, the critters will star in learning activities such as original poetry, stories, plays, and speeches. At 2 p.m., the critters and the children, led by the principal, will parade around the school grounds. Contact principal Otha Davis or news liaison Pamela Burgess, 451-2915.

- **Layton Hall Elementary** will hold an International Olympics on Thursday, May 25, at 9:30 a.m. In addition to familiar Olympic events, students will compete in games from foreign lands such as a Korean tug of war, African hoop racing, Philippine "soccer," Chinese rope kicking, and Indonesian pillow combat. Contact principal Mary Agnes Garman or news liaison Sherri D'Amato 273-1230.

(more)

Reproduced from *Media Tips*, Fairfax County Schools, Fairfax, Virginia.

Figure 11.3

241

FAIRFAX
COUNTY
PUBLIC
SCHOOLS

Robert R. Spillane
Superintendent

January 23, 1991   No. 1,055

Calendar

January

24 School Board regular meeting, 8 p.m., Jackson Intermediate

28 School Board public hearing (budget), 8 p.m., Jackson Intermediate

29 School Board public hearing (budget), 8 p.m., Jackson Intermediate

30 Custodial Services Advisory Council, 2 p.m., Woodson House

School Board work session (budget), 7:30 p.m., Jackson Intermediate

31 Support Services Employees' Advisory Council, 8:30 a.m., Personnel Services Center

Due Process Section Renamed

The Due Process Section in the Dept. of Student Services and Special Education has been renamed Monitoring and Compliance.

Look for . . .

• Middle School Conference

• Chapter 1 Electronic Newsletter

. . . on Channel 39.

See page 5 for details.

Transportation Services Phone Numbers Change

The Office of Transportation Services and the Special Education Transportation telephone numbers at Lorton Center have changed. The new number for the Office of Transportation Services is 446-2000, and the new number for Special Education Transportation is 446-2050.

Middle School Conference Scheduled

The Jan. 29 Middle School Conference will be broadcast live from 8:30 to 10:30 a.m. from Fairfax High. Twelve hundred elementary and intermediate school staff members will be in the audience at Fairfax; all other elementary and intermediate school staff members will meet at selected school sites to view the broadcast. Area superintendents and principals will determine who will attend the conference at Fairfax High, and carpooling is encouraged for those staff members.

Virginia Recertification Point System Clarified

The Virginia Dept. of Education has made an announcement regarding the Recertification Point System. Specifically, that "school of education courses in health and physical education, vocational education, or library science may also be used to satisfy the content requirement for those certificate holders with endorsements in those areas." However, holders of these endorsements cannot fulfill the content requirement for bachelor's degree holders with courses taken from schools or departments of education unless such courses include content in health and physical education, vocational education, or library science. For example, "Education 500, Learning Styles: Left/Right Brain," would not meet the content requirement for bachelor's degree holders endorsed in health and physical education, vocational education, or library science.

Based on this clarification, we will recommend, to the State Board, approval of education coursework for these endorsement holders through the spring of 1991. As of July 1, 1991, these bachelor's degree holders must apply for a waiver in keeping with the guidelines provided in the *Guide for Implementing the Virginia Recertification Point System*, page 7.

Hodgson Nominations Being Accepted

Letters from high school principals nominating students for Al and Winnie Hodgson Awards are being received until April 1. Al Hodgson was a School Board member from 1972 to 1976, and Winnie Hodgson taught and volunteered in Dranesville District schools for many years. The annual awards, each a U.S. saving bond with a $100 face value, are given to students for excellence demonstrated in one of these categories: English composition; mathematics or science (physics, chemistry, or biology); art, drama, or forensics; vocational education; or community relations. A Hodgson award will also be given to an outstanding teacher in each of these categories. The selection of teachers who will receive the awards will be handled in conjunction with the Washington Post Agnes Meyer Outstanding Teacher of the Year and the Fairfax Teacher of the Year award processes. See Reg. 3832.1 for details.

Reproduced from *Supergram*, Fairfax County Public Schools, Fairfax, Virginia, January 23, 1991.

Figure 11.4

 **Fairfax County School Board**

TYPE OF MEETING:
Regular - No. 19

DATE:
May 9, 1991

LOCATION:
Jackson Intermediate School
3020 Gallows Road
Falls Church, Virginia

I. **EXECUTIVE SESSION** (when required for matters permitted by law)   7:00

II. **MEETING OPENINGS**
   A. Call to Order/Pledge of Allegiance   8:00
   B. Certification of executive session compliance
   C. Confirmation of action taken in executive session
   D. Announcement of changes in the agenda
   E. Other announcements
   F. Resolution honoring principals

III. **PRESENTATIONS TO SCHOOL BOARD**
   Citizen participation
   (Citizens who wish to address the School Board should arrange to be
   placed on the speakers' list by calling 246-3646)

IV. **ACTION ITEMS**
   A. **Adoption of Consent Agenda** (without discussion)
      1. **Minutes** - Approve minutes of April 25, 1991, regular Board
         meeting (SB)
      2. **Language, Composition, and Literature Textbooks** - Adopt language,
         composition, and literature textbooks (IS; presented as information
         4/11/91)
      3. **Naming the Elementary School Facility at the Pender/Franklin Site** -
         Name the new school facility located at the Pender/Franklin Site
         "Waples Mill Elementary School" (Area III; presented as information
         4/25/91)
      4. **Award of Contract for Reroofing at Clifton Elementary School** - Award
         the contract for reroofing at Clifton Elementary School to J. E. Wood
         & Sons, Inc., in the amount of $65,728 (FcS; presented as information
         4/25/91)
      5. **Award of Contract for Reroofing at Floris Elementary School** - Award
         the contract for reroofing at Floris Elementary School to R. D. Bean,
         Inc., in the amount of $108,387 (FcS; presented as information
         4/25/91)

C----Communications	IS--Instructional Services	S----Superintendent
FcS--Facilities Services	MIS--Management Information Services	SSSE--Student Services & Special Education
FnS--Financial Services	PS--Personnel Services	VACE--Vocational, Adult, and Community Education
GS--General Services	SB--School Board	

Reproduced from *Meeting Agenda,* Fairfax County School Board, Fairfax, Virginia, May 9, 1991.

Figure 11.5

meeting summary

FAIRFAX
COUNTY
PUBLIC
SCHOOLS

ROBERT R. SPILLANE, Superintendent
DOLORES BOHEN, Assistant Superintendent
Office of Community Relations

10700 PAGE AVENUE
FAIRFAX, VIRGINIA

TYPE OF MEETING: Regular – No. 19
DATE: May 9, 1991
LOCATION: Jackson Intermediate School

RESOLUTION

The Fairfax County School Board adopted a resolution recognizing May 5 through May 11 as Principals' Week and honoring principals for their vital and valued efforts.

PRESENTATIONS AND COMMUNITY PARTICIPATION

The Board received presentations from Arthur Purves (family life education); Rayna Larson, Maureen Daniels—Fairfax Education Association president, Dan Warner, Robert Salisbury, Mark Glofka—Fairfax County Federation of Teachers vice president, Anthony DeBenedittis, and Joe Burnette (VRS early retirement program); Leigh Coen (naming elementary school at Pender/Franklin site); and Gloria Hwang (Asian- and Pacific-American Heritage Month).

THE BOARD APPROVED:

...Certification that the immediately preceding executive session was conducted in conformity with the requirements of the Virginia Freedom of Information Act.

...Naming the new school facility located at the Pender/Franklin site "Waples Mill Elementary School."

...Awarding the contract for reroofing at Clifton Elementary School to J. E. Wood & Sons, Inc., in the amount of $65,728.

...Awarding the contract for reroofing at Floris Elementary School to R. D. Bean, Inc., in the amount of $108,387.

...Awarding the contract for reroofing at Gunston Elementary School to Virginia Roofing Corporation in the amount of $96,960.

...Awarding the contract for reroofing at Cedar Lane Center to J. E. Wood & Sons Company, Inc., in the amount of $82,156.

...Awarding the contract(s) for replacement of boilers at Gunston Elementary and Marshall High Schools to Capitol Contractors, Inc., in the amount of $391,000.

...Awarding the contract for chiller replacement at Lake Braddock Secondary School to Tonco Mechanical Contractors, Inc., in the amount of $285,800.

...Authorizing the School Board Chairman to execute a lease agreement with the Fairfax County Water Authority involving the Poe Intermediate School site.

...Authorizing the School Board Chairman to execute with the Chesapeake and Potomac Telephone Company of Virginia an underground conduit easement involving the Forestdale Elementary School site.

...Not participating in the early retirement program under the Virginia Retirement System because of the associated long-term financial obligation.

Note: This is an information summary only, issued by the
Office of Community Relations. For further information, call 246-2991.

Reproduced from *The Fairfax County School Board Meeting Summary*,
Fairfax, Virginia, May 9, 1991.

Figure 11.6

"Speaking of Teaching..."

From Robert R. Spillane, Superintendent ■ *FAIRFAX COUNTY PUBLIC SCHOOLS*

June 1989

Dear Teachers:

As always, May and June are hectic months filled with the ambiguities of panic and relief—panic about all the things that have to get done before the last day of school and relief that the last day is finally in sight. I know that the relief always wins out over the temporary panic, so I hope that by now you are all filled with a wonderful sense of satisfaction about your accomplishments this year.

I hope that, from the perspective of your own professional development, the same can be said—that any temporary panic has been outweighed by relief and a personal sense of satisfaction about your accomplishments. Whatever might have been your individual involvement in the Teacher Performance Evaluation Program this year, the program is now fully implemented systemwide, and we are a giant step closer to our goal of making teaching the respected profession it deserves to be. Competitive salaries and an optional career ladder are realities, but they are only the beginning. Professional growth opportunities are greater than ever before, but so are the challenges.

Back in 1985, I defined the goal of professionalizing teaching as "making teachers responsible to each other and to the highest standards of the teaching profession for the quality of their teaching." I believe that, in the last three years, we have come a long way toward accomplishing this goal, but I also recognize that more needs to be done. We need to improve teachers' working conditions and increase professional opportunities, and we need to work hard to maintain and improve the quality of performance evaluation. I would be interested to hear from you about any such ideas for next year.

In August, we will resume publication of "Speaking of teaching..." and begin another school year with the characteristic optimism of most educators. Thank you for making this another successful year.

Sincerely,

Robert R. Spillane

Robert R. Spillane
Division Superintendent

WHAT IS CARB?

Once the basic structure of teacher performance evaluation was in place, I developed the Career Advancement Review Board (CARB) to help ensure the fairness of the Career Level II selection process by reviewing some cases in which teachers have applied for, but not achieved, Career Level II status. CARB consists of seven members, four of whom are teachers elected by their peers for staggered three-year terms. I appoint the other three CARB members to one-year terms. CARB examines the process by which a teacher was denied Career Level II status and makes recommendations to me as to whether the process followed published standards and procedures and was fair to the teacher. It is my responsibility to make the final decision on CARB appeals.

CARB has heard 73 appeals so far from teachers who are unsatisfied with their principals' evaluations and has made recommendations to me on these appeals. I have overturned a total of eight CARB recommendations. For the first two years of a new process, this record is very good. A summary of the CARB recommendations and actions is as follows:

CARB RECOMMENDATIONS		SUPERINTENDENT'S ACTIONS	
Grant CL II:	29	Upheld:	18
		Overturned:	8
		Pending:	3
Deny CL II:	42	Upheld:	42
		Overturned:	0
		Pending:	0
No Decision:	2	Denied CL II:	2
		Pending:	0
TOTAL:	73	TOTAL:	73

Office of Community Relations • 10700 Page Avenue, Fairfax, VA 22030 • 246-3660

Reproduced from *"Speaking of teaching . . .",* Fairfax County Public Schools, Fairfax, Virginia, June 1989.

Figure 11.7

245

The division superintendent usually has a message to teachers, often soliciting feedback or comment.

- *Partners in Education* — This quarterly publication is distributed to a mailing list in order to inform the business and professional community of the partnership activities of the school district. Businesses respond favorably to being featured in this publication — good PR for both the school district and the business community (Figure 11.8).
- *Familygram* — Five issues of this newsletter are published each year, with additional issues published to cover special topics. It is distributed to parents through the schools and to the community through mailing lists. Its primary purpose is to provide parents with information about school schedules, programs, and regulations (Figure 11.9).
- *The Apple* — This professional magazine is written by, for, and about teachers in the FCPS. It is distributed four times a year to teachers and school staffs to share innovative ideas and to recognize excellent teachers and programs. Conferences and exciting school occurrences, such as a presidential visit, are also written up. It is unusual for a school district to care enough to publish a magazine for and about teachers (Figure 11.10).
- *Bulletin* — In yet another attempt to keep the community informed, the school district issues the *Bulletin* twice a year (Figure 11.11). Its purpose is to inform the staff and the community about the district's Annual Operating Plan and the school board's priorities. One issue informs the reader of the current Annual Operating Plan, while the second issue is the annual report on the accomplishments of the past year in achieving the goals.
- *Fact Book* — The *Fact Book*, currently in its sixth edition, provides a quick reference guide to the demographics of the county and the school district (Figure 11.12). In addition to general information about the school district, such as telephone numbers, the names of the school board members, school calendar, etc., it contains information on the instructional programs; student information on membership, the past graduating class, admission requirements, the testing program, reporting to parents, pupil promotion and retention, graduation requirements; personnel information; facilities information; and financial data on the school district's budget, tuition rates for nonresident students,

FAIRFAX COUNTY PUBLIC SCHOOLS

PARTNERS in Education

SUMMER 1990 ■ A Newsletter for the Business and Professional Communities

Forging the Future of Education

By Richard Thompson
Vice President, Government Affairs
Bristol Myers Squibb
Richard Thiel
Area Manager, ROLM Company

Allen E. Murray

n April 18, almost 300 concerned Northern Virginians gathered at the McLean Hilton to look twenty years into the future. Their task was to envision the public school system in 2010 and to develop the checkpoints necessary to get there. From every indication, this day was a success.

Outlook 2010 was a one-day education forum that brought together leaders from business, education, and government. Because each of these groups has a stake in building the educational system of the twenty-first century, the goal of the conference

was to provide an opportunity to exchange views about what would be needed to meet the changing educational needs of Fairfax County and the business community. Outlook 2010 was sponsored by the Superintendent's Business/Industry Advisory Council (BIAC), a group of 35 business appointees chartered by Superintendent Robert R. Spillane. The primary

mission of the Council is to provide a channel through which the school division can express its needs to the business community, as well as to represent the interests of business and industry to the school administration.

The program was an exercise in cooperation among all of the participating groups. A high school band and color guard opened the meeting. County government and School Board officials welcomed everyone. The Division Superintendent gave his view of the student of tomorrow. The keynote speech, delivered by Allen E. Murray, chairman of the board, president, and CEO of Mobil Corporation, stressed the importance of working together to maintain educational excellence. He also described the concept of empowerment, matched with accountability, and how

Continued on page 7

The following business leaders (pictured from left) spoke and lead a discussion about the characteristics of the work force in the year 2010: Jack M. Dreyfus, TRW Systems Division; John T. Hazel, Jr., Hazel/Peterson Systems; George C. Newstrom, Electronic Data Systems; Rodney F. Page, Arent, Fox, Kintner, Plotkin, and Kahn; Maston T. Jacks, INOVA Health Systems; and Patricia M. Woolsey, Northern Virginia Natural Gas.

Reproduced from *Partners in Education,* Fairfax County Public Schools, Fairfax, Virginia, Summer 1990.

Figure 11.8

247

FAMILYGRAM

Published for citizens of Fairfax County

Robert R. Spillane, Division Superintendent — 10700 Page Avenue • Fairfax, Virginia 22030

JANUARY 1990

SUPERINTENDENT'S MESSAGE

Dear Parents:

Beginning on the front page of this *Familygram* is a description of the budget that I have proposed to the School Board for operating your school system during fiscal year 1991, beginning in July of 1990. Because of dwindling resources, this is a very tight budget; my staff and I have done everything possible to reduce or delay expenditures where possible. We have traded off budget flexibility and continuation of ongoing maintenance and replacement in order to retain program quality and increase students' opportunities at the secondary level. At all times, the welfare and academic achievement of our young people have been our highest priorities.

You may read about the budget in the accompanying article, but I would like to mention a few budget issues that I believe are most important for the community to understand. The revenue picture is critical. Federal and state revenues have declined substantially as a percentage of the school system budget over the past several years. While federal funds are a very small percentage of our funds in any case, declines in state funding have substantially restricted our budget flexibility. The actual dollar amount of total state aid to Fairfax County Public Schools (FCPS) has decreased between the 1990 and 1991 fiscal years.

What this means, of course, is that either the school system budget must decline while the school system is growing or local funds must increase to keep pace with declining federal and state revenues. In fact, the Board of Supervisors has agreed to increase their funding of the schools (the "county transfer" to the school budget) by 10 percent of the FY 1990 allocation. Combined with the decline in federal and state revenues, this means that the school budget will actually grow by 7.5 percent over this year's approved budget. Given factors such as inflation and growth in student population, this is essentially a no-growth budget with little or no flexibility to meet contingencies that may arise during the fiscal year.

The major initiative funded in this budget is the restructured school day for secondary schools, which will add a seventh period to high school and intermediate school schedules, providing students with greater opportunities and more flexibility for meeting graduation requirements. Included in this initiative are more teachers and counselors as well as more time for department chairpersons and guidance directors to ensure the quality of new instructional opportunities for students. Also included in the total cost are funds for bus drivers and bus

maintenance needed for extending the secondary school day. Less costly initiatives include eight signers/interpreters for hearing-impaired students, a bilingual specialist to assist in the Central Registration Office, two positions to support new teacher recertification requirements, and two foreign language resource teachers. Because a number of items that we consider essential could not be funded under current constraints, I have attached a list of "additional requirements" to my proposed budget.

Fairfax County public schools rank among the finest in the nation by any measure. For instance, ninety percent of the 1989 FCPS graduating class went on to postsecondary education, with the vast majority going to four-year institutions. The high quality education reflected by such statistics is maintained in a very cost-effective manner. For instance, FCPS ranks fifth in per-pupil expenditures in the metropolitan Washington, D.C., area--after Alexandria, Falls Church, Montgomery County, and Arlington. Because excellent instruction and the welfare of children are our focus, you may be sure that we will maintain the preeminence of your school system. I look forward to the support of our Fairfax County community over the next year.

Sincerely,

Robert R. Spillane

Robert R. Spillane
Division Superintendent

FY 1991 PROPOSED BUDGET

The proposed budget for Fairfax County Public Schools (FCPS) for FY 1991 (July 1, 1990, to June 30, 1991) includes seven major funds totaling just over $1.1 billion. The largest of these funds is the School Operating Fund, totaling $873.4 million, which pays for the day-to-day operation of almost 200 schools and centers. Due to the Board of Supervisors budget guidelines and projected decreases in state funding, the total school budget increase amounts to 4.6 percent for the School Operating Fund and the locally funded portion of the School Construction Fund.

Included in this budget is $15.3 million for the restructured school day at the secondary level, which was approved by the School Board in November 1989. This budget also includes funding for the fourth year of the Teacher Performance Evaluation Program, full funding to continue the increases authorized in the School Board's FY 1990 Approved Budget for support employees, and a 3 percent cost-of-living adjustment for all employees.

1

Reproduced from *Familygram*, Fairfax County Public Schools, Fairfax, Virginia, January 1990.

Figure 11.9

Figure 11.10

Reproduced from *Bulletin,* Fairfax County Public Schools, Fairfax, Virginia, November 1989.

Figure 11.11

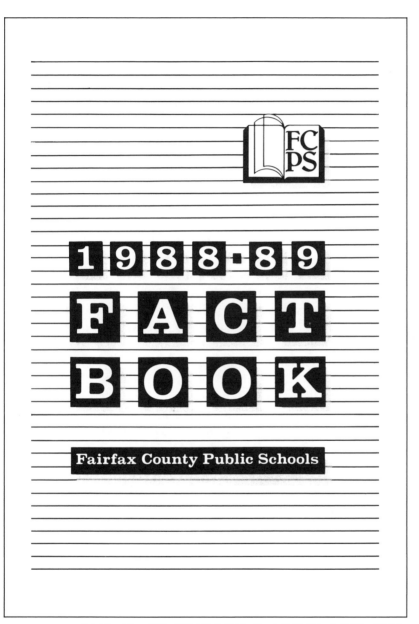

Reproduced from *1988–89 Fact Book,* Fairfax County Public Schools, Fairfax, Virginia.

Figure 11.12

school lunch prices, etc. The *Fact Book* is distributed to schools and offices for their use in responding to inquiries.

- *Handbook*—Distributed through schools, realtors, and Welcome Wagons, the *Handbook* provides basic information about the Fairfax County Public Schools. Its purpose is to inform parents new to the area. It includes such topics as: school district organization, statistics about the school district, attendance information, instruction and special programs, services provided by the school district, the FCPS school calendar, and FCPS school directory.
- *Meet Your School Board*—This publication is published annually and is available at board meetings. The Statement of Mission of the FCPS and the school board priorities are identified. The protocol used at the board's meetings is described. Pictures of the board members, the division superintendent, and the student representative are included along with a brief paragraph about each of them. Facts and figures about the school district, staff members, and student accomplishments that are bound to impress any visitor to a board meeting are included (Figure 11.13).
- *Good Schools . . . Good News*—Because there is a need to assist schools with media relations, this annual publication is distributed at orientations for school news liaisons who provide the information published in *Media Tips* (see page 239). It discusses how the media serves the schools, identifies the various media outlets, and gives staff members tips on how to sell their good news to the press (Figure 11.14).

The publications mentioned herein, as impressive as they are, pale in comparison to the tremendous effort currently expended by the Office of Community Relations and the Office of Media Services in using FCPS' public affairs cable TV Channel 21. Called *Red Apple 21,* with its own distinctive logo, it can be received by all Media General Cable and Warner Cable subscribers in the county and operates as a communication link between FCPS and the community (Figure 11.15).

FCPS produces nearly all of the programming that airs on Channel 21. Regularly scheduled shows cover topics such as:

- live, interactive teleconferences
- practical suggestions for parents on ways they can participate more fully in the education of their children
- individual school profiles

SCHOOL BOARD MEMBERS

Anthony T. Lane, Chairman
Lee District
Appointed 1/12/72; term expires 6/30/89

Mr. Lane is the intellectual property counsel for the Army. In addition to his almost seventeen years on the School Board, he has been a member and served as chairman of the Fairfax County Planning Commission, served on the Fairfax County Crime Commission, held offices in the Rose Hill Civic Association, and was the first Lee District representative to the County Federation of Citizens Associations. He also has served on boards of directors and as counsel to youth athletic clubs in the area. Mr. Lane holds both J.D. and B.E.E. degrees from The George Washington University.

Carla M. Yock, Vice Chairman
Mason District
Appointed 6/17/85; term expires 6/30/89

Before her appointment to the School Board, Mrs. Yock was a history and social studies teacher at Glasgow Intermediate School for six years and also taught in the North St. Paul, Minn., and Norfolk, Va., public school systems. She has been active as a parent, community, and teacher representative, serving on the Superintendent's Advisory Committee on Sex Bias (Title IX), local and County PTA Boards, and as an officer and member of the lobbying corps for AAUW. She is currently vice president of Phi Delta Kappa, Virginia Tech Northern Virginia Chapter. Mrs. Yock holds a B.A. degree from St. Olaf College in Minn., an M.A. in school administration from VPI&SU, and is currently enrolled in the Ed.D. program at VPI&SU.

BOARD ACTIVITIES

Citizens of the county are invited and encouraged to attend public meetings of the School to observe its deliberations.

MEETINGS

The Board holds business meetings at 8 p.m. twice monthly, usually on the second and fourth Thursdays of the month, in the Board Room at Jackson Intermediate School, 3020 Gallows Rd., Falls Church. Special meetings are scheduled as required. In accordance with the Virginia Freedom of Information Act, closed meetings are held only on certain student, personnel, property, and legal matters.

AGENDAS AND SUMMARIES

Agendas for Board meetings are prepared by the Division Superintendent in consultation with the School Board Chairman and are distributed about one week in advance of the meetings. Items are listed as "information" or "action." A summary of Board action is published the day following the meeting. For copies of an agenda or a meeting summary call 246-2991; for information about an agenda item, call 246-3646.

PRESENTING VIEWS

Citizens desiring to present their views to the School Board may submit them in writing to the Board Chairman, 10700 Page Avenue, Fairfax, VA 22030. Copies of the material will be provided to Board members for consideration.

ADDRESSING THE BOARD

Time is allowed on the agenda of each business meeting for citizen presentations. Priority is given to persons addressing topics on the meeting agenda. A person who wishes to address the Board during this part of the meeting or at a scheduled public hearing should call the School Board Office (246-3649) prior to 4:30 p.m. on the day immediately preceding the meeting day to be included on the list of speakers. Speakers are asked to provide 15 copies of their written remarks for distribution to Board members and staff. For additional information, call the School Board Office at 246-3649.

PUBLIC HEARINGS

To allow many citizens an opportunity to address a single issue, such as budget or boundaries, public hearings are scheduled by the Board at various times during the year. Presentations by representatives of countywide organizations are limited to six minutes at public hearings; all other speakers are limited to three minutes.

WORK SESSIONS

Meetings of Board committees and other work sessions are held to examine subjects in greater depth than is possible during business meetings. Several are scheduled during budget deliberations. Actions tentatively decided upon at work sessions are confirmed by the Board at regular business meetings; no action is taken by the Board at work sessions.

Reproduced from *Meet Your School Board*, Fairfax County Public Schools, Fairfax, Virginia, 1988 – 89.

Figure 11.13

good**Schools**...

good**News** 1988-1989

The Office of Community Relations
Fairfax County Public Schools
10700 Page Avenue
Fairfax, Virginia 22030
246-2991

Figure 11.14

CHANNEL 21:

NEWS AND VIEWS FROM FAIRFAX COUNTY PUBLIC SCHOOLS

Red Apple 21, the Fairfax County Public Schools' (FCPS) public affairs cable TV channel, is a relatively new and growing part of the school system's community outreach program. All Media General Cable subscribers in the county can receive Channel 21, which operates as a communication link between FCPS and the public.

CHANNEL 21 SERVICES

Videotaped Programs

FCPS produces nearly all of the programming which airs on Channel 21. Regularly scheduled shows cover topics such as:

- Practical suggestions for parents on ways they can more fully participate in the education of their children
- Individual school profiles
- Musical and dramatic performances
- Special school events
- Extracurricular activities such as clubs, service projects, and sports
- Teen ideas and interests, in a show planned by and starring high school students
- Student-produced videotapes

Channel 21 also produces a weekly TV news magazine featuring regular appearances by the Superintendent, School Board members, teachers, administrators, business and community leaders, and volunteers. Each show visits a classroom where an unusual or exemplary activity is taking place. In the reading-incentive segment of the program, students at all grade levels find creative ways to review their favorite books.

School Board Meetings

All School Board regular business meetings, public hearings, budget work sessions, and special meetings are aired live, in their entirety, on Channel 21.

Red Apple 21 Bulletin Board

This continuous electronic message service provides viewers with timely information and announcements, program listings, school lunch menus, and emergency messages about early school closings, late openings, and other schedule changes.

HOW TO USE CHANNEL 21

Publicize Events on the Red Apple 21 Bulletin Board

Events announced on the Bulletin Board are school-sponsored and open to the general public. To receive a form for submitting announcement information to the Bulletin Board, contact the Office of Community Relations at 246-3661.

Share Ideas for Videotaped Programs

We encourage school staff to let us know about upcoming activities which could be taped and featured on Channel 21. Our programming is selected in part to reflect as wide a diversity as possible in grade levels, subject matter, schools, and geographic areas. Originality and copyright considerations are also important. Program ideas are always welcome and will be considered carefully within the above guidelines and the resources available to Channel 21. Advance notice is encouraged. To suggest a program topic, call or write the cable programmer in the Office of Community Relations, Burkholder Center.

Channel 21 services are provided jointly by the Office of Community Relations and the Office of Media Services.

Figure 11.15

- musical and dramatic performances
- special school events
- extracurricular activities such as clubs, service projects, and sports
- teen ideas and interests, in a show planned by and starring high school students
- student-produced videotapes

Channel 21 features a twenty-four-hour bulletin board of school-related announcements, information, lunch menus, emergency messages, and program listings. The channel also runs a weekly TV news magazine featuring regular appearances by the superintendent, school board members, teachers, administrators, business and community leaders, and volunteers. Each show visits a classroom where an unusual or exemplary activity is taking place. In the reading-incentive segment of the program, students at all grade levels find creative ways to review their favorite books.

Following is a listing of the regularly scheduled programs produced for Channel 21 by FCPS. It is printed with permission.

(1) *School Board Meetings* — There is live coverage of all regular business meetings, special meetings, public hearings, and budget work sessions.

(2) *Superintendent's Roundtable* — Live hour-long discussion among a panel of teachers, the superintendent, and viewers (through phone-ins). Each program focuses on a specific educational issue of broad interest to teachers. "Lead Teachers: Vital Links in the Resource Chain," "Teachers Talk about Teaching Writing," and "Summertime: An Opportunity for Professional Development" are among the issues that have been discussed.

(3) *SchoolScene* — Weekly news magazine that includes three or more of the following segments:
  - *Superintendent's Forum* — National, state, and local educational leaders join the FCPS superintendent for discussion of issues ranging from teacher professionalism to restructuring the schools (monthly).
  - *Across the Board* — School board members and their guests discuss board priorities and system-wide initiatives (monthly).
  - *Montage* — This is on-location coverage of unique or

exemplary classroom activities, such as language arts programs, use of math manipulatives, invention conventions, and international celebration (weekly).

— *Teacher Feature* — This is a feature on recognition of outstanding FCPS teachers, including Teacher-of-the-Year finalists and other teachers who bring special skills and talents to their classrooms (monthly).

— *Interviews* — Conversations with outstanding parent volunteers, students, and others who have made unusual or significant contributions to the school system are featured (monthly).

— *Area Report* — News from the four administrative areas about special programs. Examples have included an art enrichment program and behind-the-scenes preparation for science fairs (monthly).

— *State Report* — This is a recap of educational actions and issues at the state level (monthly).

— *Special Event Coverage* — This is on-site coverage of selected occasions, such as a presidential visit and the superintendent's press conference (as appropriate).

— *Partners* — The Office of Business Relations hosts a review with business leaders of successful school partnership arrangements that range from Education Foundation grants to individual school ''adoptions''(bimonthly).

— *Book Beat* — Creative and colorful book reviews presented by students. Props such as stuffed animals, costumes, posters, and even food are used to help entice viewers to read the books under discussion (biweekly).

— *Administrative Reports* — News about central administrative programs and services of interest to parents, students, and the community. Topics have included nutrition in school lunches, the safety concerns of bus drivers, and the school security patrol (bimonthly).

(4) *Profile* — This is in-depth coverage of an individual school, focusing on outstanding classroom and other instructional programs, special events, interviews, parent involvement, school history, and other characteristics of the school that together present a composite view of what makes that school special (monthly).

(5) *Red Apple 21 Presents* — This program covers a diverse range of

subjects, from special issues (family life education) to special events (550-student demonstration of dance instruction in physical education) (monthly).

(6) *Students' Corner*—A show planned by and starring high school students, with stories on school-related topics of interest and concern to teens. The agonies of the college application process, voter registration among teenagers, the fall football scene, and school building accessibility for handicapped students are among the subjects that have been covered (bimonthly).

(7) *Classroom Classics*—This is a showcase for outstanding school-produced tapes (bimonthly).

(8) *Sportscene*—This covers the high school sports program, combining studio and on-location segments on steroid use among athletes, weight training programs, skills development for girls' softball pitchers, college recruitment of athletes, the unusual commitment of scholar-athletes, and other sports-related topics (triannually).

(9) *The Fifth Week*—Highlights of special school events, such as the Theatre Arts Workshop, the Journalism Workshop, and the annual Countywide Science Fair are featured (triannually).

(10) *Culminations*—An hour-long show featuring end-of-the-year activities in four school locations. Examples have included high school graduations and all-night graduation parties, writing celebrations, and other culminating events (annually).

A weekly program guide, *Channel 21 Highlights and Program Schedule*, is issued by the Office of Community Relations and distributed to the media, selected governmental agencies and educational journals, student newspapers, and key community groups. Channel 21 program listings also appear in the internal newsletter *Supergram*, in Media General Cable's monthly program guide for subscribers, and on the *Red Apple 21* text message bulletin board.

During the original franchise negotiations between Fairfax County and Media General Cable, farsighted district representatives acquired six cable channels for school system use. Channel 21, the first of the channels to be activated, began cablecasting in August 1984. Last January, the five remaining channels came on line, thanks to the installation of a unique audio/video distribution system and the establishment of the school district's central TV production facility as a cable origination site. One of the five new channels provides community instruction and staff development services. The other four channels are for internal communications; their uses include the preview, evaluation, and distribution of tapes, along with in-service training and various administrative functions.

Channel 21 has been very well received by the community. It numbers approximately 20,000 viewers according to a survey conducted by Media General Cable.

According to Superintendent Spillane, ''In the five years since its inception, Channel 21 has established itself as a major source of news and information about Fairfax County Public Schools. System-wide, staff members recognize the value of placing their messages on Channel 21. They know that information will be presented in responsible, quality productions and delivered to a receptive community, eager for news about its schools. The community response to this outreach effort has been tremendous and I foresee a great future for this already successful communications vehicle.''

In addition to the district efforts, the schools are encouraged to publish newsletters to their parents, student newspapers, and literary magazines. The intent is to publicize the efforts of the schools and give recognition to the staff and students.

There is a strong network of informal, face-to-face communications which provide for the other half of the two-way communication process and a variety of formal channels for input:

> (1) verbal testimony at Board meetings, as well as frequent written testimony submitted by organizations and individuals, (2) the approximately 60 different standing committees and councils, (3) the Superintendent's Community Advisory Council and the PTA structure, (4) daily letters and phone calls to our public response secretary, (5) letters to the editor and editorials, and (6) community surveys which we conduct periodically. . . . We actively seek input from the community as to how their schools should be operated. (Bohen, 1989)

Have the Fairfax County school district's communications/public relations efforts been recognized? The FCPS Office of Community Relations recently won three national awards for its publications. The office received an Award of Merit in the 1988 School and College Publications Contest, sponsored by the National School Public Relations Association (NSPRA), as well as a Meritorious Award and a Best of Class Award from the National Association of County Information Officers (NACIO).

The 1988–1989 handbook *Fairfax County Loves Its Schools,* a brochure for parents that provides comprehensive information about the school system's programs and services, won the NSPRA Award of Merit. The NACIO Meritorious Award also went to *Fairfax County Loves Its Schools.* The NACIO Best of Class Award was given to *The Apple,* a magazine by, for, and about teachers.

Although the Fairfax County citizens cannot vote directly on the school budget, they can, and do, make their wishes known to the Board of Supervisors. The speakers addressing the Board of Supervisors are usually very well informed; support for the school district's budget is generally excellent. The voters do have an opportunity to vote on bond referenda proposed by the school district. Fairfax County's two most recent school bond referenda totaled over $325 million and were passed with unprecedented voter approval: the 1986 referendum for $146,120,000 received a 70 percent affirmative passage vote, and the 1988 referendum for $178.9 million received a 72 percent approval vote. The school district does an excellent job of briefing the community about the district on a continuing basis, not just when a vote is needed.

If we accept the definition of school public relations as ''a planned and systematic two-way process of communication between an educational organization and its internal and external publics designed to build morale, good will, understanding, and support for that organization'' (National School Public Relations Association, 1986), then we must conclude that FCPS has in fact an outstanding public relations program. One measure of understanding and support is the financial support the system enjoys. Fairfax County is a district that values education and supports it.

As Superintendent Spillane states:

> Communication with the community is a critical element in a school system's efforts to provide every student with the best education possible. The more information that parents and taxpayers and teachers and administrators have about what we are doing, the more they will support the good we do and call us to account for anything that is not up to standards. True accountability must be based on ready availability of information and clear understanding of its context. This is what our community relations efforts develop and provide.

C H A P T E R   12

SHOWCASING: ORANGE-ULSTER BOARD OF COOPERATIVE EDUCATIONAL SERVICES

T H E Orange-Ulster Board of Cooperative Educational Services (BOCES)** is located in southeastern New York State, overseeing services to eighteen school districts with a total enrollment of some 53,000 students over an area of 875 square miles. It has a staff of 575, and conducts fifty-one different services in five facilities throughout Orange County. Although not the largest BOCES in the state, it operates the largest BOCES adult program in the state.

As described by the Bureau of School District Organization (October 1989):

> BOCES are voluntary, cooperative associations of school districts in a geographic area, which have joined together to provide educational or business services more economically than each could offer by itself. They are organized under Sec. 1950 of the Educational Law. BOCES services focus on providing education for handicapped students, vocational education, academic and alternative programs, summer schools, staff development, computer services (management and instructional), educational communications, and cooperative purchasing. As of October 1989 all but 14 of the state's school districts belonged to a BOCES.

The commitment of the BOCES to the districts it serves is clearly stated in the words of its executive officer, Emanuel Axelrod, as contained in the transmittal letter of his annual report to the component school board members, the chief school administrators, and members

---

**Emanuel Axelrod, District Superintendent of Schools, Executive Officer.

of the Orange-Ulster BOCES educational community — "At the Orange-Ulster BOCES we are proud of the quality of our programs and services and are completely dedicated to fulfilling the needs identified by our component districts. Our aim is and has always been to provide services and programs to school districts and their constituents in a most efficient and economical manner" (Axelrod, 1989).

The commitment to open lines of communication is restated in the transmittal letter when Mr. Axelrod says, "In order for this BOCES to be successful it is essential that continuous and open communication be maintained. We must know your needs and you must know how we go about attempting to meet those needs" (Axelrod, 1989). Axelrod is the first to tell you that you "need to be proactive in getting information out — aggressive, constantly getting it out in an organized way." This he does, and does very well.

The Superintendent has said time and again that "if people know what you're doing, it makes your job easier; if it's a mystery, it will be very difficult to garner support for the service." In order to let people know what is going on, he makes himself readily available to every community group, and to anyone who wants to discuss the BOCES or education in general. He is constantly speaking to community and professional organizations, and is usually out three nights a week. He attends all functions, meetings, and conventions of the New State School Boards Association and the Mid-Hudson School Study Council, serves on the Superintendents Advisory Council to the President of The College at New Paltz, State University of New York, and is Chairman of the District Superintendents' Committee on Occupational Education. Manny, as he is known to all, is the one individual who is called when there is a question related to education.

The commitment to public relations in the BOCES is such that the members of the Superintendent's staff attend countless school and community meetings. Not only do they respond to invitations, they initiate many contacts. The commitment to "let the public know what is going on" is known to the staff and acted on by them.

The Superintendent's relations with the press are such that reporters do not hesitate to call on him when they need information. He built the relationship with the press by being open, honest, and forthright. Press conferences are scheduled in order to brief the media on what is happening and to bring issues to the forefront. At the press conference, background information on action being planned or taken is discussed; explanations for the action are given; and questions are answered. A press packet is generally prepared in advance of the conference. Members of the press know that, should they have a question about educational issues, the superintendent is available; they have his home telephone number and feel free to call him. As Mr. Axelrod puts it, "We've built a bridge between the agency and the press."

The BOCES is covered by eighteen newspapers, both dailies and weeklies. The coverage is broad and includes programs, board meetings, special events, student activities, and general meetings held at BOCES. The press is briefed and knowledgeable about the Orange-Ulster district. With the assistance of a part-time public relations person, newspaper coverage of BOCES activities has tripled over the past year.

The logo of the BOCES is the shape of the two counties it covers, Orange and Ulster and carries its theme, "Serving the Needs of 18 Local School Districts" (Figure 12.1). Every publication, every communication that comes out of the central office bears this logo. Component members districts and the media readily recognize a communication from the BOCES.

BOCES Newsbrief for Board Members is a monthly publication sent to the component school board members and their chief school administrators in order to keep them informed about what is happening at the BOCES. Reports on activities, programs, awards received, and successes of students and staff are items that are routinely included, in addition to other informational items (Figure 12.2).

A monthly *Newsletter* is mailed to all 115,000 property owners and renters in the geographic area covered by the BOCES in order to keep them informed of what the BOCES is doing. It is felt that the entire community needs to know that there is a BOCES and that it is actively

Reproduced from *BOCES Newsbrief for Board Members, July 1989,* Goshen, New York.

Figure 12.1

BOCES NEWSBRIEF

FOR BOARD MEMBERS
JULY 1989

LAW DAY REPORT

The activities for Law Day, 1989 were a huge success. Ceremonies were held at the Orange County Courthouse on May 1. The Honorable David Ritter, Administrative Justice for the Ninth Judicial District, gave the opening presentation on the theme of "Equal Access to Justice." Members of the BOCES Senior Enrichment Program took part in a mock trial with Supreme Court Justice S. Barrett Hickman presiding.

Posters submitted by elementary students were on display in the main lobby of the Government Center until June 5, when they were taken down and returned to the local schools.

Awards were presented in the various categories as follows.

Clare J. Hoyt Memorial Foundation Essay Contest for Secondary Students - theme, "Equal Access to Justice":

1. Tie for first place -

$300   James Horton - Cornwall
$300   Philip Santo - Valley Central

2. Second place -

$100   Jennifer Townsend - Valley Central

Liberty Bell Award to recognize a teacher for outstanding community service that has strengthened the American system of freedom under law:

Two winners -

Simonee Tierney,   Goshen Middle School
Barbara Campbell,   Burke Catholic H. S.

Poster Contest - for elementary students:

First Place Winners -

William Keller, Grade 5, Goshen
Joseph Ribando, Grade 4, Tuxedo
Barry Whitman, Grade 2, Middletown
Lauren Barone, Kindergarten, Tuxedo

Second Place Winners -

Whitney Baird, Grade 5, Goshen
Paul Hoffman, Grade 4, Tuxedo
Dori Lerman, Grade 2, Middletown
Lisa Birish, Kindergarten, Tuxedo

Third Place Winners -

Kenneth McGrady, Grade 4, Tuxedo
Jessica Burgoyne, Grade 4, Tuxedo
Joanne Wu, Grade 2, Middletown
John Mancuso, Kindergarten, Tuxedo

VO-TECH STUDENTS TAKE TEST

Nineteen second year Vo-Tech Auto Mechanics students took the N.Y.S. Department of Motor Vehicles Certified Inspectors Test. The test was administered at the Vo-Tech Center by a representative of the N.Y.S. Division of Vehicle Safety Services.

Certification as an inspector enhances a

Reproduced from *BOCES Newsbrief for Board Members, July 1989*, Goshen, New York.

Figure 12.2

engaged in meeting the needs of the community. The course offerings of the Adult Occupational and Continuing Education program are included (Figure 12.3).

The Cooperative Board meetings are widely publicized, and they are open meetings. Staff members make presentations on some aspect of the program; the board is continually being in-serviced. The agendas are available; the public can speak. Public hearings are held as needed, and the community's comments are taken under consideration.

Wanting the BOCES to maintain as high a profile as possible, the community, county school boards, and legislators are encouraged to use the facilities for their meetings. Often this encouragement results in BOCES' staff becoming involved in the issue being discussed.

Needs assessments are done by the Curriculum Advisory Council which is composed of the assistant superintendents of the component districts. Once the needs assessment is conducted, action is recommended and generally responded to as quickly as possible.

An example of a need that was identified and met was when the entire asbestos issue became a problem for the member districts. BOCES hired a management person, who now does all the asbestos training and keeps the districts informed about the latest information available on the subject. A major area of concern was taken care of with speed and dispatch and at minimum cost to the member districts.

Crisis situations are referred to the Superintendent; he becomes involved and is generally the spokesman for the BOCES. When a member district has a suicide, an emergency, or a crisis, a call made to the Superintendent's office results in action. The response may be, for example, a team going in to work with staff and students in a building following a suicide.

With the rising cost of health insurance, the Orange-Ulster BOCES developed a self-funded health insurance plan that currently covers twenty-one school districts, including several from Sullivan County. They are able to deliver far better health insurance to their employees at far less cost. This is certainly good public relations for BOCES and for the school district.

Responding to the fact that the cost of supplies and materials was high when purchased by the individual districts, BOCES initiated a cooperative bidding service for such items as custodial supplies, paper goods, art supplies, food equipment, etc. As a result, the districts were able to purchase the items for less money. Listening to the districts has paid off.

The philosophy of saying "yes" to requests, coupled with specific

Board of Cooperative Educational Services

Sole Supervisory District of Orange-Ulster Counties

CAR-RT. SORT

RESIDENTIAL
CUSTOMER
LOCAL

Non-Profit Org.
U.S. Postage
PAID
Orange-Ulster
BOCES

| Vol. 18, No. 4 | Goshen, N.Y. | September 1989 |

CHALLENGE AND ACHIEVEMENT - SUMMER AT BOCES

Summer is a time of growth and transformation, and this held true for the summer of 1989 at BOCES. The entire BOCES Complex was alive with discovery in many challenging summer activities and programs.

The Twelve-Month Special Education Program completed its third successful summer with a substantial increase in the number of students enrolled, and the addition of a new playground built specifically for handicapped children. Running from July 5th through August 15th, the Twelve-Month Program enables those students with severe handicaps to maintain the developmental levels of learning that they have worked so hard throughout the school year to achieve. The students in the program not only benefitted from the many activities available at the Special Education Center, but they also took field trips to High Point State Park, the Orange County Fair, and went swimming and picnicking at Maple Hill Park in Middletown. The students' summer culminated with a "street fair" held at the Special Education Center for which each class maintained a booth featuring different "bazaar games" and foods. Clowns also roamed through the fair adding to the festivities.

The students in the Twelve Month Program were not the only ones enjoying themselves at BOCES this summer. The Summer Enrichment Program under the guidance of Mrs. Eileen Candito and Mr. Greg DiNunzio kept local gifted and talented students challenged through programs in puppetry and computers.

Mrs. Candito's students ventured into the world of circus entertainment; they created many puppets out of material from socks to paper mache'. The students also learned about the art of clown costuming and make-up as well as the fundamentals of juggling and sleight of hand.

Mr. DiNuzio's students also entered a new and exciting world of computer graphics in their "LOGO: Turtle Training" classes. These students learned to move a "turtle" on the computer screen to design graphic displays. As the students became more skilled, the designs became more intricate until the final creations were achieved, replete with moving images, verbal texts and music.

Adult students also had the opportunity to benefit from BOCES programs this summer. Over 700 students enrolled in more than 80 sections of adult education courses. The Adult Education Program has seen a 25% increase in enrollment in all of its classes over the past year, an increase attributed to the wide variety of timely course offerings and a newly created site in Newburgh. The Adult Education Program also works in conjunction with local businesses to train new personnel in a variety of needed skill areas.

Thus, the many summer programs at BOCES provided creative and challenging opportunities for students of all ages and backgrounds.

Three participants in the BOCES Summer Enrichment Program "clown around" as part of their activities in the "Clowns, Puppets and Magic" classes offered this summer

Students in the Special Education 12-Month Program enjoy their new playground.

Reproduced from *BOCES Newsletter,* Goshen, New York.

Figure 12.3

action, permeates the staff of the BOCES. The BOCES operates twelve months a year, six days a week, with most of the facilities being used six days a week from 8:00 A.M. to 10:00 P.M. The switchboard opens at 7:30 A.M. and closes at 10:00 P.M. Many adults who return home after work can contact the BOCES until 10:00 P.M. to have questions answered about programs and services offered at the Orange-Ulster BOCES.

Recognizing the importance of good internal communications, Mr. Axelrod maintains contact with his staff on a continuing basis. The *Newsletter* is distributed to the staff. In addition to having meetings with individual staff members, cabinet meetings; group meetings of directors; large group meetings with all administrators, directors, and assistant directors; and meetings with local superintendents are held. Getting information out and shared is a priority.

The Superintendent and BOCES administrators visit the various programs and can be seen in the school buildings all the time, stopping to talk with staff and students. Fast communication with the members of the districts is possible by means of a facsimile machine and a telephone "tree"; and to the State Education Department by electronic means. The continuous communication that takes place has a very positive impact on the community's attitude towards the BOCES.

Emanuel Axelrod has earned the highest respect and confidence of his constituents, to the point that when local school districts need to fill a vacant superintendent position, they look to him to do the search in both dependent and independent districts.

In all endeavors that are undertaken by the BOCES, there is a commitment to including and informing the community, both internal and external. An example of one of their recognized PR efforts is that which is done to publicize the Vocational-Technical Center's programs.

It is recognized that many of the vocational-technical programs that could be offered to students are by their very nature expensive to run, in that the cost of the equipment, facilities, and staffing are high, while the number of students in a school district desiring a particular program could be few in number. This disparity usually prohibits the home school district from providing the program.

The Orange-Ulster BOCES can and does offer a broad range of some twenty-eight programs in its Vocational-Technical Center (Vo-Tech Center) that are attended by students coming from eighteen school districts. There is a recognized need that enrollment in the various courses must be maintained.

In order to counter declining enrollment trends and to bolster attendance in the Vo-Tech programs, the Orange-Ulster BOCES undertook an aggressive public relations effort in order to make their program known and accepted as a viable educational option. The PR effort was all-encompassing, and included the following elements.

- *Display advertisements* — A thrust in the public relations and program promotion areas included a display advertising campaign. Ads promoting individual programs and special events were run in the local newspapers. Included in the ads were feature success stories about former students, human interest stories, and Vo-Tech program information. The ads encouraged adults, out-of-school youth, and current high school students to "prepare for work or prepare for college" with a Vo-Tech education (Figure 12.4).
- *Guidance newsletters* — Each month a newsletter highlighting a different Vo-Tech program was issued. The publication, in poster format, described the program and identified successful graduates. The newsletter is mailed to all guidance counselors and principals (Figure 12.5).
- *Vo-Tech Views* — A bimonthly publication in newspaper format that included topical information about vocational education. Each issue focused on a different vocational program and included standard features such as: editorial comments on issues of interest, articles on career opportunities, profiles of students currently enrolled, and profiles of successful program graduates (Figure 12.6).
- *Program brochures* — Program description brochures were developed to provide prospective secondary and adult students with information about specific courses, career employment opportunities, special program requirements (such as physical examinations), and education sequence requirements. School counselors received personalized copies and copies for student use (Figure 12.7).
- *Vo-Tech calendars* — The Offset Printing program designed several calendars for county distribution. The Monthly Planner Calendar and Statue of Liberty Calendar are two popular items.
- *Videotapes* — A video library was developed to include programs and twenty videotapes, each four minutes in length, highlighting Vo-Tech programs and clusters. The videotapes were distributed to high schools and middle schools serviced by the center. The

High School Students

Begin your career at the Tech Center

A Technical education gives you the opportunity to explore career choices while still in high school.

A Technical education prepares you for the job you want with the *Education that Pays.*

If you are 16 years old or older, you can sign up for next September at the Orange-Ulster Vo-Tech Center.

Course offerings include:

Business/ComputerTechnology	Health Services
Graphic Arts	Law Enforcement
Electronics	Health Occupations
Automotive Trades	Horse Care and Handling
Childhood Services	Welding
Heavy Equipment Operation/Repair	Dental Assisting
Building Trades	Culinary Foods
Computerized Machining/Robotics	Horticulture/Landscaping
Maintenance Services	Vehicle Maintenance

For further information,
contact your guidance counselor today

Figure 12.4

269

SPOTLIGHT ON THE WELDING PROGRAM

Through dark glass and a curtain of sparks, welders guide their fiery tools to fabricate, strengthen, and give form to the variety of metals in endlessly changing designs and applications. It is a demanding skill that blends artistic technique with high technology.

New York's bridges may be falling down and her highways caving in, but students who complete the Welding program at the Vo-Tech center stand to benefit from the problem -- by becoming part of the solution. That's because the State of New York is determined to certify a new generation of welders who will repair and maintain our highways and by-ways. The prize for excellence in skills is great. Those students who pass a special performance test to be Certified Welders can look forward to a job earning as much as $25.00 an hour to start!

Hands-on Skill Development

Welding students learn contemporary metal joining, cutting, and reinforcing processes for manufacturing and fabrication. Modern high-strength steel, aluminum, cast iron, and other metals and alloys are used. Introductory topics include use of metal working tools and equipment such as drills, grinders, band saws, and identification and preparation of metals. Skills are developed in various methods of joining and cutting metals: shielded metal arc (stick) welding, oxy-acetylene (gas) welding, cutting, and brazing, MIG and TIG welding, and plasma arc cutting. Metallurgy and blueprint reading and drawing are emphasized.

Career Opportunities

Outstanding career opportunities in the construction and service industries await trained welders. Second year students may participate in paid work experiences in the welding industry and may prepare for the challenging New York State Department of Transportation Welder Certification Test. Students completing the program have been employed as thermal cutters, production or construction welders, ornamental iron-workers, and metallurgical technicians. Others have chosen to further their education at technical institutes and two and four-year colleges, or to open their own businesses.

Meet some successful former students who specialize in a variety of career fields.

Scott Grausso, Class of 1987
Minisink Valley High School
Assistant Welding Foreman
Harja Metals Fabrication
Sloatsburg, New York

Tom Romanowski, Class of 1987
Middletown High School
TIG Welder
Virtis Company
Gardner, New York

Henry Noha III, Class of 1988
Construction Welder
U.S. Navy
Siganella, Italy

Figure 12.5

Vol. 2, No. 3

Vo-Tech Students Excel at State VICA Contest

From the Editor...

I am new here. And, boy, is this place busy. I would like to share my first impressions with you.

The Vo-Tech Center is earnest about its purpose--promoting quality occupational education.

The teachers definitely take pride in their specialized area and conscientiously work at passing on their knowledge. I am impressed with the variety of programs offered here, 26 in all, and the sense of professionalism in the classroom.

The students are friendly, quite respectful, and generally responsible. I mean it. Is it because they have chosen to be here? I wonder.

The Guidance Department gracefully combines effort and expertise. Much work in the area of public relations has been added to the "normal" goings-on of the Department. There is concern over the student's need to know the options available here at the Vo-Tech Center. The 8th grade information sessions with the tours of the Center, along with the 10th grade assemblies and their visitations, reflect the Department's active outreach. Home schools appreciate the Vo-Tech Center's input and visibility.

There is no reason why a student graduating from high school should not be prepared for work and/or prepared for education.

The Vo-Tech Center is dedicated to securing a student's right to that preparation. I am glad to be here and encourage open communication between you and us. We can work together to guide the next generation into their future.

Eleven Vo-Tech students were honored at the Vocational Industrial Clubs of America (VICA) annual skill Olympics of New York State held April 12-14 at the Concord Hotel in Kiamesha Lake.

John Bennett, a Commercial Art student from James I. O'Neill High School in Highland Falls, received the State Pin Award sponsored by the Vocational Teachers Association. His winning design is a variation of the VICA hands logo with a hand breaking through a piece of metal. "I wanted to represent my theme that 'You can't stop us' by having the hand break through something very hard," John explains. This design is now the VICA logo for next year and is reproduced on pins and T-shirts distributed throughout the state. John will be attending Rockland Community College in the Fall where he hopes to build on the excellent foundation he has already received: "The Vo-Tech Center has opened up career interests and possibilities I never knew existed. I feel I really have a head start in my field because of the exposure I have gotten here. Winning the Pin Contest has encouraged me a lot."

Twenty-three Vo-Tech students competed with 2500 others at the state skill Olympics. The Vo-Tech Center is proud of all its representatives. "This is the culmination of a student's two years of studies at the Vo-Tech Center, giving them the opportunity to demonstrate the skills they have learned during studies preparing them to work," said William Calabrese, Director of Occupation! Education. Adele Purcell, VICA coordinator for the Center, said, "the state skill Olympics competition requires students to demonstrate skills in vocation-

al areas ranging from auto mechanics to nursing and in performance events such as extemporaneous speaking and job interviews."

Students Triumph

Ten out of the twenty-three Vo-Tech students placed in the skill competition. Three students won first place in their respective competitions and qualified for the VICA United States Olympics to be held in Tulsa, Oklahoma, the last week in June.

Jason Curabba concentrates on plumbing specs at contest.

The students and the competitions they won are Ronald Stone of Minisink Valley, Graphic Communications; Michelle Nathan

(Continued, page 2)

BOCES

Figure 12.6

Picture Yourself.

Do you like cars?
Do you like detailed mechanical
work?
Are you willing to work hard?

Picture yourself at the
Orange-Ulster BOCES
Vo-Tech Center in the
Auto Body Repair
program!

Prepare for Work or
Prepare for College.

Each year, more than 2.5 billion dollars is spent on auto
body work. The **Auto Body** program focuses on collision
repair, metalworking, fiberglass fabrication, spray
painting, color matching, custom painting and graphics,
and welding using the latest techniques and state-of-the art
equipment as well as business management.

Students gain daily practical experience on vehicles provided by the Vo-Tech Center and the
students. Second year students may participate in a work experience in the auto body industry.

It's Education that Pays!

Gain marketable skills and the competitive edge! Students completing
the **Auto Body** program have been employed as auto body repairers,
automotive restorers, paint specialists, and sales/service representatives.

Others have chosen to further their education at technical institutes and
two and four-year colleges, or to open their own businesses

Figure 12.7

tapes are available to students and parents in each school's library or guidance department. The students are allowed to take the videos home to view with their parents. In addition, a video entitled *BOCES Program and Services — A Reflection of Needs* was developed to further promote the overall BOCES program and to educate the community regarding its functions and services.

- *Bumper stickers and decals* — Six different themes/slogans were highlighted on a series of bumper stickers for students, parents, industry sponsors, and interested others. Vo-Tech Center decals were also available (Figure 12.8). The themes/slogans are:

  - "Get a Vo-Tech education. It's the competitive edge."
  - "I'm proud to be a Vo-Tech student."
  - Prepare for College. Prepare for Work.
  - "I'm the proud parent of a Vo-Tech student."
  - Education That Pays!
  - "I support Vo-Tech education."

- *Tee shirts* — Students wore tee shirts with the slogan: Education That Pays! Orange-Ulster BOCES Vo-Tech Center.

- *Open house* — An annual Vocational-Technical Center open house was conducted. Approximately 1,000 persons toured the facilities during school hours and in the evening to observe Vo-Tech classes and skill demonstrations. The open house presents an opportunity for parents, prospective students, and employers to learn more about the scope of the Vo-Tech programs, while affording visitors a close-up view of the excellent teaching facilities housed at the center.

- *Skill demonstrations* — The Vo-Tech students were in the public eye at a major shopping plaza for three days, where they could be seen demonstrating their skills in occupational areas such as carpentry, business data processing, trade electricity, and electronics. Visitors had an opportunity to have their blood pressure taken by students from the Nursing program and their nails manicured by Cosmetology students. A highlight of the display was the on-site construction of a storage building by the Building Construction students. Vo-Tech program staff operated an information center at which members of the public could secure printed materials, view visual presentations, or receive personal answers to their inquiries about the many programs offered at the Center (Figure 12.9).

Figure 12.8

274

About the Orange-Ulster BOCES Vo-Tech Center...

Who attends the Vo-Tech Center?

Seventeen school districts in Orange and Ulster counties send students to the center. Students who choose a vo-tech program attend their home school and are bussed to the Vo-Tech Center for 2-1/2 hours of the school day.

What about credits?

Students who complete vo-tech programs may receive up to four **Regents** credits for **each** year completed as well as recommendation for sequence credit towards Regents or local high school diplomas. To receive such credit, students must complete and pass Introduction to Occupations, CORE (where required), prescribed sequence units of instruction, and the occupational proficiency exam (when available) By successfully completing a vo-tech program, students can fulfill the requirements for either a major or minor sequence.

What programs are offered at the Vo-Tech Center?

Twenty-five different programs are offered at the Vo-Tech Center, as follows:

Trade & Industrial	Agriculture	Business
Auto Body	Horse Care and Handling	Business/Computer Technology
Auto Mechanics	Horticulture-Landscaping	
Building Construction		Home Economics
Climate Control/Plumbing	Health Occupations	Childhood Services
Commercial Art	Dental Assisting	Culinary Food Trades
Cosmetology	Health Services	
Electronics	Licensed Practical	Basic Occupational
Offset Printing	Nursing	Education
Trade Electricity		Hospitality Services
Welding		Maintenance Services
Computerized Machining/Robotics		Warehousing/Vehicle
Heavy Equipment Operation/Repair		Maintenance
Law Enforcement and		
Criminal Justice		Occupational Exploration

You can prepare for work or prepare for college!

Students who complete vo-tech programs find a variety of options for the future available to them. Work experience (Capstone) positions frequently lead to permanent employment. The Vo-Tech Center has a job developer on staff who receives calls daily from employers looking for applicants. This information is always available to our students.

Many students elect to further their education at two and four year colleges or at specialized training institutes. Several programs have articulation agreements with Orange and Sullivan County Colleges, and Delhi Institute. Vo-Tech students may receive credit and/or advanced placement at these and other institutions of higher education both in and out of state.

Figure 12.9

- *Expo '89—Showcase of Skills*—On a Sunday, people of all ages attended Expo '89, an extravaganza that featured a variety of activities for the entire family which included guided tours of the facility classrooms, labs, and shops where students demonstrated their talents in such fields as offset printing, computerized machining, desktop publishing, and practical nursing. Students from the Warehousing/Vehicle Maintenance program gave free car washes. Culinary Food Trades students prepared and served fruit plates and hot dogs so no one would go away hungry. Faculty and students alike were enthusiastic in displaying and demonstrating their skills, and that same enthusiasm was felt by the visitors. One young guest visiting offset printing was overheard commenting, ''I can't wait until I'm old enough to take the printing program.'' Many adults noted that they had no idea that there were so many programs and that such extensive and modern facilities existed at the Vo-Tech Center.
- *Information sessions and grade visitations*—Information sessions were scheduled for eighth and tenth graders at which time the broad scope of programs and opportunities were presented to the students using the videotapes, presentations, and printed materials. These information sessions were followed up by grade level visitations to the facility, at which time the students could ask specific questions of the instructors of the programs they were interested in learning more about.

The Orange-Ulster Vocational-Technical Center received two outstanding honors for its public relations efforts:

(1) OCCOLADES '88 was a competition sponsored by the Information Dissemination Council of the New York State Education Department. The purpose of this award program was ''to recognize the efforts of schools, BOCES, and colleges in conducting public relations activities that promote occupational education.'' All educational institutions in New York State were eligible to submit entries (The State Education Department, 1989).

Of the approximately 125 entries received, the Orange-Ulster Vocational-Technical Center was awarded First Place for its Total Public Relations Program.

(2) The National Association of Vocational-Technical Education Communicators (NAVTEC) sponsored a nationwide competition. Of the approximately 175 entries received, the Orange-Ulster Vocational-

Technical Center was awarded Second Place honors for its Overall Promotional Campaign.

When asked whether the results are worth the time and effort put into the PR program of the district, Emanuel Axelrod will tell you that it certainly is. He remarks, ''The educational programs and support services have grown rapidly over the past fifteen years. This has come about because everyone was kept informed. An example of this occurred three years ago when a $10 million bond issue was presented to the county voters and approved by a 9 to 1 vote. I was told by many people that they supported it because we kept them informed of our growth and the need for the expansion. The ongoing public relations is important and the effort is worth it.''

CHAPTER 13

SHOWCASING: SOUTH CENTRAL SCHOOL DISTRICT NO. 406

L O C A T E D in King County, Washington, the South Central School District† provides services for over 1,700 public school students in kindergarten through grade 12, and covers an area of approximately 7.5 square miles. It has three elementary schools, a grade 6−8 middle school (Showalter Middle School), and a grade 9−12 high school (Foster High School). One of the elementary schools, Cascade View, also houses a district-supported preschool and daycare program. Seventy-five percent of the students in the district are white; the remainder are Asian, Hispanic, black, and Native American. The district employs a certified staff of 112 and a classified staff of 57 full-time equivalent positions. The five-member board of directors prides itself in parent and citizen involvement and an extensive communication program.

According to Dr. Silver, ''In the heart of our changing community, South Central Schools remain a constant. Many of our residents and employees are graduates and long-time friends. New families find the school to be one source of identity with their new surroundings. South Central Schools are an important focus in the community, and our community is important to us. We are partners with our community and see the community as a major resource for learning.''

The financial condition of the district is sound, with a healthy fund balance and the prospect for continued stability. The Seattle-Tacoma International Airport; Longacres Racetrack, a major regional shopping center; Boeing Aerospace; and other high-tech installations are nearby or in close proximity to the school district. Approximately 11,000 people reside in the South Central School District.

†Michael Silver, Ph.D., Superintendent of Schools.

The community values education and has a long history of supporting tax levies. Hundreds of parents and other patrons volunteer their time in the schools each year, serving on committees, assisting teachers, and working on a one-to-one basis with students. The passage of a $16 million bond issue in 1988 to build a new high school replacing the existing one is the most recent example of community support for the schools.

Following the defeat of a $32.9 million bond election in May 1988, careful planning, involving the community, was begun. Prior community meetings were held to gain input and to determine why the bond failed, what priorities should be set for the long-range facilities plan, and what additional information was needed by voters.

The community felt that the $32.9 million effort to build the new high school, modernize the other four schools and the administration building, build a new daycare facility, and purchase computers and high technology equipment for all schools, was too extensive (and expensive) for the district to undertake at that time. The board listened and voted to place a $16 million bond issue for a new high school, computers, and high technology in all schools and a $1 million bond issue for a new daycare facility on the ballot in November 1988. A Bond Steering Committee was formed and a timeline was developed to accomplish the goal of passing the bond in three months (Table 13.1).

An intensive marketing effort was undertaken to communicate effectively with staff and patrons about the bond issue. A fact sheet, informational flyers, a brochure, a community tabloid newsletter, yard signs, campaign buttons, news releases, newspaper ads, and staff and key communicator publications were utilized (Figures 13.1 – 13.7).

The success of the efforts was clearly evidenced when the bond issue of more than $16 million was approved by 63 percent of the voters in an election run on the general election date in November 1988. Within a six-month period, the district was able to turn a 60 percent negative vote to a 63 percent positive vote to support the improvement of school facilities!

Communication with the staff and community did not stop with the passage of the bond referendum. The district published a newsletter called *Focus on Foster* (Figure 13.8) in order to keep the community and staff informed about the progress of planning the newly approved high school.

The public relations effort of the district is largely accomplished by the Superintendent of Schools, Dr. Michael Silver, and a part-time School/Community Relations Specialist.

Table 13.1.

Project	Due Date
Fact sheet	9/15
Questions and answers	9/23
#1 Flyer (basic information)	9/26
#2 Flyer (w/sketch of Foster)	10/7
(Both flyers—send home with elementary students; send home by mail to middle and high schoolers)	
Voter registration booths	
Elementary open houses	9/27,28,29
FHS football games	9/23,30,10/17
Weekly news releases to media	weekly
South Central News	10/15
To all residents and businesses	
Brochure	10/27
Postcards	
SCEA	10/31 − 11/7
Parents to neighbors and non-parents	10/31 − 11/7
Speakers Bureau—to speak to:	now until 11/8
Professional organizations	
Community organizations	
Staff groups	
Parents	
Personal signs	9/30 − 11/8
Yard signs	10/25 − 11/8
Campaign buttons	9/30
Endorsements	10/10
Publish in printed material	
News release	
Buy ad in newspaper?	
Doorbelling	
Speak to residents or leave flyer on door	
Booth at Larry's Market	10/29
	11/5,6
Telephone reminders to parents	11/7,8
using class lists only	

SOUTH CENTRAL SCHOOL DISTRICT NO. 406

November 8, 1988 Bond Election

"LET'S FOSTER EXCELLENCE"

ANSWERS TO YOUR QUESTIONS

1. What is the bond issue for?

Proposition I would pay for the construction of a new Foster High School and computer and technology equipment for all five district schools.

Proposition II would provide for construction of a day care center located in a separate one story building on the Foster High School campus.

2. What is the cost of the bond issues?

The total cost of Proposition I is $16,063,000. The average tax rate for the proposal is $1.57 per $1,000 of assessed valuation.

The total cost of Proposition II is $1,135,000 and would carry an average tax rate of 11¢ per $1,000.

3. What will the new Foster High School look like?

The new Foster High School will be a two-story building located on the site of the present high school. An artist's sketch of what the new school would look like is on display at the Administration Building, 4640 South 144th Street. (Beginning September 28th). Also, a written description of the facility listing proposed classrooms is available at each school and the administration building.

4. Why do we need a new Foster High School?

The present high school was built inexpensively 35 years ago to house the post-war baby boom. It is now showing its age. Leaky roofs, cracked beams, broken heating pipes, inadequate wiring, and asbestos make Foster a less than desirable facility in which to educate our young people.

Figure 13.1

November 8, 1988 Bond Election

Proposition I
•for construction of a new Foster High School on the site of the present high school

•for the purchase of computer equipment and technology for students in all five district schools

Proposition 2
•for construction of a day care facility on the Foster High School campus (relocation of the district's existing child care center from the overcrowded Cascade View Elementary School)

Costs:
Proposition 1 •$16,063,000
($1.30 estimated average tax rate per $1,000 of assessed property value)

Proposition 2 •$1,035,000
(9 cents estimated average tax rate per $1,000 of assessed property value)

(These estimates have been provided by the King County Assessor's Office.)

Financing the bond:
Individual homeowners in South Central pay 25 cents of each school tax dollar because of South Central's large industrial tax base. In this district, businesses will pay 75% of the cost of the bond issue.

Homeowners with a home valued in 1990 at $100,000 would pay an estimated average tax of $130 per year for Proposition I and $9.00 per year for Proposition 2. If approved, the tax will begin in 1989.

For further information, call Cynthia Chesak, 244-1270 or Gary Shearer, 244-4736 (Bond Steering Committee co-chairpersons) or Dr. Michael Silver, superintendent, 244-2100.

South Central School District #406
4640 South 144th
Seattle, WA 98168

Figure 13.2

South Central School District **news release**

For Immediate Release

4640 South 144th
Seattle, WA 98168

Phone: 244-2100

October 21, 1988

Chamber Board Supports South Central School District's November 8 Bond Issue

At their October 6 meeting, the Tukwila/SeaTac Chamber of Commerce Board of Directors unanimously approved two separate motions in support of South Central School District's November 8 Bond Election.

The board members voted unanimously to support Proposition I for a new Foster High School and computer technology for all schools. The directors said they would like to be involved in future meetings and have asked the school district for periodic updates.

A motion was unanimously passed by the board to support the construction of day care facilities at Foster High School to serve the community's needs, including families who live in the area and employees who work in the area. In a letter to the school district, Gene Jaeger, Chairman of the Board, said the chamber applaud's the district's plan, which includes using high school students to work with children as part of their education in an effort to help them learn about child development and parenting skills.

The Tukwila/Sea Tac Chamber of Commerce, according to the letter, hopes that these two propositions are perceived by the voters as responsible investments in our future generations.

Figure 13.3

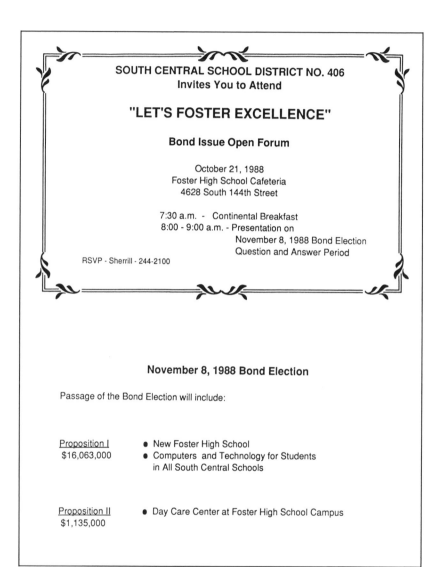

SOUTH CENTRAL SCHOOL DISTRICT NO. 406
Invites You to Attend

"LET'S FOSTER EXCELLENCE"

Bond Issue Open Forum

October 21, 1988
Foster High School Cafeteria
4628 South 144th Street

7:30 a.m. - Continental Breakfast
8:00 - 9:00 a.m. - Presentation on
                        November 8, 1988 Bond Election
                        Question and Answer Period

RSVP - Sherrill - 244-2100

November 8, 1988 Bond Election

Passage of the Bond Election will include:

Proposition I   ● New Foster High School
$16,063,000   ● Computers and Technology for Students
                            in All South Central Schools

Proposition II   ● Day Care Center at Foster High School Campus
$1,135,000

Figure 13.4

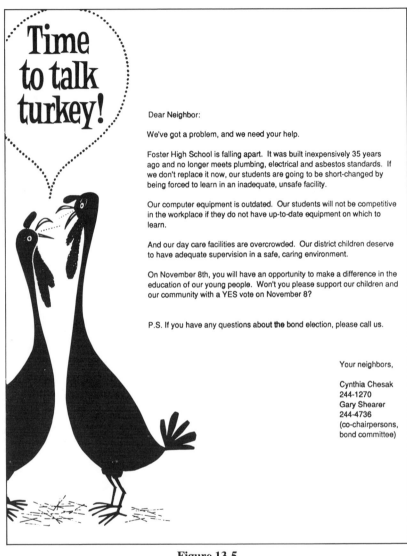

Figure 13.5

Figure 13.6

Don't Forget

TO VOTE TOMORROW

Tuesday, November 8, 1988

School Bond Facts

Proposition I
•for construction of a new Foster High School on the site of the present high school

•for the purchase of computer equipment and technology for students in all five district schools

Proposition 2
•for construction of a day care facility on the Foster High School campus (relocation of the district's existing child care center from the overcrowded Cascade View Elementary School)

Costs:
Proposition 1 •$16,063,000
($1.30 estimated average tax rate per $1,000 of assessed property value)

Proposition 2 •$1,035,000
(9 cents estimated average tax rate per $1,000 of assessed property value)

(These estimates have been provided by the King County Assessor's Office.)

For further information, call Cynthia Chesak, 244-1270 or Gary Shearer, 244-4736 (Bond Steering Committee co-chairpersons) or Dr. Michael Silver, superintendent, 244-2100.

South Central School District #406
4640 South 144th
Seattle, WA 98168

Figure 13.7

288

Focus on Foster

March 31, 1989

BOARD SELECTS FOUR ARCHITECTURAL FIRMS FOR INTERVIEW FOR NEW FOSTER HIGH SCHOOL

At a special board meeting held on Wednesday, March 29th, the South Central Board
of Directors selected four architectural firms for interviews for the New Foster
High School. The firms will make presentations to the Board at a special board
meeting on Wednesday evening, April 5, 1989 beginning at 6:00 p.m. in the Board
Room of the Administration Building. The four firms are:

- Bassetti/Norton/Metler/Rekevics
- GTde Weisenbach
- The BJSS Group
- Rue.Butler.Marshall.Lamb

The Board will also select architectural firms for the design competition for
the New Foster High School at the April 5th meeting.

UPDATE AND PUBLIC HEARING HELD

Sixty-two people attended an Update and Public Hearing on the new Foster High
School on March 14, 1989 at Showalter Middle School. Participants received
information and discussed design, program and space issues planned for the new
high school.

Information was presented on:

- technology planning for K-12
- Schools for the 21st Century
- school visitations
- educational program/space allocations
- general building considerations
- auditorium definition
- career-vocational education
- new Foster central kitchen

ADMINISTRATIVE PLANNING

District administrators are at work on the following areas in regard to the
construction of the new high school:

- budgeting
- applying for state funding
- scheduling the planning and construction process
- student housing for 1990-91

(over)

South Central School District

Figure 13.8

The board's commitment to continue parent and citizen involvement and an extensive communication program can be readily seen in the ''Proposed 1988−89 District Goals'' (Figure 13.9).

The district's logo and/or a distinctive masthead is used on all district publications. This helps the receiver recognize that the communication is from the school district.

In order to let the community know what is going on in the school district, a newsletter *South Central News*, is published bimonthly ''in the interest of better understanding of the South Central School District'' (Figure 13.10). It is mailed to all residents and postal addresses, to include businesses, in the district. The topics included in the newsletter are timely and informative, e.g., district-wide test results, planning in progress, a section called Profiles in Achievement featuring a staff member, People in the News, Alumni News, an article from the superintendent addressing a specific topic, Upcoming Calendar of District Events, and the sports schedule. Community members can also find the telephone numbers of the schools and district offices in *South Central News*, should they want additional information.

Meetings of the Board of Directors of the district are listed in the calendar included in the *South Central News*. The board's meeting agenda is available to individuals requesting it prior to the meeting and at the board meeting. Following the board meeting, the Office of the Superintendent issues *Board Briefs* (Figure 13.11), which is distributed to all staff members and community key communicators. It contains the presentations made to the board, discussions that took place at the meeting, and the action and information items considered at the meeting.

The Key Communicator (Figure 13.12), is issued from the Office of the Superintendent of Schools on a monthly basis and is distributed to a predetermined group of community leaders called key communicators.

Key communicators are community members who talk to others in the community. They have a reputation of being a reliable source of information about the community and events taking place within it. Some key communicators are in positions of authority or officially recognized leaders in civic organizations, task forces, churches, agencies, or local government. Others are friends and neighbors within the community.

Key communicators pass along information to others in the community about the South Central School District during the course of their normal activities. The work of the key communicators is done every time they tell someone they know about the South Central School District: over coffee with a neighbor, at the grocery store, at church, at work, at club or organization meetings.

SOUTH CENTRALSCHOOL DISTRICT NO. 406
4640 South 144th Street
Seattle, Washington 98168

PROPOSED 1988-89 DISTRICT GOALS

1. Review, develop and implement a plan addressing staff growth and development to promote student motivation and self-esteem.

   - Review and develop a personnel plan emphasizing career development.

   - Continue to implement district staff development and promote staff training emphasizing equity issues and student achievement.

2. Review and develop school level programs to promote excellence in teaching and learning.

   - Continue to develop a plan for early childhood and primary education emphasizing developmental principles for human growth.

   - Review the elementary program as part of the self-study and accreditation process.

   - Implement and evaluate the middle school instructional and curriculum program using the team process.

   - Implement a plan of action for high school improvement responding to the high school self-study and accreditation process and evaluate the plan.

3. Review, develop and improve district-wide curriculum programs and programs which meet students' special needs.

   - Implement the School Scholars Program.

   - Continue to review student support services and implement recommendations for improvement.

   - Continue to develop and implement a K-12 program articulating thinking skills and study skills in the curriculum.

   - Maintain the on-going curriculum review and development cycles.

4. Review, develop and implement school-community partnerships and improve school-home-community communications.

   - Continue to develop staff, parent and community participation through committees, task forces, and school volunteer service programs.

   - Continue to develop and improve programs supporting parents and responding to the changing family structure, parental involvement in schools, parent education and orientation to parents new to the district.

5. Review the long-range facilities/building improvement plan, prioritize facilities needs and seek funding to implement the facilities plan priorities through a bond election.

Figure 13.9

South Central News

Volume 9, No. 4   South Central School District • 4640 South 144th • Seattle, WA 98168   March 1989

Foster High debate team participates in national forensics tournament

Five Foster students traveled to the University of California at Berkeley to take part in a forensics tournament involving over 1,000 high school students. They are, standing, left to right: Dawn St. Clair, Kristen Chesak and Darren Wellington. Seated: Mark Mullet and Teresa Gebaroff. See page three for the story.

Reproduced from *South Central News*, South Central School District, Seattle, Washington, March 1989.

Figure 13.10

Board **BRIEFS**
From the office of the superintendent

South
Central
Schools

Regular Meeting
Board of Directors
November 22, 1988

PRESENTATIONS/DISCUSSIONS

Sandi McCord, Assistant Superintendent for Curriculum and Instruction, reported to the Board on 1988-89 staff development goals and activities. Staff development offerings through November have included sessions on first aid, physical education, teaching the writing process, thinking skills, whole language instruction and cluster teaching. Sandi reported on the cluster teaching pilot program of grouping highly capable students together within a class at each grade level for grades 1-5. Clustering groups of highly capable students in classes allows more opportunities for the students to work together on activities which extend classroom learning.

Susan Gulick, Program Supervisor for Waste Reduction and Recycling for King County Solid Waste Division, reported on King County's proposed waste reduction and recycling goals. King County is considering a goal of achieving 65 percent waste reduction and recycling within twelve years. Interim goals of 35 percent within three years and 50 percent within six years are also recommended. Schools are among the targeted groups for developing in-school recycling programs, waste reduction efforts, and educational programs for students.

Superintendent Michael Silver reported to the Board on the results of the November 8, 1988 Bond Election. Proposition I received 2489 962.27%) YES votes and 1508 (37.73%) NO votes. Proposition II had 2119 (53.39%) YES and 1850- (46.61%) NO votes.

The Board of Directors discussed proposals for financing the bond-issue for Foster High School to meet expenses for 1989. The Board set a special meeting date of December 2, 1988 at 5:00 p.m. to consider action on bond funding through a bond anticipation note for 1989.

Superintendent Michael Silver outlined a five-phase plan for designing a new high school and developing a plan for the computer/technology funding.

ACTION ITEMS

The Board approved South Central's 1988-89 Affirmative Action Plan.

The Board authorized the replacement of the district's food/delivery step van.

The Board approved a resolution to rollback the General Fund Maintenance and Operations excess levy for 1989 from the amount of $1,663,348 approved by the voters on February 4, 1988 to $1,557,737 in accordance with Washington levy lid law, the state's WAC 392-1319. The 1989 tax rate for South Central will be $1.85 down from $2.42 in 1988.

INFORMATIONAL ITEMS

The Board reviewed the district's financial status report, the Children's Center financial report and the district's investment report.

The next regular meeting of the Board of Directors will be on December 20, 1988 at 5:30 p.m. in the Administration Building.

Figure 13.11

293

The **KEY COMMUNICATOR**

From the office of the superintendent

South
Central
Schools

Bond Campaign underway

Cynthia Chesak and Gary Shearer are co-chairpersons of the Citizen's Steering Committee for the November 8 Bond Election. Over the next two weeks, bond materials will be published by the Citizen's Steering Committee and the Advisory Council.

King County Assessor's Office announces tax rates for school bond issue

The King County Assessor's Office has issued its estimates for tax rates on South Central School District's bond issue propositions for the November 8 election.

According to the assessor's office, the estimated average tax rate for Proposition 1 (A new Foster High School and district-wide computer technology at a total of $16,063,000) would be $1.30 per thousand dollars of assessed property value. The estimated rate is what a property owner would have to pay each year in additional taxes to support the bond issue.

The assessor's office's estimated tax rate on the Proposition II issue of $1,135,000 for a day care center is estimated at nine cents per thousand dollars of assessed property value. Both estimates by the King County Assessor's Office are lower than the estimates provided by the school district which were $1.57/$1,000 for Proposition I and 11¢/$1,000 for Proposition II.

District submits asbestos plan to state

In compliance with the federally legislated Asbestos Hazard Emergency Response Act, the district has submitted an initial management plan to the State on October 12, 1988. The plan includes the inspection report of asbestos materials for all district buildings. This preliminary report is available for review at the District Administration Building, 4640 South 144th Street, Seattle, during the business hours of 8:00 a.m. and 5:00 p.m., Monday - Friday. Individual building reports are also available for review at each school administration office during school operation hours.

The management report is not final until approved by the State and appropriate responses determined by the district during the upcoming 180 days. Within the next six months, the district will provide additional information to employees and parents concerning asbestos awareness and action taken to remove asbestos from our schools. Maintenance and custodial employees will receive more extensive training.

Questions and concerns may be directed to the district's AHERA Designation Person, Terri Patton at 244-2100.

(over)

Reproduced from *The Key Communicator*, South Central School District, Seattle, Washington.

Figure 13.12

Key communicators are kept informed of issues and events within the district on a regular basis. One source of information is the newsletter, *The Key Communicator*. It generally contains information about district issues, events, decisions, or plans that can be used by the key communicators as background information as they speak informally with other community residents about the schools.

406 Focus is yet another publication issued from the Office of the Superintendent of Schools in an effort to communicate with all district staff members. It is issued biweekly (Figure 13.13).

News releases (Figure 13.14) are issued as needed in order to inform the press of happenings in the district that might interest them. The name of the individual who is closest to the item covered in the news release is identified so that the media may obtain additional information, if needed.

Media coverage has been generally positive, and tends to reflect the values held by the community. Actions of the board, special programs and ceremonies such as the annual School Scholars Recognition Ceremony and Reception, and the task forces' progress and reports, are covered by the local news media. The district often issues an information sheet that gives the media additional information on a topic so that they can be better informed (Figure 13.15).

The pride that the district has in its schools can be readily seen in an informative flyer that is distributed to people desiring information about the school district. It has as its motto "Great Expectations . . ." (Figure 13.16).

Coverage and recognition of the fine educational program has gone beyond the confines of the Greater Seattle, Washington area. In the December 1987 issue of *Money* magazine, Foster High School was among the ten schools in the country singled out for their course in personal finance by the magazine and included in *Money* magazine's "financial first string." This was a great public relations accomplishment for so small a school district!

The district's early childhood education program has brought national attention to the district as a result of the program's inclusion in "The Public School Early Childhood Study" by Bank Street College of Education; "The Great Preschool Debate, When, What, and Who?" (Bridgman, 1988); and accreditation by the National Academy of Early Childhood Programs. Such national recognition and publicity helps the district when it applies for grants and support from industry and funding agencies.

406 FOCUS

From the office of the superintendent

South Central Schools

February 24, 1989

In Memoriam

Aileen Felker, a South Central School District employee for 15 years, died Sunday from cancer. She was 45.

Aileen was a playground aide at Tukwila Elementary from 1974-84 and a daycare teacher at the South Central Children's Center at Cascade View Elementary from 1984-89.

She taught the two to three year old class and was like a second mother to many of the children. She worked the early shift, opening the school at 6 a.m. She loved the children and the children loved her.

Aileen always had a hug and a ready smile for the children as well as the staff and parents. She will be remembered for her positive attitiude and helpful manner.

Aileen was also an active parent at Foster High School, where her five children went to school. Last year she helped coordinate the all-night trip for seniors following graduation. Her youngest daughter, Laurie, is a senior at Foster this year.

Aileen was born and raised in Hawaii. Besides her mother and two sisters who live in Hawaii, she is survived by her husband, Jon, sons John, Robert and Jim, and daughters Judy and Laurie.

A service will be held Saturday at 11 a.m. at St. Thomas Church.

Employee Benefits - Preferred Vendors

If your doctor (medical, vision or dental) or your pharmacy does not appear on the current preferred list, it would be to your benefit to call your medical companies to see if they inadvertently left the name off before changing doctors or pharmacy.

Celebrate Success

South Central celebrates Black History Month

In recognition of Black History Month in February, the South Central School District is hosting the Seattle Children's Theatre's touring production of the internationally acclaimed Most Valuable Player. The tour is funded by grants from the George L. Argyros/Mariner Youth Baseball Foundation, King County, and Washington State Arts Commission's Cultural Enrichment Program.

Performances were held at Tukwila Elementary School and Showalter Middle School on February 21 and will be held at Thorndyke Elementary on March 3 at 10:00 a.m. and 1:00 p.m.

Most Valuable Player recounts the life of one of America's greatest contemporary legends, Jack (Jackie) Roosevelt Robinson. Robinson broke professional baseball's color line in 1947 when he was contracted to play with the Brooklyn Dodgers. Robinson became the first black man to participate in what had been white-only professional sports in America.

Most Valuable Player brings to the stage all the passion, rage, and excitement of Jackie Robinson's life with the Brooklyn Dodgers and his bitter struggle against prejudice. Accepting his role as the first black man to play major league baseball took tremendous courage. His strength as a player was awesome -- during his career he held a lifetime batting average of .311, stole over 200 bases (including home plate 20 times), and scored over 100 runs in a season six times during his ten year career with the Dodgers. Such athletic feats earned him the Most Valuable Player Award in 1949 and a permanent place of honor in baseball's Hall of Fame.

Reproduced from *406 Focus,* South Central School District, February, 24, 1989.

Figure 13.13

South Central School District news release

For Immediate Release

4640 South 144th
Seattle, WA 98168

Phone: 244-2100

FOSTER HIGH NAMED TO "FINANCIAL FIRST-STRING"

Foster High School, in the South Central School District, is one of the top ten high schools in the nation in regards to the teaching of economics, according to MONEY magazine.

In its December 1987 issue, the magazine published its pick for the "Financial First-String" of high schools. The schools were selected because they offer "great courses in personal finance." besides Foster, the other schools named were: Great Neck North High, Great Neck, N.Y.; William Penn High, New Castle, Del.; Northeast High, St. Petersburg, Fla.; Shaker Heights High, Shaker Heights, Ohio; Louisville Collegiate, Louisville, Ky.; Homewood-Flossmoor High, Flossmoor, Ill.; Park High Richardson, Texas; and Mills High, Millbrae, California.

The selections were based on nominations from education association, teachers and school superintendents; consultation with branches of Federal Reserve banks which are active in education; the recommendations of nonprofit groups such as the College for Financial Planning and the Joint Council on Economic Education; along with research by MONEY's staff.

At Foster, the applied economics course is taught by Mike Shannon. Unlike the elective courses offered at most other schools, Foster's economics course is a graduation requirement. "Foster is one of the few schools in the state to

Continued......

Figure 13.14

297

Program: Challenging Students to Succeed: a business-school partnership program

Purpose: To bring business people and teachers together to develop partnership activities

Analysis:

The South Central School District, in cooperation with the Southwest King County Chamber of Commerce and a neighboring school district, Highline, sponsored a business-school partnership forum on February 6, 1989. The goal of the forum was to initiate a "grassroots approach" to building activities by utilizing teachers and business people. The forum was held after a careful examination of the need to establish mutually beneficial relationships between the business community and the schools.

Planning:

Planning for the forum was accomplished by the Southwest King County Education Committee which includes staff members from the South Central and Highline School Districts and business persons from the Chamber. The goals and outcomes for the forum included the following:

l. To develop instructional and educational linkages between business/industry and classrooms, utilizing the human resources within the community for instructional purposes in order to enrich learning experiences.

2. To provide experiential opportunities for students within the business community, including work study programs as well as high school internships in professional fields.

3. To build rapport and support for the schools with the business community.

Execution and Communication:

South Central and Highline School Districts selected a combined total of 50 teachers (K-12) to attend the forum. A letter was sent to each teacher planning to attend the forum. Business persons responded to a brochure sent to all members of the Chamber. Fifty business persons were matched with the teachers attending the forum. During the forum, teachers and business persons met in pre-arranged pairs to formalize agreements for business partnership activities. "Contract" were signed. (A packet containing information for each of the forum participants is enclosed.) At the closing luncheon, a representative from each table reported on the activities agreed to by teachers and business persons seated at the table.

Evaluation:

An evaluation form was completed by participants. Evaluations indicated an overwhelming number of "smiling faces." (See evaluation form) The greatest indicator of the forum's success was that 90 contracts were finalized. These activities will be completed between February and June, 1989. We believe our success was due to the inclusion of a wide variety of business representatives and the support received by the district's teachers and administrators as well as the school district and Chamber boards of directors.

Figure 13.15

SOUTH CENTRAL SCHOOL DISTRICT

Great Expectations...

South Central School District

4640 South 144th
Seattle, Washington 98168
(206) 244-2100

Reproduced from *Great Expectations. . .*, South Central School
District, Seattle, Washington.

Figure 13.16

Recognizing the many advantages of bringing business people and teachers together in partnership activities, the district teamed up with the Highline School District (a neighboring school district) and the Southwest King County Chamber of Commerce in sponsoring a forum "to initiate a 'grassroots approach' to building activities by utilizing teachers and business people." The program "Challenging Students to Succeed: a Business-School Partnership Program" grew out of a school-business partnership committee and was named SUCCESS: Schools United with Chambers of Commerce to Establish Success for Students. It had as its purpose "To bring business people and teachers together to develop partnership activities." A fact sheet on the program contained a section on planning, which included the anticipated goals and outcomes of the program:

> Planning for the forum was accomplished by the Southwest King County Education Committee which includes staff members from the South Central and Highline School Districts and business persons from the Chamber. The goals and outcomes for the forum included the following:
>
> 1. To develop instructional and educational linkages between business/industry and classrooms, utilizing the human resources within the community for instructional purposes in order to enrich learning experiences.
> 2. To provide experiential opportunities for students within the business community, including work study programs as well as high school internships in professional fields.
> 3. To build rapport and support for the schools with the business community.

The need to continue to build rapport and obtain support from the business community is recognized by the district, as is the need to continue to build rapport and obtain support from the community at large and to reflect the community it serves. A South Central 2000 Planning Council composed of twenty staff members, parents, and community and business representatives met for a period of five months to study the trends and educational implications for the educational program of the district and reported on recommendations for South Central.

A section of the "South Central 2000 Recommendations for the Educational Program prepared especially for the South Central School

Board'' by the South Central 2000 Planning Council (South Central, 1989) included recommendations entitled ''Community Partnership'' and these were as follows:

- Implement a Community Education Concept, including the following:
  - Adopt a policy ''community is the classroom.''
  - Develop a homework outline.
  - Offer school-age child care at all elementaries.
  - Develop collaborative programs and services within and outside the standard school day (recreation/education/social and health/cultural) for all community residents.
  - Increase use of school facilities for the delivery of collaborative programs and services.
  - Allow space-available access for community to use school facilities and classrooms during school hours.
  - Initiate a school-volunteer program.
  - Initiate a youth community services course.
  - Expand school/business partnerships.
  - Provide programs for parents including literacy, ESL and parenting skills.
  - Provide after-school or evening classes for the community (cost to be underwritten by tuition, and credit to be given to current high school students).
- Develop expanded educational options outside of the school district:
  - consortium developed with other school districts
  - partnerships with area businesses
  - partnerships with area colleges and universities
- Expand latch-key after-school program in combination with state agencies, municipalities, and community volunteers.

Following the issuance of the recommendations, the district has implemented several new programs including:

- The Washington State Early Childhood Education and Assistance Program (ECEAP). The district has become a site for ECEAP which serves eighteen preschool-age children and their families. The program is offered free to children from low-income families that qualify under federal income guidelines. It is similar to the federally funded Head Start Program. Among the services provided to students in the program are: developmental screening and services, social service referrals and social and educational experiences with children their own age. Parents have the opportunity to work with other parents to learn parenting skills and are involved in shaping their child's education.

- In an effort to expand school-business partnerships, the school district and the city of Tukwila are partners in the ECEAP program in providing matching funds for the program's operation. The city of Tukwila's Parks and Recreation Department also is using the school district's gym facilities at several schools for student and adult recreation programs.
- It introduced parenting classes at all three elementary schools taught by the district's social worker.
- It introduced eighth grade middle school students to the concept and activities of youth community service through a semester course called "Skill for Adolescence."
- It expanded its after-school child care program.

The district's emphasis on school-community interaction is identified in the core values of the school district which are associated with the district's mission statement. The South Central mission statement is:

Our mission is to help learners develop the visions, skills and confidence to manage and enhance their own lives and contribute to society.

The three core values supporting the mission statement are: caring, challenging, and dedication. In defining these values, the description for caring highlights the ongoing relationship between the schools and the community:

CARING

In South Central, we *care* . . . for our learners, our staff, our parents, and our community. Every employee teaches and shows the care that has become a trademark of South Central. We strive to know each student and family personally. We welcome them into a caring environment that encourages involvement.

The commitment to the involvement of parents, teachers, and community in the educational program of the district, can also be seen as reflected in one of the four areas of focus contained in the Vision Statement of Foster High School:

Foster develops pride by:

- Involving parents
- Promoting student spirit
- Acknowledging supportive teachers
- Encouraging support of local businesses
- Forming active alumni groups

Dr. Cheryl Hansen, Foster High School Principal, explains Foster Pride this way: "Developing Foster Pride is an ongoing objective. The students and community should be proud of their high school. Pride is established by recognizing students for their achievements and celebrating successes at student assemblies. It is developed by acknowledging the successful achievements of Foster alumni through the Foster Greats program. Finally, the school could not be a source of pride without the ongoing recognition of the teachers who make learning happen."

South Central School District No. 406 cares about the physical, social, and mental health of its total community — employees, students, and parents — and recognizes the need to maintain optimal wellness. The district feels that "a healthy employee is more productive; a healthy student achieves more; an informed community supports the maintenance of both."

The district developed a comprehensive Wellness Program in order to assist the staff, students, and total community. A Wellness Advisory Board to the Superintendent was appointed. A publication, *Focus on Wellness*, is issued quarterly by the school district and distributed to staff members (Figure 13.17). The work of the Wellness Advisory Board has been pervasive, resulting in:

- a revised school board policy on alcohol and other drugs (the policy addresses issues of prevention, intervention, after-care support, and discipline)
- the adoption of a tobacco-free policy for students and staff on all school grounds and buildings
- the adoption of revised goals and objectives for the district's physical education curriculum
- the implementation of an employee health and fitness evaluation program provided through a partnership with a local hospital
- the offering of an aerobics class for staff held after school in a school gym three times a week

FOCUS ON WELLNESS

Published by the South Central School District

April, 1989

It's a Stitch!

Have you ever been running or walking rapidly when you suddenly get a sharp pain, called a "stitch," in the side?

A stitch is the diaphragm in spasm, and it is very much like a leg cramp.

These are the steps you can take to help prevent getting a stitch:

- Wait 30 minutes or more after a meal to begin exercising.
- If you plan to increase the intensity of your exercise, do it gradually.

If you do get a stitch, you can (1) take deep breaths and exhale slowly; (2) slow down or stop exercising; or (3) reach above your head to stretch your stomach muscles.

The more aerobically fit you are, the less likely you are to get a stitch.

Know the warning signs of a heart attack! 1. Uncomfortable pressure, fullness, squeezing or pain in the center of your chest lasting two minutes or longer. 2. Pain may spread to the shoulders, neck or arms. 3. Severe pain, dizziness, fainting, sweating, nausea or shortness of breath may also occur. If you show these symptoms, the American Heart Association says "Get help immediately!"

The Many Types of Anxiety

Mental health experts say that a little anxiety keeps us better attuned to the world around us. "Anxiety" refers to mental tension that has no apparent identifiable cause, and it is as much a part of life as eating and sleeping.

In the right context, anxiety is beneficial because it heightens alertness and readies the mind and body for action. However, sometimes people suffer from anxiety so intense that it interferes with work and family life.

There are various types of anxiety. For example, when the heart races and breathing is difficult, it's called a "panic attack." Other types of anxiety include "agoraphobia," or fear of leaving home, and specific phobias such as fear of elevators,

flying, animals, or whatever.

"Social phobia" keeps people from speaking in public, dancing, dining in restaurants, and meeting new people.

An "obsessive disorder" is usually a thought you can't get out of your mind. A "compulsive disorder" is something you do frequently — but know is strange.

"Posttraumatic stress disorder," once called "battle fatigue," is experienced by people who have seen violence, abuse, or terrible accidents.

"Generalized anxiety" is experienced by people who just feel anxious most of the time.

You can test your own general anxiety level by answering the questions in the box below.

ARE YOU ANXIOUS?

1. Do you ever have a sudden racing of the heart, dizziness, or shortness of breath?

2. Have you visited a hospital fearing a heart problem but found there was none?

3. Do you suddenly fear something terrible will happen?

4. Do you avoid travel on buses, trains, or airplanes?

5. Are you afraid to leave home alone?

6. Do you avoid crowds or places like shopping malls?

7. Do you spend much time worrying about bad things that might happen?

8. Do you feel tense and anxious most of the time?

9. Do you get extremely anxious when you are the center of attention?

10. Are there things you do repeatedly, like washing your hands or checking the door?

11. Do you feel you must drink or take tranquilizers before social occasions or performances?

12. Do thoughts you can't stop, but that make little sense, occupy your mind?

If you answered yes to any of these questions, your physician or employee assistance counselor could help you identify the cause and get some relief.

Figure 13.17

304

The district forms task forces in order to address areas of concern. One such area is equity education. A South Central Equity Education Task Force was organized to assist the district in planning curriculum activities, board policies and procedures, cultural awareness activities, and parent involvement activities, and to act as a resource for the district administration and the school board. The task force is comprised of staff, parents, and community members from each of the district's schools who indicate an interest in promoting an equitable education for all students through the task force. The task force issues a publication entitled *Equity News* on a quarterly basis to staff and parents (Figure 13.18).

The work of the equity task force has led to school board adoption of policies on malicious harassment and sexual harassment, the training of all certified staff in a twenty-hour staff development program called "Gender Expectations and Student Achievement," the district's participation in a cultural awareness curriculum program called "Global Reach," and the district sponsorship of a cultural fair for middle school students. The involvement of staff, parents, and community members furthers the district's efforts to involve key support groups.

Fully appreciating the contribution of advisory boards and committees, and desiring to improve their public relations efforts beyond the current status, Superintendent Silver formed a Public Relations Advisory Board, asking them to do the following.

- Give counsel on public relations strategies, general public relations, and other topics as requested by the school board or administration.
- Give feedback on ongoing public relations programs in the district.
- Give advice on short- and long-range school/community relations plans and projects affecting the community.
- Share information about public perceptions of the district and bring related matters to the district's attention at bimonthly Public Relations Advisory Board meetings or as needed.

The Public Relations Advisory Board consists of eleven community members and four staff members, including Superintendent Silver. The community members are professionals in the field of public relations and include public relations managers/directors/specialists from industry and government, as well as presidents and vice presidents of industries. The district representatives, in addition to the Superintendent of Schools, include a board member, the district's School/Community Relations

EQUITY NEWS

A publication of the Equity Task Force
South Central School District #406

Equity Education Task Force Formed

January, 1989

A South Central Equity Education Task Force was formed last year to discuss equity issues, review Multicultural education and act as a resource for the district administration and School Board.

The Task Force is comprised of representatives from each school staff and parent service organizations, as well as community patrons. The Task Force is co-chaired by Tammy Rabura, ESL teacher and Tavo Quevado, a Showalter parent. Current Task Force members include:

School staff

Tamera Rabura, Scott Desmond, Sue Ness, Dick Fain, Sandi McCord, Larry Green, Lisa Thorne, Kristi Skanderup, Kay Evey, Della Grainger, Bruce Zahradnik, Elsie Gardner and Michael Silver.

Parents and community patrons

Tavo Quevado, Paul and Denise Johnson, Marsha and Alfonso Marsh, Jeanelle Baldwin, Tom Kilburg, Renee Baron and Hinh Luong.

Resource assistance

Gilbert Hirabayashi, U.S. Department of Justice and Al Aragon, Center for National Origin, Race and Sex Equity.

Interested parents may contact any of the district offices for additional information.

GEESA Training for Teachers

Teachers and instructional assistants in South Central School District will receive training in GEESA - Gender/Equity Expectations Student Achievement. GEESA examines teacher-student interactions. It utilizes research-based instructional strategies and resources to eliminate any biases that may exist. GEESA is based on the premise that in order to ensure quality and excellence on an equitable basis, school districts need to directly confront the issues of gender and ethnic bias in teachers' interactions with students.

GEESA training will begin with a presentation on the January 30th teacher workshop day. The presenter will be Dee Grayson, the GEESA program author. The workshop will be held in the Foster High School cafetorium from 8:00 - 11:30 a.m. Additional staff training will be provided each month through May.

Board Adopts Malicious Harassment Policy

A new policy regarding malicious harassment written by the Equity Task Force has been adopted by the South Central School Board. The purpose of the policy is to maintain a learning environment that is free from any form of harassment related to a person's race, religion, gender, culture or ethnicity. Copies of the policy are available through the schools or the South Central Administration Office.

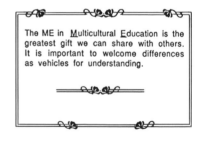

The ME in Multicultural Education is the greatest gift we can share with others. It is important to welcome differences as vehicles for understanding.

Reproduced from *Equity News*, South Central School District, January 1989.

Figure 13.18

Specialist, and a member of the South Central Advisory Council. (The South Central Advisory Council is composed of parent representatives from all schools serving as an informational support network and is the coordinating group for school levy and bond campaigns.)

The Public Relations Advisory Board looked at the district's planning efforts, giving special attention to developing a school communications marketing plan for each of the following groups:

(1) Parents
(2) Non-parents — single, young couples, parents of preschool-age children, senior citizens, and past presidents
(3) The business community
(4) The city of Tukwila
(5) Media

Each school issues a monthly newsletter to parents.

The district receives input from the community in a variety of ways:

(1) All regular board meetings have a time provided for citizen comment and communications (scheduled and unscheduled).
(2) The district holds special board meetings such as public hearings, i.e., bond issue discussions.
(3) The district uses surveys designed to gauge the community's attitudes about the schools.

The school/community public relations efforts of the South Central School District are paying off in many areas. The support of the community for the district's programs, a very low turnover of staff, a very low percentage of students leaving for private or parochial schools, and a reduced dropout rate are evidence of the community's level of satisfaction with the school district.

Additionally, the National School Public Relations Association 1989 Golden Achievement Awards were given to the district for its successful 1988 bond election campaign and the coordination of a school-business partnership program.

It has been possible to receive this level of support only as a result of a Superintendent of Schools and Board of Directors who are committed to the principle of inclusion, openness, and two-way communication. The size of the district in no way hampered the efforts that were made; size was not an excuse for not having a first rate public relations program!

NEEDS ASSESSMENT

Dear Community Members:
School District Employees:
Students of Grades 6-12:

The University City Schools would like your assistance to help the public schools do a better job of meeting students' needs. We ask your cooperation in completing this questionnaire. There are no right or wrong answers. The purpose of the questionnaire is to help us know how you feel toward your school district's programs and procedures. We want your thinking about the school system as a whole, not about a particular school at this time. The schools will be surveyed individually.

When you have completed this questionnaire, please mail it on or before Monday, September 12 in this self-addressed postage paid form, or give it to any teacher or administrator in the University City Schools. Your 13¢ stamp on this mailer will be a great help to the district. It is not necessary to sign your name. It is necessary to return it by September 12 as we want to begin new efforts at once toward establishing the district's priorities as shown in this needs assessment.

Sincerely,
School District of University City

Irene M. Lober
Superintendent

INSTRUCTIONS

Please complete Section I which gives us background information needed in this study of our schools. Other sections contain several items. On each item please circle the numeral 1, 2, 3, 4, or 5 according to the instructions for each part.

SECTION I
Please complete the part that best describes yourself and circle the numeral(s) before the appropriate responses.

COMMUNITY MEMBERS:

I am a: 1. Parent of public school child or children
          2. Parent of private school child or children
          3. Citizen having no children in grades K-12

My child or children (if any) are in grade(s) or level(s):
1. Preschool   4. Junior high, 8-9
2. Elementary, K-5   5. Senior high, 10-12
3. Middle school, 6-7

SECTION V

These questions can be answered yes, no, or don't know.
Please mark your opinion on each one.

(circle one)

(a) Do you believe that high school students should pass a state or national examination before they can graduate?
    Yes   No   Don't Know

(b) Should schools teach moral behavior?
    Yes   No   Don't Know

(c) Do you believe that drug abuse is a problem in our schools?
    Yes   No   Don't Know

(d) Do you believe that teachers should assign homework?
    Yes   No   Don't Know

(e) Should the schools require higher standards of school work?
    Yes   No   Don't Know

(f) Are you able to keep well-informed about what is going on in the schools?
    Yes   No   Don't know

(g) Should students be given fewer electives or choices and more required courses?
    Yes   No   Don't Know

SECTION VI

PLEASE ADD YOUR COMMENTS

What would you most like to see improved in this District?

_____

_____

_____

_____

_____

OPTIONAL

If you would like to work with a task group on a high priority need of the District, please give your name and telephone number or address, and the topic you would prefer.

Topic or Area _____

Name _____

Address _____

Telephone _____

FIRST CLASS
Permit No. 10997
St. Louis, Mo.

BUSINESS REPLY MAIL
No Postage Necessary If Mailed In U.S.A.

POSTAGE WILL BE PAID BY

SUPERINTENDENT'S OFFICE
UNIVERSITY CITY SCHOOL DISTRICT
725 KINGSLAND AVE.
UNIVERSITY CITY, MISSOURI 63130

Side One

Side Two

(circle one)

I have lived in University City:
1. Less than a year
2. 1-5 years
3. 6-10 years
4. More than 10 years

My age is:
1. Under 30
2. 30-50
3. 51-65
4. Over 65

I live in this subdistrict, or it is my nearest public elementary school: (To parents: If in doubt, choose the school your child attends.)
1. Daniel Boone
2. Delmar Harvard
3. Flynn Park
4. Jackson Park
5. McKnight
6. Nathaniel Hawthorne
7. Pershing
8. University Forest

My race is:
1. Black   2. White   3. Other

My sex is:
1. Female   2. Male

SCHOOL DISTRICT EMPLOYEES

I am a:
1. Teacher, counselor, librarian, specialist
2. Administrator, supervisor
3. Other employee (all support services)

My work is:
1. Preschool
2. Elementary K-5
3. Middle school 6-7
4. Junior high 8-9
5. Senior high 10-12
6. Districtwide

I have worked in the District:
1. Less than a year
2. 1 to 5 years
3. 6 to 10 years
4. More than 10 years

My race is:
1. Black   2. White   3. Other

My sex is:
1. Female   2. Male

STUDENTS

I attend:
1. Brittany Middle School
2. Hanley Junior High School
3. Senior High School

My race is:
1. Black   2. White   3. Other

My sex is:
1. Female   2. Male

SECTION II

WHAT SHOULD THE SCHOOL DISTRICT'S PRIORITIES BE?

Grade Each Item:
1 = Very high priority
2 = High priority
3 = Moderate priority
4 = Low priority
5 = Don't know

STUDENTS SHOULD BE ABLE TO:

(circle one)
1 2 3 4 5 (a) Read materials which contain directions and information.
1 2 3 4 5 (b) Read for enjoyment and to learn new ideas.
1 2 3 4 5 (c) Use basic mathematics in daily life.
1 2 3 4 5 (d) Use standard English in writing and speaking.
1 2 3 4 5 (e) Listen and comprehend information needed in daily life.

(circle one)
1 2 3 4 5 (f) Express themselves clearly in oral communications.
1 2 3 4 5 (g) Write clearly and effectively.
1 2 3 4 5 (h) Understand and get along with other people.
1 2 3 4 5 (i) Think, reason, and solve problems for themselves.
1 2 3 4 5 (j) Become good citizens, helpful to others, well-behaved.
1 2 3 4 5 (k) Accept responsibility for self-discipline.
1 2 3 4 5 (l) Participate in extracurricular groups.
1 2 3 4 5 (m) Participate in student government.
1 2 3 4 5 (n) Develop creative abilities.
1 2 3 4 5 (o) Prepare for jobs.
1 2 3 4 5 (p) Get into advanced schooling or college.
1 2 3 4 5 (q) Prepare for work that will be faced in advanced schooling or career choice.

SECTION III

HOW WELL ARE WE DOING?

Next are areas of emphasis that the schools offer now. Please give your opinion of the quality of each one by grading the school district on how well it is doing in each of the areas listed below.

Grade Each Item:
1 = Excellent quality
2 = Good quality
3 = Fair quality
4 = Poor quality
5 = Don't know

HOW WELL IS THE SCHOOL DISTRICT DOING IN:

(circle one)
1 2 3 4 5 (a) Working cooperatively between schools and parents.
1 2 3 4 5 (b) Giving individual attention to each student's special learning needs.
1 2 3 4 5 (c) Providing adequate education and career counseling advice to students.
1 2 3 4 5 (d) Offering personal assistance with problems.
1 2 3 4 5 (e) Providing for orderly behavior in the schools.
1 2 3 4 5 (f) Demanding good work, good achievement in school.
1 2 3 4 5 (g) Providing high quality teachers.
1 2 3 4 5 (h) Providing high quality teachers.

(circle one)
1 2 3 4 5 (i) Providing meaningful teacher-parent conferences.
1 2 3 4 5 (j) Offering worthwhile meetings for parents and other citizens to learn about the schools.
1 2 3 4 5 (k) Making the school libraries available to students.
1 2 3 4 5 (l) Bringing experts, visiting artists, and other community resource people into the schools.
1 2 3 4 5 (m) Providing worthwhile field trips for students.
1 2 3 4 5 (n) Providing effective assistance from teacher aides.
1 2 3 4 5 (o) Producing excellence in school newspapers.
1 2 3 4 5 (p) Providing sufficient opportunities for students to participate in the performing arts.
1 2 3 4 5 (q) Providing frequent and attractive art exhibits of student work.
1 2 3 4 5 (r) Using audio-visual resources wisely.
1 2 3 4 5 (s) Developing sincere respect for personal differences (race, sex, abilities).
1 2 3 4 5 (t) Maintaining adequate communication with the public.
1 2 3 4 5 (u) Challenging advanced students.
1 2 3 4 5 (v) Assisting remedial students.
1 2 3 4 5 (w) Teaching about science and technology for a changing world.

SECTION IV

WHICH SUBJECT FIELDS NEED MORE ATTENTION?

Please rate each subject field according to your view of how well it is taught in the school district.

Grade Each Item:
1 = Outstanding
2 = Satisfactory
3 = Needs improvement
4 = Should be reduced in amount
5 = Don't know

(circle one)
1 2 3 4 5 (a) Art (painting, ceramics, etc.)
1 2 3 4 5 (b) Athletics and sports
1 2 3 4 5 (c) Black studies
1 2 3 4 5 (d) Business and commercial
1 2 3 4 5 (e) Dance
1 2 3 4 5 (f) Dramatics, plays, theater
1 2 3 4 5 (g) Driver education
1 2 3 4 5 (h) Foreign languages
1 2 3 4 5 (i) General music (vocal, choral)
1 2 3 4 5 (j) Grammar/English
1 2 3 4 5 (k) Health Education
1 2 3 4 5 (l) Home economics
1 2 3 4 5 (m) Industrial arts
1 2 3 4 5 (n) Instrumental music
1 2 3 4 5 (o) Mathematics
1 2 3 4 5 (p) Penmanship
1 2 3 4 5 (q) Physical education
1 2 3 4 5 (r) Pre-school programs
1 2 3 4 5 (s) Reading
1 2 3 4 5 (t) Science
1 2 3 4 5 (u) Sex education
1 2 3 4 5 (v) Social studies
1 2 3 4 5 (w) Spelling
1 2 3 4 5 (x) Vocational/work experience
1 2 3 4 5 (y) Writing effectively

BIBLIOGRAPHY

Altman, M. 1989. Private communication, Wasilla High School, Wasilla, AK.

American Association of School Administrators. 1983. *Building Public Confidence in Our Schools.* Arlington, VA.

American Association of School Administrators. 1950. *Public Relations for America's Schools.* Washington, DC.

American Management Association (undated). *How to Make Winning Presentations.* Saranac Lake, NY.

Association of School Business Officials, International (ASBO, International). 1986. *Custodial Methods and Procedures Manual.* Reston, VA.

Axelrod, E. 1989. Private communication, Orange-Ulster Board of Cooperative Educational Services, Goshen, NY.

Axelrod, E. 1989. "Report by the Orange-Ulster BOCES Executive Officer for the 1988-89 School Year," Goshen, NY.

Bingaman, C. E. 1985. *How to Deliver Winning Presentations.* Saranac Lake, NY: American Management Association.

Bingaman, C. E., R. Graham and M. Wheeler. 1983. *Communication Skills for Managers, Second Edition.* Saranac Lake, NY: American Management Association.

Bohen, D. 1989. Private communication, Fairfax County Public Schools, Fairfax, VA.

Bortin, V. 1981. *Publicity for Volunteers.* New York, NY: Walker Publishing Company, Inc.

Brady, L. 1989. "Principals in Good and Problem Secondary Schools in Ohio Report Interaction with the External Environment," Ph.D. dissertation, The Ohio State University.

Brown, L. 1961. *Communicating Facts and Ideas in Business.* Englewood Cliffs, NJ: Prentice-Hall, Inc.

Brownell, C. et al. 1955. *Public Relations in Education.* New York, NY: McGraw-Hill Book Company.

Bureau of School District Organization. 1989. Communication, State Education Department, Albany, NY.

Chopra, R. K. 1989. "Meetings: Call to Order," *The Executive Educator.* Alexandria, VA: National School Boards Association.

Chrysler Corporation. 1989. *Learning in America.* Washington, DC: Mac-Neil/Lehrer Productions – WETA/PBS.

Davies, D. 1980. "School Administration and Advisory Councils: Partnership or Shotgun Marriage?" *Bulletin.* Reston, VA: National Association of Secondary School Principals.

Educational Research Service. 1989. *Wages and Salaries Paid Support Personnel in Public Schools.* Arlington, VA.

Fink, S. 1986. *Crisis Management.* New York, NY: American Management Association.

1988. "Saving the Schools," *Fortune Magazine,* November 7.

Gallup, A. M. and S. M. Elam. 1988. "The 20th Annual Gallup Poll of the Public's Attitude toward the Public Schools," *Phi Delta Kappan.* Bloomington, IN: Phi Delta Kappa Educational Foundation.

Grensing, L. 1988. "Start the Presses," *Piedmont Airlines,* May.

Hamburg, S. K. 1987. "Children in Need: Investment Strategies for the Educationally Disadvantaged," Committee for Economic Development.

Hogencamp, D. "Dual Language Communication Grid," unpublished paper, 1990, Beacon, NY.

Huseman, R. C., J. M. Lahiff and J. D. Hatfield. 1976. *Interpersonal Communication in Organizations.* Boston, MA: Holbrook Press Inc.

Kendall, R. M. "Public Relations and Open Communication with Parents of Special Needs and Handicapped Children," unpublished paper, 1990, Winthrop College, Rock Hill, SC.

Kindred, L. W., D. Bagin and D. R. Gallagher. 1984. *The School and Community Relations, Third Edition.* Englewood Cliffs, NJ: Prentice-Hall, Inc.

Leahy, P. E. 1990. Private communication, Newburgh Enlarged City School District, Newburgh, NY.

Lifton, H. J. 1990. "The Meeting Society, Part II," *Human Resources Forum.* New York, NY: American Management Association.

Manning, G. and K. Curtis. 1988. *Communication – The Miracle of Dialogue.* Cincinnati, OH: South-Western Publishing Co.

Mealy, D. H. 1984. *Effective Building for Managers.* New York, NY: American Management Association.

Mercury, Y. A. "Photography," unpublished paper, 1990, New Paltz, NY.

Mitchell, T. R. and J. R. Larson, Jr. 1987. *People in Organizations.* New York, NY: McGraw-Hill Book Company.

Morris, J. O. 1980. *Make Yourself Clear!* New York, NY: McGraw-Hill Book Company.

National Association of Retired Federal Employees (NARFE). 1987. *Public Relations Handbook for NARFE Chapters and Federations*. Washington, DC.

National Institute of Business Management. 1987. ''Body Language for Business Success,'' New York, NY.

National School Public Relations Association (NSPRA). 1986. *Planning Your School PR Investment*. Arlington, VA.

National School Public Relations Association (NSPRA). 1986. *School Public Relations: The Complete Book*. Arlington, VA.

New York State Education Department. 1989. *Handbook on Requirements for Elementary and Secondary Schools, Education Law, Rules of the Board of Regents and Regulations of the Commission of Education, Second Edition*. Albany, NY.

New York State Education Department. 1989. *Occolades '89*. Albany, NY: The Information Dissemination Council.

New York State Education Department. 1987. *Resource Monograph on the Middle Grades*. Albany, NY: Office of Elementary, Secondary and Continuing Education.

Newburgh Enlarged City School District. 1982. *Handbook of General Regulations and Practices*. Newburgh, NY.

Newburgh Enlarged City School District. 1988. *Newburgh Free Academy Student Handbook, 27th Revision*. Newburgh, NY.

Olivo, T. L. 1989. Private communication, Monroe-Woodbury Central School District, Central Valley, NY.

Palmer Gould, N. ''Early Childhood Administration: Are They Using Planned Communication to Reach Key Publics?'' unpublished paper, 1989, New Paltz, NY.

1989. *Poughkeepsie Journal*, August 3.

Roberts, H. M. 1951. *Roberts' Rules of Order, Revised*. Glenview, IL: Scott, Foresman and Company.

Saxe, R. W. 1984. *School-Community Relations in Transition*. Berkeley, CA: McCutchan Publishing Corporation.

Shyer, C. H. ''Communication Grid,'' unpublished paper, 1989, Rhinebeck, NY.

Sobel, M. ''Magnet School Office Communication Grid,'' unpublished paper, 1990, Newburgh Enlarged City School District, Newburgh, NY.

Sorenson, T. C. 1965. *Kennedy*. New York, NY: Harper & Row Publishers, Inc.

St. John, W. D. 1986. ''Tips for Principals from NASSP,'' Reston, VA: National Association of Secondary School Principals.

Stanton-Cuevas, G. A. 1989. ''Special Education Department Orientation Guide, 1989 – 1990 School Year,'' Newburgh Enlarged City School District, Newburgh, NY.

Stauffer, H. 1957. "How to Work with Citizen Advisory Committees for Better Schools," New York, NY: Metropolitan School Study Council.

Stellar, A. W. February 1989. "Raising Levels of Public Confidence in the Schools," *Phi Delta Kappan.* Bloomington, IN: Phi Delta Kappa Educational Foundation.

U.S. House of Representatives Select Committee on Children, Youth, and Families. 1989. "U.S. Children and Their Families: Current Conditions and Recent Trends," Washington, DC.

United States Postal Service. 1988. *Creative Solutions for Your Business Needs, Third-Class Mail Preparation.* Publication 49. Washington, DC.

Unruh, A. and R. A. Willier. 1974. *Public Relations for Schools.* Belmont, CA: Lear Siegler, Inc./Fearon Publishers.

Walling, D. R. 1982. *Complete Book of School Public Relations.* Englewood Cliffs, NJ: Prentice-Hall, Inc.

Wayson, W. D. and C. Achilles, et al. 1988. *Raising Levels of Public Confidence in the Schools.* Bloomington, IN: Phi Delta Kappa Educational Foundation.

Wherry, J. D. January 1979. "Building Public Confidence Starts with Your School," *Bulletin.* Reston, VA: National Association of Secondary School Principals.

Winston, M. B. 1982. *Getting Publicity.* New York, NY: John Wiley & Sons, Inc.

Zampolin, R. G. "School-Community Relations," unpublished paper, 1985, Nyack, NY.

INDEX

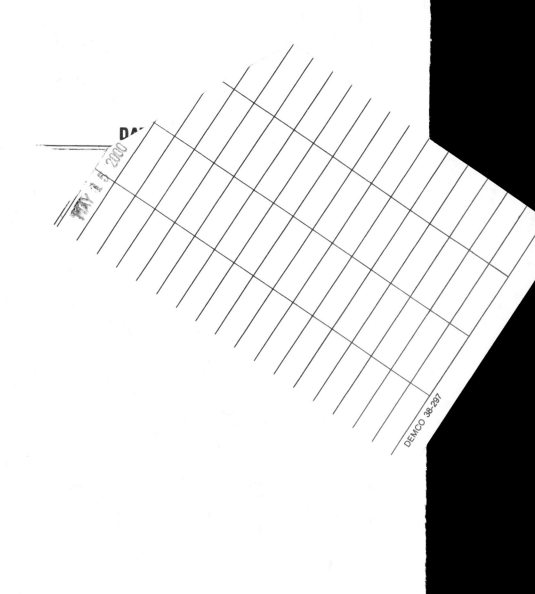

DEMCO 38-297